ALL CHILDREN CAN LEARN

ALL CHILDREN CAN LEARN

*Lessons from the
Kentucky Reform Experience*

Roger S. Pankratz

Joseph M. Petrosko

Editors

JOSSEY-BASS
A Wiley Company
San Francisco

Jossey-Bass books and products are available through most bookstores. To contact Jossey-Bass directly, call (888) 378-2537, fax to (800) 605-2665, or visit our website at www.josseybass.com.

Substantial discounts on bulk quantities of Jossey-Bass books are available to corporations, professional associations, and other organizations. For details and discount information, contact the special sales department at Jossey-Bass.

Manufactured in the United States of America on Lyons Falls Turin Book. This paper is acid-free and 100 percent totally chlorine-free.

Library of Congress Cataloging-in-Publication Data

All children can learn: lessons from the Kentucky reform experience / Roger S. Pankratz and Joseph M. Petrosko, editors.
    p. cm.—(The Jossey-Bass education series)
Includes bibliographical references and index.
    ISBN 0–7879–5523–X
 1. School improvement programs—Kentucky—Evaluation.
2. Educational law and legislation—Kentucky. I. Pankratz, Roger.
II. Petrosko, Joseph M., 1947– III. Series.
LB2822.83.K4 A44 2000
371.2'009769—dc21   00–011517

HB Printing   10 9 8 7 6 5 4 3 2 1   FIRST EDITION

The Jossey-Bass Education Series

To Donna
for her enduring
confidence and support

AND

In memory of
Mary Petrosko
1917–2000

CONTENTS

ACKNOWLEDGMENTS

WE, THE EDITORS, THANK THE MEMBERS of the board of directors of the Kentucky Institute for Education Research (KIER) for their confidence in us and for their support of a two-year effort to produce *All Children Can Learn*. We also thank KIER staff Ruth H. Webb and Sandy Jackson for their help with administrative logistics.

KIER was created by executive order of the governor in November 1992 but for the past eight years was supported as an independent non-profit organization by The Annie E. Casey Foundation. Under that support, KIER was able to conduct more than twenty statewide research studies related to Kentucky's education reform effort and to produce four reviews of research on school reform in Kentucky. *All Children Can Learn* has been a foundation-supported culminating project of this eight-year effort.

On behalf of the KIER board of directors, the editors express their sincere appreciation to The Annie E. Casey Foundation for its investment in research and in Kentucky's reform efforts. Without the foundation's assistance, *All Children Can Learn,* and much of the research on which the book is based, would not have been possible. Also, we offer a special thanks to Tony Cipollone, vice president of the foundation, who believed in Kentucky's reform program early on and who has remained a strong supporter of evaluating and communicating the results to a variety of audiences, both inside and outside of Kentucky. For this support, both KIER and Kentucky are grateful.

We offer our special appreciation to Holly Holland, who advised and assisted us in editing a book with multiple authors. Her expertise and guidance added much to the technical quality of the manuscript. Also, we thank the many readers of the chapters, especially Jacob Adams, Robert Sexton, Lois Adams-Rodgers, Audrey Carr, Susan Leib, and Jack Foster, who reviewed the chapters for accuracy.

For their many long hours of word processing, editing, copying, communicating with authors, and checking references, we express our gratitude to Gaye Jolly and Cathie Bryant, two very important members of our Western Kentucky University team.

Finally, we express our appreciation to the staff at Jossey-Bass, especially Leslie Iura, Christie Hakim, and Alice Rowan, for their congenial guidance through a set of rather arduous tasks to ready this book for publication.

THE EDITORS

ROGER S. PANKRATZ is professor of teacher education at Western Kentucky University and director of the Renaissance Group Institution's Partnership for Improving Teacher Quality. Pankratz is former executive director of both the governor's Council on School Performance Standards and the Kentucky Institute for Education Research (KIER). Under his direction KIER published three annual reviews of research on the Kentucky Education Reform Act of 1990 and more than twenty statewide studies that evaluated the progress and results of school reform initiatives.

JOSEPH M. PETROSKO is professor of education at the University of Louisville, specializing in statistics, research, and evaluation. He has studied school reform in Kentucky since the passage of the Kentucky Education Reform Act of 1990. Petrosko is codirector of the University of Louisville Nystrand Center of Excellence in Education and the Kentucky Institute for Education Research.

THE CONTRIBUTORS

JACOB E. ADAMS JR. is associate professor of education and public policy at Peabody College, Vanderbilt University, and a research fellow with the Peabody Center for Education Policy. He is chairman of the board of directors of the Kentucky Institute for Education Research. His research focuses on the policy context of education, with particular attention to the ways in which finance policies, implementation practices, and accountability mechanisms shape school capacity.

BONNIE J. BANKER, professor of education and director of graduate education, teaches at Asbury College in Wilmore, Kentucky. She has been actively involved in the development of a professional portfolio system and the use of generated data for candidate and program improvement at Asbury. She has served on and chaired several committees for the Education Professional Standards Board and has provided leadership in training, chairing, and serving on numerous board of examiners' teams.

STEPHEN K. CLEMENTS is assistant professor in the Department of Educational Policy Studies and Evaluation at the University of Kentucky. His doctoral work at the University of Chicago, Department of Political Science, focused on the politics of the creation and passage of the Kentucky Education Reform Act of 1990. His research areas include state-level school reforms enacted since the mid-1980s, the role of political culture in state education changes, the status of the teacher workforce in Kentucky, and data needs for effective education policymaking.

PAM COE has recently retired from AEL, Inc. in Charleston, West Virginia, where she collaborated with Patricia J. Kannapel on studies of school reform in Kentucky. She received her master's degree in cultural anthropology from Columbia University and her doctorate in foundations of education (with an emphasis on educational ethnography) from Michigan State University. She is currently working independently as a consultant. Since 1990 her research has focused on the effects of state-mandated education reform on rural school districts in Kentucky.

TOM CORCORAN is codirector of the Consortium for Policy Research in Education at the University of Pennsylvania. His research has focused on the improvement of education for poor and minority children. His current work addresses strategies for replication of effective programs, the use of empirical studies to inform policy and practice, the effectiveness of different approaches to professional development, and whole-school reform. He has studied the implementation of the Kentucky Education Reform Act for the past eight years, first for the National Science Foundation and currently for the Partnership for Kentucky Schools.

JANE L. DAVID is director of the Bay Area Research Group in Palo Alto, California. Her research and evaluation activities focus on the connections between education policy and the improvement of school quality and equity. She has studied the implementation of the Kentucky Education Reform Act of 1990 for over nine years, first for the Prichard Committee for Academic Excellence and currently for the Partnership for Kentucky Schools.

JACK D. FOSTER served as secretary of the education and humanities cabinet in Kentucky state government from 1988 to 1991 and was a member of the Task Force on Education Reform when the Kentucky Education Reform Act of 1990 (KERA) was developed and enacted. During his professional career, he has been a consultant, university professor, social scientist, public policy analyst, author, and clergyman. He received his doctorate from Ohio State University and is author of *Redesigning Public Education: The Kentucky Experience,* on the history of KERA.

PATRICIA DAVIS GOLDBERG is assistant professor of teacher education at Hanover College in Indiana. From 1988 to 1999 she was an elementary school teacher in Kentucky. During those years, she was involved in all aspects of implementing the Kentucky Education Reform Act of 1990, including her school's site-based management council, and was a writing portfolio leader for her school and district. Her research has been supported by the Spencer Foundation and focuses on metacognition and performance assessment.

HOLLY HOLLAND is author of *Making Change: Three Educators Join the Battle for Better Schools* and editor of *Middle Ground* magazine, published by National Middle School Association. A former reporter at *The Courier-Journal* in Louisville, she now works as a freelance writer and editor specializing in education coverage.

PATRICIA J. KANNAPEL is a research and development specialist for the AEL, Inc. in Charleston, West Virginia. She received her master's degree in anthropology from the University of Kentucky. Her master's thesis examined the development of the Kentucky Education Reform Act during the 1990 legislative session. She is director of AEL's ten-year qualitative study of the implementation of the Kentucky Education Reform Act of 1990. Her research has focused on the effects of state educational policy on rural school districts.

SUSAN FOLLETT LUSI is assistant commissioner for support services in the Rhode Island Department of Education. She is author of *The Role of State Departments of Education in Complex School Reform,* which reports her research on the state departments of education in Kentucky and Vermont. She has worked with state departments of education in a number of consulting and assistance capacities in addition to working for the Annenberg Institute for School Reform and the Coalition of Essential Schools.

G. WILLIAMSON MCDIARMID is professor of educational policy and director of the Institute of Social and Economic Research at the University of Alaska Anchorage. He has been studying the experiences of Kentucky teachers with professional development since 1993. His other research interests include preservice teacher learning, the effects of standards and assessments on curriculum and instruction, and teacher education reform.

JOHN P. POGGIO is codirector of the Center for Educational Testing and Evaluation (CETE) and professor of educational psychology and research at the University of Kansas. As director of CETE, Poggio works with a research team on grants and contracts in areas involving K–12 student assessment, university and program admissions testing, educational program evaluation, and monitoring school improvement for education agencies. Poggio has served as a consultant on student testing and school accountability and as an expert witness in litigation involving teacher testing. He is a former member of Kentucky's National Technical Work Group and currently serves as vice chair of the Commonwealth Accountability Testing System's National Technical Advisory Panel on Assessment and Accountability.

JAMES RATHS is professor of education in the School of Education at the University of Delaware. Since 1992 Raths and his colleagues have conducted three reviews of the progress that teachers in Kentucky have made in improving the primary school, its curriculum, and instruction. His work has been underwritten by the Prichard Committee for Academic Excellence and the Kentucky Institute for Education Research. His research areas include the evaluation of educational programs and teacher preparation. Raths serves as an executive editor of the *Journal of Educational Research*.

ROBERT F. SEXTON has been the executive director of the Prichard Committee for Academic Excellence since its inception in 1980. He has been widely recognized for his leadership in education reform, and has received the Dana Award for Pioneering Achievement and honorary degrees from Kentucky colleges. He serves on numerous national and state boards and commissions, is an advisor to foundations and other states, and is the founder of several initiatives, such as Kentucky's Governor's Scholars Program. He is currently working on a book about the Prichard Committee and its role in education reform.

ALL CHILDREN CAN LEARN

INTRODUCTION

AN AMBITIOUS PLAN FOR IMPROVING SCHOOLS

THIS BOOK DESCRIBES the goals, experiences, and results of the nation's most comprehensive and longest-running statewide school reform initiative. Seventeen authors (nine from Kentucky and eight from outside Kentucky), all of whom have been deeply involved in research or policy development associated with school reform, relate the important events and insights that shaped the Kentucky Education Reform Act of 1990 (KERA).

Other books and articles about KERA have been written by people who helped to create or implement the reforms. Although they are essential reading for those who seek to understand the impact of systemic school reform movements, they do not present the full picture of education reform. Equally important are the more long-term and global effects of school restructuring, results that are both positive and negative. The goal of this book is to provide a broader perspective.

We wrote this book primarily for education practitioners and policymakers. We wanted teachers and administrators to understand how their work fits into the broader realm of school reform. We wanted policymakers, including state government staff, local and state school board members, and legislators, to realize what certain policies and practices can and cannot do to improve teaching and learning. We wanted parents and citizens who wish to use their energy and influence to expand educational opportunities for children to know how they can contribute to the democratic process of reform. And we wanted to share new models of instruction and professional development with teacher educators and policy researchers who are preparing the next generation of school leaders.

KERA: Origins, Features, and Results

KERA did not emerge or exist in isolation. A number of prominent law-suits, for example, preceded Kentucky's effort. Prior to *Rose v. Council for Better Education, Inc.* (1989) in Kentucky, seven states had overturned school finance systems because of inequities in the distribution of resources across school districts. The Washington State and West Virginia courts decided their school finance cases not just on the basis of relative distributions of resources but also in terms of the level of resources needed for students to achieve desirable outcomes; this was important for Kentucky. These cases certainly influenced the framers of Kentucky's legal action and gave hope to the plaintiffs.

In curriculum, too, other states preceded Kentucky in reform efforts. California produced a series of instructional frameworks and changed the content and format of the state assessments. Vermont pioneered changes in assessment and new standards for instruction. Other states—South Carolina, Connecticut, Delaware, and Arizona—were trying different strategies of reform at different levels. Outside the policy arena in the 1980s, the Coalition for Essential Schools, Accelerated Schools, and the New Standards Project provided other examples of national movements to improve instruction (Cohen, 1995). In the late 1980s and early 1990s there was also progress at the federal level in pushing systemic reform in public education: the governors' meeting with President Bush at Charlottesville in 1989 (where Governor Wilkinson of Kentucky was a prominent player), the work of the National Goals Panel, the groundwork for Goals 2000, and the reauthorization of Title 1. According to O'Day and Smith (1993) systemic reform in most states focused on creating new policy instruments to enact reform and reducing the regulations of bureaucracy that would impede reform. These two elements were very prominent in KERA as well. O'Day and Smith identified four additional areas of focus for new policy instruments: new content standards, new assessments that include intellectually authentic student tasks, more ambitious curricula, and changes in teacher education that support new standards. Again, Kentucky's reform act addressed all four areas but gave far more attention to new standards for learning and new "authentic" assessments. Although it is true that reform efforts in other states and at the national level heavily influenced the framers of Kentucky's school change model, none went as far to alter the experiences of every school and every student.

KERA has three unique features. First, it was the nation's most radical and far-reaching reform in a decade, and it inspired school change initiatives throughout the United States. States began to engage in a wide range of philosophical and political discussions about academic standards, school accountability, standardized testing, financial equity, school governance, and the professional training and licensure of educators. The 1990s produced an abundance of policies and projects designed to boost the performance of America's public schools. And yet, as researchers and writers have remarked over and over again, no state went as far as Kentucky in trying to put all the pieces together. An article about KERA in *Financial World* aptly observed, "Unlike many states that have responded to well-documented concerns over America's educational crisis by instituting piecemeal changes, Kentucky has virtually started from scratch" (Barrett & Green, 1992, pp. 56–58). By tackling curriculum, governance, and school finance issues simultaneously, Kentucky gave the world a window to watch how all these pieces can individually and collectively either advance or impede academic achievement. (Exhibit I.1 provides a brief overview of the major KERA initiatives.)

Second, KERA required schools to introduce many educational innovations, such as high-stakes performance assessments and multiage elementary school classrooms, which many states subsequently tried or considered. Kentucky's experience with these models thus provides evidence for those seeking to validate the best thinking about school transformation for the twenty-first century.

Third, KERA has endured for a decade, with most of its original initiatives intact. That kind of longevity is virtually unheard of in an era marked by politicians' partisan bickering and the public's limited patience with broad social change. Kentucky defied the odds and provided the world with a detailed record of its accomplishments and failures. This book, which examines those accomplishments and failures, has the potential to advance understanding of school reform far beyond previous levels.

The core belief of the legislative Task Force on Education Reform, which designed KERA, was that all children can learn. That belief inspired the subsequent choices regarding programs and spending that Kentucky's public schools have been grappling with ever since. After ten years of steady work to revive its educational system, Kentucky has not proved that all children can learn, but it has demonstrated that many, if not most, can. Opponents of KERA would call that a hollow victory. However, supporters of school change, such as the Prichard Committee for Academic Excellence, a statewide public advocacy group, argue that Kentucky has shown enough progress to merit continuation of what it started. In *Gaining Ground,* its recent report on the first decade of KERA, the Prichard Committee for Academic Excellence (1999) put the debate into perspective:

Exhibit I.1. An Overview of Major
Kentucky Education Reform Act of 1990 Initiatives.

The Kentucky Education Reform Act of 1990 (KERA) is 946 pages of law that re-created Kentucky's public schools in response to a 1989 state supreme court decision declaring the previous system to be inequitable, inefficient, and inadequate. A legislative task force on school reform with three subcommittees was formed to recommend policies and initiatives related to curriculum, governance, and finance. The task force adopted twelve principles to guide its deliberations and recommendations. "All children can learn and most at high levels" appeared at the top of the list. Of the new initiatives mandated in the 1990 law, the following were the most significant.

Curriculum

Schools were required to expect high levels of achievement in six areas: basic communication and mathematics skills; core concepts of mathematics, the sciences, arts and humanities, social studies, and practical living and vocational studies; self-sufficiency; responsible group membership; thinking and problem solving; and integration of knowledge.

The state was required to develop a primarily performance-based assessment system that would hold schools accountable for student performance. The Kentucky Instructional Results Information System was developed and implemented as a "high-stakes" system that provided cash rewards for schools that met biennial improvement goals and sanctions for schools that fell short of their goals. Schools whose accountability indices declined significantly over a two-year cycle received financial assistance and a "distinguished educator" (today called a "highly skilled educator") as a consultant.

Two major curricular initiatives specified in the law were a preschool program for all four-year-old at-risk children and an ungraded primary school program for students in kindergarten through grade 3. The reform law intended to eliminate early failing of students by placing them in multiage, multiability groupings where they could make continuous progress. Students were to enter grade 4 only after successful completion of the primary school program.

To support at-risk students and reduce barriers to learning, KERA created the Extended School Service Program, which provided tutoring outside of regular school hours, and family resource and youth service centers, which provided greater access to social and medical services.

To build the capacity of educators to help children reach higher levels of learning, KERA greatly increased funding for instructional technology and professional development. The law required 65 percent of professional development funds to be spent at the school level, with decisions made by a school council consisting of the principal, three teachers, and two parents.

Governance

KERA ended 152 years of school governance by an elected state superintendent of public instruction and mandated an appointed commissioner of education who was to serve at the behest of the board of education. Under the new commissioner, the department of education was given the authority to take over failing schools and districts and to enforce strong antinepotism regulations. The new law also decentralized the authority of local boards of education by requiring school councils to decide on policies and issues related to curriculum and instruction. A third shift in governance was the creation of the teacher-dominated Education Professional Standards Board, which was to exercise independent authority over teacher licensure and certification and over approval of teacher preparation programs. Finally, KERA created a special legislative oversight structure, the Office of Education Accountability (OEA), to monitor compliance in all reform mandates statewide to report directly to the Kentucky General Assembly.

Finance

KERA provided significant increases in financial support for schools. The Support Education Excellence in Kentucky (SEEK) fund was established. It was designed to narrow the gap in per-pupil expenditures between richer and poorer districts in the state. It was to designate a guaranteed amount of state money per pupil based on the previous year's average daily attendance. SEEK funds were to be adjusted to reflect a local district's costs for transporting students and educating children who were at risk or disabled. In addition, the new finance law gave districts the discretion to collect and use local resources to increase their per-pupil expenditures. Finally, KERA provided for substantial increases in teacher salaries.

"We won't be happy until every child is learning to his or her full potential. But that isn't happening anywhere in America, and it never has. As a result, a more reasoned goal is to move toward that point with the hope of getting there and making every effort to do so" (p. 12). Therefore, we believe the title of this book is still as appropriate as the belief of the Task Force for Education Reform was ten years ago.

Overview of the Contents

As editors of this book, we were required to make very difficult decisions about what to include and what to leave out. It was not possible to address in a meaningful way all of the initiatives contained in the 946 pages of House Bill 940, which created KERA. Therefore we decided to highlight those features of the reform that had been the focus of thoughtful research and analysis, that provided new insights, and that offered lessons with the potential to inform future practice. Four important and successful initiatives were contenders for the chapters in this book: Kentucky's preschool program, the Extended School Services Program, the

Family Resource and Youth Services Center Program, and Kentucky's increased support for and use of technology in schools. Each of these certainly deserves a place in discussions of the Kentucky story. However, we decided to limit the focus of this book to nine other reform initiatives. We apologize for any omissions and hope others, in future books, will fill the gaps.

This book has four parts. Part One describes the foundation for Kentucky's reform law. In Chapter One, Roger S. Pankratz, former executive director of Kentucky's Council on School Performance Standards, chronicles the events in the courts, governor's office, and the legislature that produced what Stanford University professor Mike Kirst (1992) called "the most broad-based and systemic legislative initiative in the recent history of education reform" (Barrett & Green, 1992, p. 56). In Chapter Two, Jacob E. Adams Jr., finance policy expert at Vanderbilt University, focuses more specifically on the debate and actions in the courts to require an equitable and adequate education for every child in Kentucky. Adams also reports on the uneven progress in turning that vision into a reality in the state's classrooms. In Chapter Three Jack D. Foster, former secretary of Kentucky's education and humanities cabinet and Governor Wallace Wilkinson's representative on the legislative Task Force on Education Reform, recalls the law's intent from the perspective of those who designed it. Part One concludes with the highlights of a recent interview with Joe Wright, state senate majority leader at the time KERA was introduced. Wright, who helped shepherd the school restructuring initiative through the Kentucky General Assembly in 1990, considers its passage the highlight of his political career.

Part Two describes KERA's impact on teaching and learning in the state during the past decade. In Chapter Five John P. Poggio, researcher and member of Kentucky's National Technical Review Panel for the Commonwealth Accountability Testing System, presents an analysis of the Kentucky Instructional Results Information System, the state's assessment and accountability plan, which many considered to be the driving force behind KERA and which was perhaps its most controversial feature. In Chapter Six Stephen K. Clements, an education policy analyst at the University of Kentucky, examines the Kentucky Department of Education's efforts to develop a curriculum framework that would help schools realign their instruction with Kentucky's new core content standards. Clements describes the difficult time the state had in trying to communicate to teachers what students need to know and be able to do, especially in the climate of fear that followed the introduction of high-stakes assessments. In Chapter Seven James Raths, a researcher and curriculum expert at the

University of Delaware, presents the mixed results of Kentucky's primary school program. Although there is evidence that teaching and learning in Kentucky's early elementary grades have improved, Raths points out that the progress fell short of reformers' expectations. Part Two concludes with an eastern Kentucky high school student's personal experience of learning from teachers who were still struggling to understand a new set of assessments, curricula, and standards brought on by KERA.

Part Three describes the three major initiatives of KERA to build the capacity of educators. In Chapter Nine researchers G. Williamson McDiarmid of the University of Alaska and Tom Corcoran of the Consortium for Policy Research in Education provide a thoughtful analysis of Kentucky's struggle to advance the standards of instruction through professional development. Ongoing forums involving researchers, department of education officials, individual school leaders, and university faculty have yielded promising results in the effort to implement more productive practices. In Chapter Ten Patricia J. Kannapel and Pam Coe, researchers at AEL, Inc., share their findings on the effectiveness of Kentucky's Distinguished Educator Program (today the Highly Skilled Educator Program). They also point out the factors that their research suggests are the most important in helping schools to get results. In Chapter Eleven Roger S. Pankratz and Bonnie J. Banker, both teacher educators and researchers, examine the efforts of the Kentucky Education Professional Standards Board to reshape teacher preparation programs and raise the quality of instruction throughout the state. Part Three concludes with in-depth conversations with a teacher and a school administrator who share their views on the professional challenges KERA presented and the ongoing struggle to match practice to policy.

Part Four features three initiatives of KERA that were designed to bring new players into school governance and support. In Chapter Fourteen Jane L. David of the Bay Area Research Group shares her analysis of Kentucky's attempt to create democratic site-based councils in more than thirteen hundred Kentucky schools. Although the particular model Kentucky chose is one of several possible alternatives, David finds significant progress in the state's effort to make parents, teachers, and administrators full partners in education. Chapter Fifteen describes Kentucky's ambitious plan to reorganize the department of education under an appointed commissioner and how the restructuring affected the implementation of various KERA initiatives. Susan Follett Lusi, assistant commissioner of education in Rhode Island, and her colleague Patricia Davis Goldberg discuss the department of education's attempt to balance school scrutiny with school support. In Chapter Sixteen Robert F. Sexton, executive director of the Prichard Committee for Academic Excellence, tells a remarkable story of a group of citizens who led the fight for better schools in Kentucky and who continue to be a powerful voice for change today. The group's work symbolizes the important role that parents and other citizen activists can play in transforming public schools. Part Four concludes with an account of one parent's journey from directing bake sales to persuading other parents and educators to collaborate on a multitude of school governance issues.

Finally, in the Conclusion the book's editors, Roger S. Pankratz of Western Kentucky University and Joseph M. Petrosko of the University of Louisville identify and highlight twelve important lessons from Kentucky's systemic school reform movement. Pankratz and Petrosko present these dozen insights as evidence of KERA's profound impact on the state's public schools and as key principles to guide future efforts to improve education throughout the United States.

October 2000   ROGER S. PANKRATZ
                                                  Bowling Green, Kentucky

                                                   JOSEPH M. PETROSKO
                                                     Louisville, Kentucky

REFERENCES

Barrett, K., & Green, R. (1992). E for effort in education: Kentucky. *Financial World, 161*(12), 56–58.

Cohen, D. K. (1995). What is the system in systemic reform? *Educational Researcher, 24*(9), 11–17, 31.

O'Day, J., & Smith, M. (1993). *Systemic reform and educational opportunity.* San Francisco: Jossey-Bass.

Prichard Committee for Academic Excellence. (1999). *Gaining ground: Hard work and high expectations for Kentucky schools.* Lexington, KY: Author.

Rose v. Council for Better Education, Inc., 790 S.W.2d 186 (Ky. 1989).

PART ONE

THE GROUNDWORK FOR STATEWIDE REFORM

I

THE LEGAL AND
LEGISLATIVE BATTLES

Roger S. Pankratz

APRIL 11, 2000, marked the tenth anniversary of Governor Wallace Wilkinson's signing House Bill 940, more commonly known as the Kentucky Education Reform Act of 1990 (KERA). The headlines of the *Lexington Herald-Leader* one decade ago read, "Governor Signs Historic Education Bill" (Stroud, 1990, p. A1). Wilkinson called it "the most important legislation enacted in the state since the adoption of its constitution" (Jennings, 1990, p. A1). *Education Week* said, "It was one of the most comprehensive restructuring efforts ever undertaken by a state legislature" (Walker, 1990, p. 1). *The New York Times* labeled it "the most sweeping education package ever conceived by a state government" ("Starting Over," 1990, p. 35). Even President Bush singled out Kentucky as a state that used "creative thinking" to transform its public schools ("Bush Lauds Kentucky," 1990).

Educators and policymakers both in and outside Kentucky agree that KERA was the beginning of a new age for public education in Kentucky. To this day the major players who created and influenced the passage of KERA say they still cannot believe it really happened. Since 1990 other states have passed major education reform legislation, but no legislation has approached in magnitude what KERA did as far as holding schools accountable for student learning, awakening public attention to education, and increasing financial support for its schools.

Prior to 1990 Kentucky ranked nationally in the lowest 25 percent of almost every national comparison of educational performance. As a state,

Kentucky was very near the bottom in functional literacy and had one of the lowest percentages of citizens completing a high school education. (Bureau of the Census, 1985, p. 134, Table 217).

In the 1970s and 1980s many people made a number of attempts to raise the level of state funding for education, but it seemed that every time the Kentucky General Assembly took a step forward, it would follow with two steps backward (*Rose v. Council,* 1989). In 1985 Governor Martha Lane Collins called a special session on education, and the General Assembly passed several new support measures and programs for education but then failed to persuade legislators to fund them. As former governor Bert Combs put it in 1991 while serving as the chief litigator in Kentucky's historic court case *Rose* v. *Council for Better Education, Inc.,* "Most successful politicians run from the word 'taxes' like the devil runs from holy water" (Combs, 1991, p. 13).

How then was Kentucky, with some of the poorest school districts in the nation and worst track records for providing educational opportunities for its children, able to transform its public schools and find $1.3 billion of additional monies every two years to support them? The remainder of this chapter will describe the critical events that have put Kentucky in the national spotlight for its school reform over the past decade. This summary will show how ordinary Kentuckians acted with extraordinary vision, persistence, and courage in the courts, the governor's office, and the legislature to make school reform a reality in Kentucky.

The Courts Set a Solid Foundation

It all began in early 1984 when Arnold Guess, a thirty-year veteran of school finance in the Kentucky Department of Education, was fired by the newly elected state superintendent of public instruction, Alice McDonald. Guess, who had supported the wrong candidate, was forced into early retirement (Dove, 1991, pp. 5–6). However, in his new life he was able to give attention to the terrible inequities he had observed in the poor, rural schools in eastern Kentucky. As chief budget officer for the department of education and an employee of the state, he had been limited in what he could do to challenge these inequities; but as a private citizen, he saw new possibilities. Because he knew the facts behind the poor educational opportunities for students in Appalachia, he saw the legal system as a tool he could use to good effect.

Guess began to share with superintendents of some of the poorest Kentucky school districts his vision of a successful lawsuit. They were in strong agreement with his goal to leverage support for poor districts, but they were less certain about his belief that they could win a fight against Kentucky's powerful General Assembly, governor, and State Board for Elementary and Secondary Education. Very soon Guess gained the support of Kern Alexander, a longtime friend and colleague, and a Kentucky native with a national reputation for expertise in school finance. Alexander was a professor at the University of Florida and served as educational policy coordinator for the governor of Florida. Alexander's credibility provided a boost to Guess's efforts, but he needed more. On May 4, 1984, he invited selected superintendents who shared his vision to the first meeting of a group that became known as the Council for Better Education (Dove, 1991, pp. 5–6). At that meeting two school finance experts explained the basis for possible legal action. The superintendents appointed a steering committee to recruit new members and seek legal counsel.

In October Guess and several superintendents paid a visit to former governor of Kentucky Bert Combs. Combs, a partner in one of Kentucky's largest and most prestigious law firms, had held many prominent positions in Kentucky (Dove, 1991, pp. 7–8). But he had graduated from a poor rural school district in eastern Kentucky and was sympathetic to Guess's quest. However, Combs also knew the obstacles a lawsuit would face against Kentucky's well-oiled political machine. At first Combs was reluctant to commit the resources of his firm because of the risk to his law partners and clients. Combs had found the transition from governor to private attorney difficult. As Combs (1991) later told the *Harvard Journal of Legislation,* "I needed to sue the governor and General Assembly about as much as a hog needs a side saddle" (p. 3). Guess and his friends persisted. They reminded Combs that at one time "he had claimed to be Kentucky's education governor and the General Assembly had never financed the state's public schools" (Combs, p. 3). "Children of Kentucky," in their view, "were being deprived of their constitutional right to a decent and equal education and . . . we as onlookers were wasting our 'seed corn' for the future" (Combs, p. 3). After the group's third or fourth visit Combs told them that if they could get 30 to 40 percent of the school districts to join the effort, he would consider the case. Again, through hard work and persistence, Guess and his group persuaded 66 of Kentucky's 178 districts to join the Council for Better Education. They brought the evidence to Combs, and he agreed to take the case (Dove, pp. 8–9).

Combs worked pro bono, but he needed support from three attorneys and an education law expert to draft the complaints and research procedural issues. The sixty-six school districts of the Council for Better Education assessed their members $.50 per student to support the lawsuit.

Rounding out Combs's legal team were attorneys Ted Lavit, Thomas Lewis, and Debra Dawahare (Dove, 1991, pp. 9–10). Dawahare served as cocounsel to Combs in all stages of the case, and Kern Alexander was their consultant on school finance.

On May 8, 1985, the Council for Better Education announced its intentions to sue the state (Dove, 1991, pp. 9–10). Kentucky's political machine reacted to this initial threat as expected. State superintendent Alice McDonald threatened reprisals for school leaders who participated. Leaders of the General Assembly were quick to remind the public of all their efforts to fund public education in spite of the local mismanagement of funds in poor rural districts. McDonald said she would get a court injunction for the misappropriation of funds. The chairmen of the House and Senate Education Committees agreed and made a joint statement to the media. Kern Alexander, who in November 1985 had become president of Western Kentucky University, was told that if he continued to help the Council for Better Education, Western Kentucky University's funding could be in jeopardy (Dove, pp. 35–36).

However, the process Guess had started in 1984 persisted and gained momentum, thanks to unusual expertise and courage. Combs and his legal team chose a strategy of building a clear factual history of failed reforms and the evolution of a warped school finance system. They showed that the ratio of tax allocations per pupil in the ten richest districts to tax allocations per pupil in the ten poorest districts was about six to one. School tax rates per $100 of assessed property value ranged from $1.14 to $.24, depending on the locality. The amount of annual tax revenue raised per pupil ranged from $3,186 in Anchorage, the wealthiest district, to about $120 in Elliott and Owsley, two of the poorest districts (Wilkinson, 1995, p. 211; Loftus, 1989, p. A3).

On November 20, 1985, the legal team filed a complaint, *Council for Better Education, Inc.* v. *Collins,* in Franklin Circuit Court. The plaintiffs were the Council for Better Education, seven local school boards, and twenty-two public school students, suing on behalf of themselves and the class of all students in poor districts. The named defendants were the governor, the superintendent of public instruction, the state treasurer, the president pro tempore of the Senate, the Speaker of the House of Representatives, and members of the State Board for Elementary and Secondary Education. The plaintiffs alleged that the funding for local schools was "inadequate and inequitable" and in violation of Kentucky's constitutional provision requiring an "efficient system of common schools throughout the state" (Chellgren, 1985). With a solid case of funding inequities and neglect of poor rural schools, Combs and his team were concerned that even if the courts ruled in their favor, the plaintiffs would not respond, on the grounds of the separation of powers between the three branches of government. They feared the case would result in a standoff between the courts and the General Assembly (Combs, 1991, pp. 5–8).

The lawsuit infuriated many legislators, who believed they had made extraordinary efforts to develop programs and find funds to support better schools. In a special session of the General Assembly a bill was introduced to make it illegal for school boards to use state funds to sue the legislature. The bill died in committee: the chair of the House Education Committee was a representative from a plaintiff school district (Roser, 1986). The leadership of Kentucky's House and Senate employed attorney William Scent to defend them against the lawsuit. Attorneys from the department of education assisted.

The case did not come to trial for almost two years. During this time, with the help of the media, public sentiment in favor of doing something about Kentucky's system of public education grew. On August 4, 1987, the case was finally heard by Judge Ray Corns, one of two judges in Franklin County Circuit Court, located in the state capital. The brief and civilized trial included Combs's eloquent descriptions of a school system that had deprived poor children of their right to a proper education. School finance experts, school officials, and students supported his claim. For his part Scent defended the past efforts of the governor and General Assembly, blaming the poor districts for failing to tax citizens appropriately and for mismanaging their schools. The defendants tried to show that good schools were possible even with a low-tax effort, but they made the mistake of using a wealthy district as their model (Dove, 1991, pp. 15–16).

The court took a six-month recess to consider the evidence. During this time Kentucky elected a new governor and superintendent of public instruction. The new superintendent, John Brock, had attended schools in poor eastern Kentucky and, soon after taking office, notified the courts that he was joining the cause of the Council for Better Education. The plaintiffs also received support from an amicus brief filed by the Prichard Committee for Academic Excellence, an influential grassroots citizen advocacy group, which pointed out that the waste and mismanagement claimed by the defendants was more reason for the state to act to rectify the situation.

On May 31, 1988, the first bombshell exploded. Judge Corns ruled in favor of the plaintiffs, and the Kentucky General Assembly was taken to task for not providing equitable and efficient education. In his decision Corns ruled that Kentucky's school finance system was "unconstitutional and discriminatory" (*Council for Better Education, Inc. v. Wilkinson,* 1988). He also outlined nine requirements for an efficient, equitable school system and in his final ruling defined an "efficient" system of school finance (*Council for Better Education, Inc. v. Wilkinson,* 1988). The decision stunned the leaders of the General Assembly and their attorney.

Two days following Corns's ruling, top legislative leaders, government officials, and their attorney met. House Speaker Donald Blandford and Senate president pro tempore "Eck" Rose emerged from the meeting saying they would appeal the decision to the Kentucky Supreme Court. Blandford was quoted as saying, "Even if I agreed with it—which I don't—I think we would want the highest opinion we could get" (Cropper, 1988). The supreme court heard arguments on the case on December 7, 1988. This was less than two months after Judge Corns's ruling. Defense attorney William Scent argued again that the General Assembly had provided for an efficient system and that the former trial court had violated the doctrine of the separation of powers. Combs countered by stressing the immorality of neglecting Kentucky's neediest children. Although no one could predict from the trial how the justices would rule, the media continued to advocate greater measures to improve the performance of Kentucky's schools. Also, in the interim, newly elected governor Wallace Wilkinson (1995, pp. 133–136) agreed with the plaintiffs and stepped up his own rhetoric about the need for change. Again the court took six months to make its final ruling.

On June 8, 1989, the second bombshell exploded. Saying that "the children of the poor and of the rich . . . must be given the same opportunity and access to an adequate education," Robert Stephens, chief justice of the supreme court, ruled that Kentucky's "entire public school system [was] unconstitutional." In his opinion Stephens endorsed the trial court's ruling, saying, "It is crystal clear that the General Assembly has fallen short of its duty to enact legislation to provide an efficient system of common schools" (*Rose v. Council,* 1989). Furthermore, the court ordered the General Assembly to create a new system of public education by the close of the 1990 legislative session.

Bert Combs, chief counsel for the plaintiffs, told an audience, "My clients asked for a thimble full and instead they got a bucket full" (Dove, 1991, p. 21). On June 8 the headline on the front page of *The (Louisville) Courier-Journal* proclaimed in bold, "Court's Sweeping Decision Orders State to Build New, Equitable School System" (Loftus, 1989, p. A1). There was unanimous agreement among the media, politicians, and the public that this was truly a landmark decision that had put the responsibility squarely on the shoulders of Kentucky's General Assembly. Immediately below the bold headline in *The Courier-Journal,* staff writer Bob Garrett (1989, pp. A1, A12) asked the question that was on the minds of politicians, educators, and citizens: "Will Kentucky seize the moment?" His front-page analysis reminded Kentucky's leaders that earlier efforts at reform had come up short. Would the supreme court's unprecedented ruling encourage unprecedented actions by the General Assembly?

Governor and Legislative Leaders Join Forces to Respond

On the day following the supreme court's official release of its decision, House Speaker Blandford, President Pro Tempore Rose of the Senate, and Governor Wilkinson met to determine their response. The meeting, as described by Wilkinson (1995), was "wide-ranging, conciliatory, and somber in the face of the enormous challenge before [them]" (pp. 199–201). Although the supreme court clearly gave the responsibility of recreating Kentucky's schools to the General Assembly, both Blandford and Rose agreed that it was essential for the governor to be a key player. After the meeting, they held a press conference. John Brock, superintendent of public instruction, joined the three men as they stood together in the rotunda of the capitol in a show of unity. Each pledged his commitment and support to the tremendous task before them (Wilkinson, 1995, pp. 199–201).

In their initial meeting Blandford, Rose, and Wilkinson had agreed that a joint executive-legislative task force would be responsible for designing a new plan; they knew the task was too important to leave in the hands of the people responsible for the existing system. To accomplish their plan they agreed to appoint a task force to do the work but made sure each of the three of them retained private veto power over any structures or processes the group proposed. They wanted their differences to be worked out behind closed doors to avoid any public debate of differences (Wilkinson, 1995, pp. 199–201). The group they created was named the Commonwealth Task Force on Education Reform, later called the Task Force on Education Reform.

After considerable discussion about the composition of the task force, they agreed the governor would appoint six members and that Blandford and Rose each would appoint eight members from the House and Senate. Wilkinson named his secretary of the cabinet, chief of staff, budget director, the secretary and deputy secretary of the education and humanities cabinet, and one additional member from the governor's administrative staff. Blandford and Rose appointed all the members of the House and Senate leadership, the chairs of the Education Committee and the

Appropriations and Revenue Committee, and the minority leaders of the House and Senate.

The Task Force on Education Reform held its first meeting on July 12, 1989, just thirty-four days after the supreme court ruling. The task force included three committees: curriculum, governance, and finance. Each of the committees was chaired jointly by House and Senate leaders. Blandford and Rose cochaired the combined task force. Each of the committees selected national consultants to present options and to guide their deliberations. The curriculum committee selected David Hornbeck, the governance committee selected Luvern Cunningham and Lila Carol, and the finance committee chose John Augenblick (Foster, 1999). The committees worked independently on their respective issues but shared working documents. The committees circulated working papers and conducted public hearings to obtain public reaction and comments. All three committees worked long hours right up to the 1990 legislative session, which began in January. The committees presented final reports to the combined task force in mid-February. Ideas, structures, and processes that the task force approved were translated into legislative language by the staff of the Legislative Research Commission. On March 7 the Task Force on Education Reform approved 946 pages of draft legislation. In its final form this legislation became House Bill 940 (KERA).

Governor's Office Provides Strong Reinforcement

Wallace Wilkinson was a populist governor who stunned his opponents and the political establishment when he won the Democratic primary election in May 1987. Early on, Wilkinson took up the challenge issued in a 1983 editorial in *The (Louisville) Courier-Journal*: "It's inconceivable that a legislature by itself could initiate a strong program of educational improvement. It's almost equally inconceivable that a majority of Kentuckians would march on Frankfort—at least verbally—and demand that a 'play it safe' governor or rudderless General Assembly raise their taxes if necessary in order to improve the schools. Without strong leadership, the field is likely to be left once more to those citizens who think the education system costs too much already" (Wilkinson, 1995, p. 131).

Wilkinson objected to the piecemeal reform process the General Assembly wanted to follow. Wilkinson thought that, rather than changing one program at a time, the whole system should be abolished and reconstructed. Although he could not articulate or communicate exactly how that new structure would look, Wilkinson's vision and rhetoric were clearly congruent with the position taken by Kentucky's courts in 1988 and 1989. To help him develop his vision for education, Governor Wilkinson appointed Jack Foster to be his secretary of the cabinet for education and the humanities. Foster was director of a private consulting firm in Lexington and had introduced school reform initiatives in Mississippi, where a friend of Wilkinson's was governor.

Wilkinson's first plan for reforming education, developed by Foster, proposed granting bonuses to schools that could demonstrate high levels of student achievement. The plan was described in a twelve-page document distributed to Kentuckians in February 1988 (Wilkinson, 1995, p. 141). The plan called for schools to report scores on standardized tests annually. High-performing schools would get cash rewards for their efforts. Wilkinson's staff estimated the cost at about $70 million per year. Because state revenues were in short supply and Wilkinson had promised not to increase taxes, he could not rouse the leadership of the General Assembly. They already considered the programs created in the earlier 1985 special session on education sufficient.

A bill laying out Wilkinson's plan was passed in the Senate and sent to the House. With directives from the Democratic leadership the bill died in a House committee. The failure of the House leaders to support the governor's plan set up a showdown between the governor and legislative leaders. Wilkinson threatened to call a special session on education. To lay the groundwork for such a session, he distributed another public document in the summer of 1988: a question-and-answer dialogue about his new plan for education in Kentucky (Office of the Governor, 1988). As Kentucky moved toward a potential 1989 special session, Wilkinson released two more documents under the title *A Plan to Restructure Schools in Kentucky.* One was a detailed framework and the other, proposed legislation (Wilkinson, 1989). Neither the education establishment, including the Kentucky Education Association, nor the political leaders in Kentucky gave Wilkinson's plan much attention. Something more had to happen.

In early 1989 legislative leaders organized an education summit in Lexington and invited about four hundred policymakers and educators to discuss the goals of education in Kentucky for the year 2000. The featured document of the two-day summit was *Working Paper on Educational Improvement—The Next Step!* (Kentucky General Assembly, 1988), the so-called Red Book. The Red Book was a compendium of programs for which various legislators and their constituencies were trying to gain support. At the front of the Red Book were eleven goals for the year 2000.

Without linking programs to goals, more than forty new and continuing initiatives were presented for consideration and support. The governor was invited to speak at the summit. In his remarks at the summit Wilkinson said, "Our schools need more money. I've never denied that. And I'm willing to spend more money on schools. I'm willing to find more money but not until we are willing to make a commitment to change the system so we can show people that they are truly paying for improvement. To put it bluntly, if we are not going to change the system, I'd rather spend less to be last than more to be last" (Wilkinson, 1995, p. 184). Wilkinson's vision for the education reform that was to come was very much on target. However, apparently neither he nor Secretary Foster possessed the political skills or strategies to sell this vision to educators or politicians.

To launch an offensive against the continued efforts by legislative leaders to simply fund and mandate more programs as a strategy to improve public education, Wilkinson created the Council on School Performance Standards on February 16, 1989. The council included two chief executives from business, three state school board members, three school administrators, two classroom teachers, Foster, and Superintendent Brock (Wilkinson, 1995, p. 181; Council on School Performance Standards, 1989). The group was chaired by J. D. Nichols, a real estate developer from Louisville. The mission of the council was straightforward: to determine what students in grades K–12 should know and be able to do and how their learning should be assessed. The Council on School Performance Standards was to complete its work by August and report its findings and recommendations to the governor, the State Board for Elementary and Secondary Education, the Kentucky Council on Higher Education, and members of the General Assembly. The council employed a staff of professionals and created five working task forces: elementary school, middle school, high school, vocational education, and assessment of student learning. I served as executive director.

The council selected task force members from the ranks of elementary, secondary, and higher education based on demonstrated leadership and expertise. The council initially conducted six focus groups of business leaders, local government officials, school administrators, teachers, parents, and students in six geographical locations across the state to determine the skills high school graduates in the year 2000 would need to be successful. Based on ten themes that emerged from the focus groups, the council conducted a twenty-two-minute telephone interview with a scientific sample of Kentucky citizens across the state (Council on School Performance Standards, 1989, p. 1). In addition, the assessment task force members employed a state testing official from North Carolina, a measurement consultant from New York, and a test developer from Iowa to help them address how learning should be assessed in Kentucky.

Three months after the council's five task forces began their work, the Kentucky Supreme Court issued its ruling and told the Kentucky General Assembly to re-create a system of public education that was both equitable and efficient. The supreme court ruling gave new meaning and purpose to the council's work. It had been unclear how the council would resolve the struggle between the governor and the legislative leaders over reforming education. Now the court's decision and mandate provided a clear need that the council and its task forces could fulfill. All five task forces worked diligently through the spring and summer of 1989 and completed their report in September.

The report of the Council on School Performance Standards (1989, pp. 2–5) contained four key recommendations:

Kentucky should adopt a new common core of learning for elementary, middle, high, and vocational schools with an emphasis on the application of basic skills and knowledge and on student performance. The council further recommended that the common core of learning should have six goals. The goals recommended in the report later became the six learning goals named in KERA.

Kentucky should launch a major effort to assess student performance beyond what can be measured by paper-and-pencil tests. The council specifically recommended establishing a statewide school assessment plan to ensure local school accountability for the common core of learning and creating a statewide support system to strengthen ongoing assessments in local schools.

Kentucky should encourage and support innovative efforts to adopt new professional roles, organizational structures, and institutional strategies that promote student achievement of the common core of learning. Specific recommendations included new roles for principals and teachers in teamwork and decision making, school-based management that encourages professional judgment and accountability, greater parent involvement, greater use of all forms of technology, and greater use of interdisciplinary teams to plan and deliver instruction. The council gave specific recommendations for strengthened local student assessment programs that provide current information on each student relative to the common core of learning and for school structures and strategies that guarantee successful experiences for every student.

Kentucky should initiate two intensive long-range development efforts that support the new common core of learning. Specifically, the council recommended the development of assessment instruments that measure student performance related to the six goals of the common core of learning and a program to provide incentives and assistance for curriculum reform in local schools. Furthermore, the council recommended a six-year time frame for the development of assessment instruments that address student performance.

The Council on School Performance Standards presented its report and recommendations to the curriculum committee of the legislative Task Force on Education Reform on September 23, 1989. However, more than a month earlier David Hornbeck, chief consultant to the curriculum committee of the task force, requested drafts of the council's report to review for his recommendations for curriculum reform. If one examines the specific recommendations of the Council on School Performance Standards and compares these to the wording of House Bill 940, it is evident that the work of the council made significant contributions to the eventual recommendations of the curriculum committee of the legislative task force and to House Bill 940. The six goals for schools, the design of a statewide assessment system, and the six-year development schedule came directly from recommendations in the council's report. Thus what began in February as Wallace Wilkinson's new strategy to advance his school incentive plan became a major resource and contribution to the work of the legislative task force—a joint effort between the governor's office and the leaders of the General Assembly to re-create Kentucky's public schools.

Governor and Legislative Leaders Compromise to Pass KERA

The governance, finance, and curriculum committees and their consultants worked through the fall of 1989 and into the 1990 session of the Kentucky General Assembly. The governance committee recommended a new structure for the state board of education, an appointed commissioner of education, school councils for local decision making, and an education professional standards board. The finance committee tested new models of funding schools that would narrow the resource gap between poorer and richer districts of the state. A new program, Support Education Excellence in Kentucky, was to replace Kentucky's old minimum foundation and power equalization programs. The curriculum committee held three days of statewide hearings on the report of the Council on School Performance Standards. The primary purpose was to collect input and reactions from stakeholders on the recommended common core of learning, the statewide assessment plan, and school accountability for learning.

As task force committees agreed on specific elements of the new design for schools in Kentucky, Legislative Research Commission staff crafted the structures and strategies into legal language that eventually became House Bill 940. Although the legislative session officially began in early January, the final report of the legislative task force was not adopted until mid-February, halfway through the 1990 legislative session. On March 12 House Bill 940, which included 907 pages of text, was filed as an official response to the supreme court's order to re-create Kentucky public schools. Although the governance, finance, and curriculum components came from different committees, the members of those committees developed mutual feelings of trust and an acceptance of all the work. The governor's office and the leadership of the House and Senate felt a sense of accomplishment over the education reform act they had helped to create.

But House Bill 940 was only half of the battle. Now the General Assembly had to find a way to pay for the new structures, processes, and programs described in the new school reform law. Budget experts in the Kentucky Department of Education, the legislative research commission, and the governor's office projected the cost of KERA to be about $1.2 billion per biennium above existing funding levels for Kentucky schools (Wilkinson, 1995, p. 190). Throughout the 1980s the people of Kentucky had been told the coffers for funding new programs were empty, and Wilkinson had been adamant about not raising taxes. If KERA was to be implemented, new revenues had to be generated. Early proposals from legislators included an increase in the state sales tax and a use tax that everyone would pay. Wilkinson (1995, pp. 246–247) strongly believed sales tax was a regressive tax that penalized low-income families. Instead he proposed a plan to reform the state property tax, adjust personal income tax, broaden the sales tax to include services, and increase taxes on cigarettes. Wilkinson's tax plan dug deeply into the pockets of special interest groups. The services and cigarette industries are among the most powerful in Frankfort. At one point in the public debate over how to fund education, Wilkinson (1995) said at a press conference:

> This debate is not about good times. It's not about parties. It's not about receptions. It's not about the good old boys over at Flynn's [a Frankfort eatery favored by politicians and lobbyists]. It's not about

schmoozing around in friendly relationships. This fight is about and between the daddies and the mammas who take their children fishing on Saturday morning and the lobbyists who take legislators golfing on Wednesday afternoon. The fight is about whether you are going to be on the side of special interests or going to be on the side of working men and women in this Commonwealth. (p. 245)

The press accused the governor of deliberately picking a fight with legislators, but these comments truly represented how he felt about increasing a tax that would get more money from Kentucky's common folks.

The governor pushed the Democratic leadership to support his plan, but it quickly became clear that the executive and legislative branches of government had reached a serious impasse that threatened any hopes to fund what House Bill 940 promised. In the chambers of the House legislators began talking about "going it alone," but veterans of Kentucky politics knew the vote for the sweeping changes proposed in KERA would be close even with all the help the governor could muster. House leaders caucused and agreed to make one last effort to convince the governor to change his mind about the one cent increase in the sales tax. The candidate chosen to accomplish this mission was Greg Stumbo, the eastern Kentucky floor leader of the House and a friend of Wilkinson's. What really happened in that meeting with the governor only Stumbo and Wilkinson will ever know, but in the end they struck a compromise. Wilkinson agreed not to oppose the increase in the sales tax in exchange for additional money for road repair and community development. Both men acknowledged that the compromise would never have been reached had they not believed the future of Kentucky's children was at stake. To this day sources close to the former governor say that his concession to raise the sales tax was and is against his strongest beliefs (Jack Foster, personal communication, September 1, 1999).

On the very next day the leaders of both the House and Senate were summoned to the governor's office to secure the compromise. Although there could be no absolute guarantees, all agreed to work diligently for passage of House Bill 940 and the accompanying tax package. Even with this compromise and joint support for KERA, everyone knew the vote in the House would be close. Legislators from the two wealthiest school districts, Louisville and Lexington, were not sure how they would benefit from giving more money to districts in eastern Kentucky. At the same time, legislators from Appalachian districts, where public education is the largest employer, did not like the restrictions on nepotism and the stronger measures for accountability in the law. Although the reform bill provided more money for teachers' salaries, it severely limited any involvement of teachers in local school board elections.

By the time House Bill 940 was scheduled for debate in the House, fifty-seven amendments had been attached (*Kentucky Legislative Record,* 1990). House leaders had strategized and rehearsed for this debate—the most critical performance of their entire political career. Greg Stumbo, representing Floyd County, would introduce House Bill 940. Kenny Rapier, the majority whip, would present arguments for the bill and try to defeat unfriendly amendments. House Speaker Donald Blandford believed he had fifty-eight of the one hundred votes needed to stop debate and call for a vote when needed. After an opening speech, Stumbo presented amendments to House Bill 940 one by one, beginning with those brought by members who most needed to be heard to gain support for the total package. Rapier had prepared arguments explaining why each amendment would be an unwise addition to the original bill. To keep their end of the bargain with the governor and keep the reform package intact, legislators had to defeat all amendments that would threaten the integrity or passage of the original legislation. The floor debate was proceeding as planned, with Speaker Blandford masterfully managing the debate.

Then, in a surprise development, Representative Pete Worthington, a Democrat, attached an amendment to reduce the requirement that poorer school districts collect more property taxes. House leaders knew this development meant losing all support for KERA from Lexington and Louisville, dooming the entire legislative package. Blandford telephoned Stumbo on the floor of the House, and Stumbo called a twenty-minute recess. During the recess House leaders made a heroic effort to persuade their colleagues to defeat the amendment they had just passed. A call went out for anyone who could help "bail water" out of the sinking ship. House leaders told Worthington they would recall his amendment and that this time he must not object. After the recess the damaging amendment was recalled and defeated. As Representative Louie Mack, a Democrat from Lexington, put it, the legislators then "put the train back on the track" (Howington, Jennings, & Wilson, 1990).

After more than three hours of sometimes hostile debate, the House considered thirty-four amendments and approved fourteen. At that point Blandford decided the debate had gone on long enough. Because the remaining amendments were hostile to the bill, he called for a vote on House Bill 940. It passed, fifty-eight to forty-two (Howington, Jennings, & Wilson, 1990). But it left a number of very angry Republicans without an opportunity to have their voices heard. Republican legislators, and even some Democrats, accused Blandford of demagoguery, but many supporters of KERA called it his finest hour. Regardless of how it was judged, the House had just passed a comprehensive legislation package that would change forever the way schools were operated in Kentucky.

On March 29 the Senate considered several additional amendments and voted thirty to eight to support House Bill 940 and the $1.3 billion tax increase over the next two years. On the following day the House gave its final approval to all changes made by the Senate. On the floor of the House, Stumbo ended his speech to his fellow legislators with these words:

> When you look at the part of this state that I come from, and the fact that kids all too often start out behind in life and all they do is get farther behind, and I think that what we have a chance to do today is to see that that never happens again—that no child in Kentucky will ever have to look back and say that he or she didn't receive the full educational opportunity that he or she is entitled to by the Constitution of this state.
>
> Mr. Speaker, I move you sir that the House concur in all Senate amendments and that we treat all Senate amendments as one amendment on concurrence. (Stroud, 1990)

There was an immediate and sustained standing ovation.

To this day the most active players in the development and passage of KERA say they can't believe that anything so comprehensive, so bold, and so expensive could have made it through the twists and turns of Kentucky politics. It is all the more amazing when considering the historically low priority Kentucky placed on public education. Ten years later the vision of ordinary people performing extraordinary levels of public service may have faded from our collective consciousness. But the legacy of their achievements endures. Some had vision, some contributed their expertise, some showed their persistence against all odds. But all showed courage to do what was right for Kentucky's children and their future.

REFERENCES

Bureau of the Census, U.S. Department of Commerce. (1985). *Statistical abstract of the United States 1986*. Washington, DC: Author.

Bush lauds Kentucky for efforts to reform schools. (1990, April 5). *Lexington Herald-Leader*, p. A8.

Chellgren, M. (Associated Press). (1985, November 21). Sixty-six school districts sue state over funding for education. *Lexington Herald-Leader*, p. A1.

Combs, B. T. (1991). *Creative constitutional law: The Kentucky school reform law.* Lexington, KY: Prichard Committee for Academic Excellence.

Council for Better Education, Inc. v. Collins, No. 85-CI-1759, filed November 20, 1985 in Franklin Circuit Court. (Franklin Circuit Court, KY, May 31, 1988).

Council for Better Education, Inc. v. Wilkinson, No. 85-CI-1759 [Findings of Fact, Conclusions of Law, and Judgment] (Franklin Cir., May 31, 1988).

Council on School Performance Standards. (1989). *Preparing Kentucky youth for the next century: What students should know and be able to do and how learning should be assessed: Vol. 1. Executive summary, recommendations, and technical report.* Frankfort, KY: Author.

Cropper, C. M. (1988, June 3). Legislators to appeal school ruling; court's authority in case questioned. *The (Louisville) Courier-Journal,* p. A1.

Dove, R. G., Jr. (1991). *Acorns in a mountain pool: The role of litigation, law and lawyers in Kentucky education reform.* Lexington, KY: Prichard Committee for Academic Excellence.

Foster, J. D. (1999). *Redesigning public education: The Kentucky experience.* Lexington, KY: Diversified Services.

Garrett, B. (1989, June 8). Will Kentucky seize the moment to improve schools? *The (Louisville) Courier-Journal,* pp. A1, A12.

Howington, P., Jennings, M., & Wilson, R. (1990, March 22). House passes reform bill after heated debate. *The (Louisville) Courier-Journal,* p. A10.

Jennings, M. (1990, April 12). School reform and tax bill becomes law. *Louisville Courier Journal,* p. A1.

Kentucky General Assembly, Interim Joint Committee on Education. (1988). *Working paper on educational improvement—The next step!* Frankfort: Author.

Kentucky Legislative Record. (1990, March 21).

Loftus, T. (1989, June 8). Kentucky's entire system is unconstitutional. *Louisville Courier Journal,* pp. A1, A3

Office of the Governor. (1988). *A plan to restructure schools in Kentucky.* Frankfurt, KY: Author.

Office of the Governor. (1988). *Q.A.: Improving Kentucky schools, a conversation with Governor Wallace G. Wilkinson.* Frankfort, KY: Author.

Rose v. Council for Better Education, Inc., 790 S.W.2d 186 (Ky. 1989).

Roser, M. A. (1986, February 9). Kentucky suit aimed at helping poor school districts. *Lexington Herald-Leader,* p. A1.

Starting over. (1990, April 8). *The New York Times,* Section 4A, p. 35.

Stroud, J. S. (1990, March 30). Education reform sent to Governor. *Lexington Herald-Leader,* p. A8.

Stroud, J. S. (1990, April 12). Governor signs historic education bill. *The Lexington Herald Leader,* p. A1.

Walker, R. (1990, April 4). Lawmakers in Kentucky approve landmark school reform bill. *Education Week, 9* (28), 1, 34–35.

Wilkinson, W. G. (1989). *A plan to restructure schools in Kentucky.* Frankfort, KY: Office of the Governor.

Wilkinson, W. G. (1995). *You can't do that, Governor!* Lexington, KY: Wallace's Publishing.

2

RESOURCE EQUITY AND EDUCATIONAL ADEQUACY

Jacob E. Adams Jr.

EVERYONE STOOD as the justices of the Kentucky Supreme Court entered the room. Robed in black, carrying sheaves of paper, the justices stood before their high-backed, wood and leather chairs, arranged in a straight row across the dais.

"Open court," instructed the chief justice, Robert J. Stephens.

"*Oyez! Oyez!*" intoned the clerk. "Silence is commanded for the justices of the supreme court of Kentucky while they are sitting. All those having pleas to make or causes to prosecute, draw nigh and ye shall be heard. This court is now in session. God save the commonwealth. God save this honorable court."

The case before the high court that day in 1988 was *Rose v. Council for Better Education, Inc.* Known then as "Kentucky's school finance case," *Rose* would come to be regarded as among the most sweeping school finance decisions in U.S. history and as the progenitor of the nation's boldest education reform legislation—the Kentucky Education Reform Act of 1990 (KERA).

At the moment, however, John Rose, president pro tempore of the Kentucky Senate, and Donald Blandford, Speaker of the House of Representatives, were appealing a lower court's ruling that the Kentucky school finance system was unconstitutional. Counsel for the appellants (defendants) and the appellees (plaintiffs) sat at hardwood desks, awaiting instructions from the chief justice. Each side had one hour to present its arguments. Warning lights at the podium would help speakers keep track of time. This case was particularly important. Indeed, as the chief justice would soon write on behalf of the court, "[W]e are ever mindful of the immeasurable worth of education to our state and its citizens, especially to its young people" (*Rose v. Council,* 1989, p. 189).

William Scent, counsel for the state, approached the podium. He argued against the trial court's ruling that Kentucky's school finance system was unconstitutional. He rejected the facts and supposed constitutional violations that supported the lower court's conclusions. Moreover, he devised legal rationales to derail the case: plaintiffs failed to state a claim against defendants, the court had no jurisdiction because the subject matter was "political," plaintiffs lacked standing to bring the action, local school boards had no legal authority to sue the state, the class action filed on behalf of public school students was improper.

In his turn Bert Combs too addressed the justices from the richly polished podium. With white hair made brighter by his dark blue suit, half-glasses perched on his nose, the former Kentucky governor and federal judge, now counsel for the plaintiffs, rebutted Scent's arguments. He reviewed the plaintiffs' claims, the violations of constitutional principle they represented, and the significance of the case.

But it was Combs's associate, Debra Dawahare, who turned the discussion back to the inequitable and inadequate school conditions that brought them to court that day. "No one," she asserted, "can get around the fact that some kids in poor schools are going to school in trailers, they're using lavatories without doors, they [couldn't] take advanced courses if they wanted to, and they're studying routine science courses in things that resemble some kind of medieval alchemist's lab" (Brown, 1989, Court Video Reel 3, at 2616).

Refereeing the legal parley, justices frequently interrupted the attorneys, probing and challenging the arguments, exploring the legal basis on which their eventual decision would turn. At this point in the judicial process, however, no one—not the plaintiffs, defendants, attorneys, experts, or observers—could have anticipated the scope and importance of the supreme court decision that was about to be handed down.

Constitutional Challenge

The case before the court that day originated in a complaint filed in the Franklin Circuit Court in 1985 by sixty-six school districts, seven local boards of education, and twenty-two public school students, collectively known as the Council for Better Education. Plaintiffs argued that school funding in Kentucky was *inequitable* and *inadequate*—inequitable because some school districts had much more money than others to support education and inadequate because of Kentucky's low level of educational achievement. As a result, plaintiffs charged, the state system of school funding failed to provide equal educational opportunities for Kentucky's children. Moreover, that system was not "efficient," as required by the education clause of the state constitution. Attorneys argued that because the school finance system failed to comply with the constitutional requirement for efficiency, the system should be declared unconstitutional and the General Assembly should be directed to enact new legislation to make the system sound. Judge Ray Corns, presiding at trial, would decide whether the facts of the case supported the plaintiffs' charges and what remedy, if any, the law required.

An Inequitable School Finance System

Evidence at trial demonstrated that property-rich school districts—those with a relatively large property tax base—raised as much as fifteen times the amount of funding locally as did property-poor districts. Combined state and local education funding differed between rich and poor districts by as much as one and a half times, and this 50 percent discrepancy amounted to a difference of more than $23,400 per classroom. Evidence further indicated that funding discrepancies of this magnitude affected educational quality. Poor school districts, for example, offered fewer and "markedly deficient" courses, operated larger classes and smaller libraries, employed less qualified teachers, and held classes in dilapidated buildings, some of them constructed by the depression-era Works Progress Administration.

Plaintiffs also showed a statistical correlation between school district wealth and student achievement, meaning that students in rich districts tended to have higher achievement scores whereas those in poor districts had lower scores. School district differences aside, evidence also portrayed Kentucky as having one of the most severely deficient educational systems in the nation, with high rates of adult illiteracy and the highest number (forty-six) and percentage (26 percent) of undereducated counties in the country. In the judge's words, Kentucky suffered from "an extreme case of educational malnutrition" (*Council v. Wilkinson,* 1988, p. 11).

After examining the evidence, Judge Corns concluded that the quality of education in a school district is contingent primarily on the money it has to invest in education. "While marginal differences in revenue per student may not create undue educational disadvantage," he wrote, "it is apparent that revenue differentials as large as those which exist between the more affluent and the poor districts in Kentucky create an inefficient and unequal system of common schools" (*Council v. Wilkinson*, 1988, p. 11). As a result, Kentucky's school finance system bore "no rational relationship to the State's duty to provide an efficient system throughout the Commonwealth" (*Council v. Wilkinson*, 1988, p. 7). That efficient system, the judge determined, required substantial uniformity, substantial equality of financial resources, and substantial equality of educational opportunity for all students (*Council v. Wilkinson*, 1988). Kentucky's method of funding schools fell short of these criteria. Furthermore, the system "invidiously discriminated" against a substantial percentage of students on the basis of their place of residence (*Council v. Wilkinson*, 1988, p. 14). The judge concluded, "This is an unnatural distinction with no reasonable relationship to the state's duty to provide all Common School students with a substantially equal, free public education" (*Council v. Wilkinson*, 1988, p. 15). Kentucky's school finance system was unconstitutional, and the legislature was directed to establish a new, efficient system as soon as reasonably possible.

Kentucky in Perspective

At this juncture, pending review by the state supreme court, Kentucky's school finance case looked much like equity cases in other states. Since the early 1970s, courts in forty-three states have heard equity challenges similar to the one brought by the Council for Better Education. In nineteen of these cases plaintiffs won at the state supreme court level, and finance systems were overturned. Courts upheld another twelve finance systems. Plaintiffs lost before reaching the supreme court in nine states but subsequently filed modified actions. As of 1999, supreme courts had yet to rule in three other suits (Minorini & Sugarman, 1999).

In all of these cases plaintiffs made similar complaints: that state school finance systems deliver more money to some school districts than to others. Why? Funding disparities arise because states support education with a combination of state and local tax revenues. Local revenues come primarily from property taxes, but property tax bases in school districts vary widely. A higher tax base allows a school district to raise more money, with equal or even lower tax rates, than its property-poor neighbor. Such a disparity disadvantages a poor district's students and taxpayers, the former through lower revenues and the latter through higher tax rates. If a state's school finance formula—which dictates how much money school districts receive, how much of that money comes from state and local sources, and how much leeway school districts have to tax and spend above the state-determined amount—does not compensate for wealth variations among school districts, funding disparities result. Inequitable systems deny students equal protection under the law, or they violate education clauses that require "substantially uniform," "efficient," or similar distributions of tax revenue. In this regard Kentucky's school finance case was typical of its predecessors.

Shortfalls of the School System

The Kentucky Supreme Court agreed that the state's education funding was inequitable and inefficient. The chief justice wrote, "[T]he overall effect of appellants' evidence is a virtual concession that Kentucky's system of common schools is underfunded and inadequate; is fraught with inequalities and inequities . . . is not uniform among the districts in educational opportunities" (*Rose v. Council,* 1989, p. 197). But what did this conclusion mean legally?

The central legal issue in the case revolved around the court's interpretation of the constitutional term *efficient.* In defining this term, the Kentucky court broke new ground in school finance law. An efficient system of common schools, the court ruled, is the sole responsibility of the General Assembly, is free to all, is available to all, is substantially uniform throughout the state, and provides equal educational opportunities to all children, regardless of location or economic circumstances. Also according to the court the premise for the existence of common schools is that all children in Kentucky have a constitutional right to an adequate education and to funding that is sufficient to provide each child with an adequate education. The supreme court further determinded that an adequate education develops seven capacities (*Rose v. Council,* 1989):

- Sufficient oral and written communication skills to enable students to function in a complex and rapidly changing civilization
- Sufficient knowledge of economic, social, and political systems to enable students to make informed choices
- Sufficient understanding of governmental processes to enable students to understand the issues that affect their community, state, and nation
- Sufficient self-knowledge and knowledge of their mental and physical wellness
- Sufficient grounding in the arts to enable students to appreciate their cultural and historical heritage

○ Sufficient training or preparation for advanced training in either academic or vocational fields to enable all students to choose and pursue life work intelligently

○ Sufficient levels of academic or vocational skills to enable students to compete favorably in academics or in the job market with their counterparts from surrounding states

In short the supreme court defined an efficient education as substantially uniform, equal in opportunity, and adequate, with adequacy defined as student knowledge and skills in prescribed areas. No court before had so clearly defined an adequate education, nor had any court so clearly articulated a citizen's right to an adequate education anchored in learning.

Having defined its guiding principles, the Kentucky Supreme Court ruled on the one legal issue in the case, deciding that the legislature had failed to establish an efficient system of common schools. Thus the court declared the state's *entire* elementary and secondary school system—not just the school finance system—to be inefficient and unconstitutional. In the court's words, "This decision applies to the entire sweep of the system—all its parts and parcels. . . . the whole gamut of the common school system in Kentucky" (*Rose v. Council*, 1989, p. 215). With this judgment the Kentucky high court launched the state into the realm of new law, new policy, and new opportunity.

Policy Response

"This is the first time in the history of Kentucky," noted Bert Combs, "when all three branches of government have attempted to do something about the school system" (Brown, 1989, Reel 2 at 5235). In declaring Kentucky's educational system to be unconstitutional, the state supreme court also directed the General Assembly to create a new network of common schools. Within a year policymakers had completed their work on KERA, which restructured the school finance system in Kentucky. In addition to restructuring the school finance formula, KERA provided new money to support school construction projects and it created grants-in-aid programs to support its larger learning goals—programs such as after-school tutoring, teacher professional development, and family resource centers.

Regarding school finance, the text of KERA states that the intention of the General Assembly is to "assure substantially equal public school educational opportunities . . . but not to limit nor to prevent any school district from providing educational services and facilities beyond those assured by the state supported program. The program shall provide for an efficient system of public schools throughout the Commonwealth . . . and for the manner of distribution of the public school fund among the districts" (*Kentucky Revised Statutes,* 1996, p. 701). To give a practical effect to these ambitions, the General Assembly created a new school funding formula known as Support Education Excellence in Kentucky (SEEK). This new formula encompassed the whole legislative response to the court's demand for greater equity, equal educational opportunity, and adequacy in Kentucky's school system.

SEEK provides a state-guaranteed minimum amount of funding, called the "base guarantee," for every student in the state. SEEK then adjusts the base guarantee by providing additional money to assist economically disadvantaged and exceptional students, to support students whose health impairments require hospitalization or convalescence, and to reimburse school districts for the cost of transporting students who live a mile or more from their schools. In 1990–91, SEEK's first year, the base guarantee equaled $2,305; by 1998–99 the base guarantee had risen to $2,839 (Office of Education Accountability, 1999).

SEEK also controls state and local contributions to education funding by requiring that every school district levy a uniform tax ($.30 per $100 of assessed property value). Because of differences in school district property wealth, some districts raise more money than others through this uniform tax. The state's contribution to education funding makes up the difference between a district's adjusted base guarantee and its local contribution. In this way state support varies according to school district wealth. Rich districts receive less state funding and poor districts more, which equalizes the total support for education.

School districts that wish to spend more than their adjusted base guarantee have two options. Under a program known as Tier 1 they can increase their allotted amount by as much as 15 percent through additional local taxes. To ensure that these extra funds do not have an unbalancing effect on the whole system, the state also provides "equalization funds" to poor school districts that participate in the Tier 1 program. Equalization funds guarantee that all districts in this program will raise the same amount of money with an equal tax effort regardless of their tax base. A similar program, Tier 2, allows school districts that want to raise more money still to raise up to 30 percent more revenue, again through additional local taxes. This option requires a vote of the local electorate, and no equalization funds are available. Tier 2 effectively puts a cap on total state and local revenue, allowing variation in total funding across districts of up to 49.5 percent.

From a national perspective, KERA's school finance provisions did not break new ground. The revised formula used known strategies and policies to address specific shortcomings of the old finance system. The base guarantee established a minimum level of funding for all children. Formula adjustments provided extra money for special student needs. The required local tax equalized effort among taxpayers while state support, varying with school district wealth, equalized funding across school districts, within allowable bounds. Categorical grants supported curricular programs. Revenue options tailored spending to local concerns, again within allowable bounds. Like other public policies, KERA's finance provisions attempted to balance competing demands and interests.

Compared with other components of KERA, school finance reform proved relatively simple to implement. For the most part, policy changes required adaptations in an arithmetic formula controlled by the state. School board members adjusted tax rates as needed and chose whether to add Tier 1 and Tier 2 monies. (Forty-seven percent of districts operated with tax rates lower than the KERA-imposed minimum and so were required by statute to increase their effort.) Nowhere was finance implementation as uncertain or as problematic as attempts to implement governance and curricular initiatives that required changes in individuals' behavior. The central question regarding Kentucky's new school finance policy was whether SEEK would be able to effect the improvements required by the court.

Lessons from Practice

"You're suggesting that we tell [the General Assembly] to 'do better,' and that's not much of a remedy," complained Judge Leibson, associate justice of the Kentucky Supreme Court, hearing arguments in *Rose*.

"To devise a remedy that works," responded Debra Dawahare, counsel for the appellees. "And I believe that remedy can only be tested by its results" (Brown, 1989, Reel 3 at 1330).

In 1997 the Kentucky General Assembly convened the Task Force on Public Education. With work divided among a series of issue groups, task force members set about to determine what progress had been made on education reform. The Finance Issue Group examined a number of practices but focused particularly on SEEK. Was it working? According to the group, yes. In fact, they were "tempted to declare victory on the issue of 'equitable' funding for school districts" (Task Force on Public Education, 1997, p. 2).

Postreform analyses of school finance practice by the Office of Education Accountability (1999)—the state's education oversight agency—and independent researchers (Adams & White, 1997) substantiate this victory to a degree. However, the supreme court defined an efficient public school system as uniform, equal in opportunity, *and* adequate. Kentucky has made clear progress on uniformity and opportunity; it has made little progress on adequacy. With advances in equity but not adequacy, Kentucky's new school finance system resembles an unbalanced ledger, with the court's high standard on adequacy defining the state's unmet liabilities.

Among its strengths and weaknesses school finance practice in Kentucky reveals five broadly applicable lessons for reformers:

○ Finance policy can compensate for variations in school district tax capacity and effort, improving system equity (uniformity) and opportunity.

○ Finance policy creates both opportunities and constraints for educators, which need to be managed.

○ Both technical and political considerations affect finance policy's success.

○ Education reform requires a new school finance accounting.

○ Adequacy requires more than marginal increases in school funding; it requires an entirely new approach to school finance.

Greater Uniformity and More Equal Opportunity

With all the attention given to inequities in Kentucky's school finance system, the obvious postreform finance question is whether the policy changes create more equity in education funding. How uniform is the new system?

At some point all the complaints, legal rationales, judicial opinions, and policy decisions about equity reduce to a set of statistical measures that indicate exactly how much equity exists in a school finance system. The statistics track equity improvements from three perspectives: the funding differences between the richest and poorest school districts, the distribution of education funding across all districts, and the comparative funding levels across categories of school districts grouped by property wealth.

At its widest the range of education funding between rich and poor school districts in Kentucky narrowed by 22 percent. If the upper and lower extremes of the range are omitted, as school finance analysts recommend, then the "restricted range" comparison shows that, before reform, those in the ninety-fifth percentile of funding received 77 percent more money than those in the fifth percentile, but only 38 percent more afterward. In both range calculations equity improved (Adams & White, 1997).

When all school districts are included in the equity calculation, the state again appears to be more equitable. One can visualize this kind of improvement by imagining a bell-shaped curve. In an inequitable school system the bell shape would be wide and low, as if someone had flattened it, indicating that school districts receive widely differing amounts of funding. In an equitable system the bell shape would be narrow and high, indicating that school districts receive similar amounts of money. Short of truly equal funding, equity is a judgment call. School finance experts have defined an equitable system as one in which two-thirds of the bell shape fall within 10 percent of the average funding level, represented by the vertical centerline of the bell (Odden & Picus, 1992). Two-thirds of Kentucky's funding distribution fell within 22 percent of the average before reform but within only 11 percent after reform, approaching the narrow, high shape that represents equity (Adams & White, 1997).

Another way to examine the equity impact of school finance reform is to array finance data by wealth quintiles. Wealth quintiles group students according to the amount of property wealth available to them. Each quintile contains approximately 20 percent of a state's students. In a uniform system the quintile analysis would show no variation in education funding across the quintiles and no discernible pattern in funding levels, up or down, across the quintiles. Before reform, students in Kentucky's quintile 5, the richest, received 1.63 times as much funding as students in quintile 1 received. Furthermore, students in each quintile received more funding than their peers in the quintiles below, indicating that variation in revenue was related to wealth. This gap narrowed by 31 percent after reform. Variation existed after reform, but within a narrower range, indicating more uniformity across the system (Adams & White, 1997).

The Kentucky Supreme Court ruled that an efficient school finance system required more equity but also more equal educational opportunity. In school finance equal opportunity is measured in terms of the statistical relationship between education funding and school district property wealth. If a relationship exists, students receive unequal educational opportunities—different amounts of money—simply because of where they live, an unconstitutional situation. Kentucky's new school finance policies cut the relationship between funding and district property wealth in half, weakening the link between revenue and wealth. Thus Kentucky's new finance policies also produced more equal educational opportunity (Adams & White, 1997).

From these perspectives Kentucky's school finance system exhibits more equity and educational opportunity today than it did before reform. The lesson here is that school finance policies can improve equity and educational opportunity. This lesson is notable because conventional wisdom from school finance studies of the 1970s and 1980s held that finance reforms produced few substantial improvements in system equity (Berne, 1988).

Opportunities and Constraints

Besides improving equity and equal opportunity, Kentucky's school finance reform also increased education funding, enabling some school districts to make new investments in educational programs. How did funding change?

During the first three years of reform implementation, education funding increased by approximately 34 percent (19 percent when adjusted for inflation). With new revenue available, school districts increased spending across most functions—the accounting categories that denote what spending supports, such as instruction, administration, and maintenance. Interestingly, resource allocation patterns—the balance among different spending categories—were virtually identical before and after reform. Salaries went up, but not as fast as spending overall. Most reform dollars appear to have been devoted to instruction (Adams, 1997).

What did reform dollars buy? There is little systematic evidence on this count. One early study (Adams, 1994) provided an initial look at spending in high- and low-wealth school districts. In rich and poor districts alike, reform dollars addressed long-standing needs for classroom supports, particularly instructional materials, technology, and professional development. They compensated teachers, and they funded new categorical programs in extended school services, preschool for at-risk youngsters, and family resource and youth service centers. These opportunities existed for districts regardless of size, location, demographics, or wealth. In fact, postreform changes in district expenditures were not measured as much in terms of spending increases and declines as by the magnitude of increases.

Nevertheless, administrators in these districts variously portrayed the new formula as providing opportunities *and* constraints. For example, the superintendent in a low-wealth district remarked that KERA provided "an opportunity to have resources to do things for kids here that I could only dream about before. I kept telling myself what we're gong to be able to do, and I've not been disappointed" (Adams, 1994, p. 383). In contrast, his counterpart in a high-wealth district argued that the new funding formula was "pulling us down and backwards as fast as you're bringing other people up. The formula hobbles us and will not let us grow comparable to our wealth" (Adams, 1994, p. 383). Their different perceptions about opportunities and constraints in Kentucky's new school finance system led one superintendent to conclude that "you're going to see . . . more of a gulf developing between the haves and have nots, in [terms of] attitudes and ability to work together" (Adams, 1994, p. 383).

The lesson here is that policy changes create winners and losers, whether real or perceived. Policies have consequences. They elevate some values over others; they allocate benefits and costs. A state's constitutional responsibility to operate an equitable public school system may prevent some localities from using the full range of resources available to them to support education. Unintended policy consequences or negative perceptions that diminish local enthusiasm can increase conflict and negatively affect reform progress, particularly when reform requires sustained support and effort over a number of years. Whether constraints are grounded in fact or image, they become part of the climate of reform and may be worthy of state policy attention.

Technical and Political Choices

The benefits of Kentucky's school finance reform—more equity and opportunity—came as a direct result of policy changes enacted by the legislature, as did the remaining inequities. The gains and limitations of finance reform arose from the balancing of technical and political considerations that characterize policy development in school finance.

Before reform, state education funding failed to account for variations in school district property wealth. Allocating state aid to school districts without regard to wealth had an unbalancing effect on the whole system. The policy challenge in school finance reform was to make the distribution of state aid more sensitive to local wealth so that the higher a school district's property wealth, the less state aid it received. Legislators used foundation programs, guaranteed tax bases, required local efforts, and other school finance technology to craft a policy solution to this problem. Yet local funding options still allowed 49.5 percent variation in education funding. Additional, marginal gains in equity could be achieved by raising the base amount or by tinkering with Tier 1 guarantees, but these gains would come at considerable cost.

The lesson here is that school finance equity is both a technical and a political issue—political in the sense of demanding choices among competing values. Kentucky's postreform school finance system is more uniform and provides more equal educational opportunity than its predecessor system did. But it could accomplish more. Its limitations derive from political choices enacted in policy. In crafting that policy, legislators had to balance competing interests of high- and low-wealth school districts, taxpayers and students, education and other public services, state and local control. Did the policy accomplish enough? Short of another judicial review, there is no way to know whether Kentucky's equity gains satisfy the court's interpretation of an efficient system. Certainly, more equity could be gained, but such gains would require new investments and a rebalancing of the values that support the system. The trade-offs are inevitable, a normal requirement of democratic policymaking. Good policy balances the amount of equity that is technically possible with the amount that is politically feasible. Making these trade-offs explicit helps stakeholders to anticipate the changes that follow policy adoption.

A New School Finance Accounting

Policymakers designed KERA's finance components to complement the state's overhaul of the whole school system. These policies changed the distribution of education funding, introduced new programs—the categorical grants—to support teachers, students, and families, and raised funding levels overall. These changes represent major investments of public resources. Are reform dollars promoting reform? No one knows exactly. The role of school finance in this reform is obscured by conventional, audit-oriented means of accounting for education dollars.

Kentucky school districts, as those elsewhere, account for dollars in terms of functions and objects—the things dollars buy—such as teachers, books, and buses. Dollars reported in this nonprogrammatic fashion ensure the fiscal integrity of school districts, but they are essentially useless for tracking expenditures on reform, ascertaining local response to reform, or promoting educational productivity. In contrast, program-based accounting would serve the public's desire to promote educational reform and productivity, providing an education-oriented accounting. Without such a change school finance and program reforms can never become fully integrated.

The lesson here is that significant, sustained education reform may demand new education accounting systems that better integrate finance and program reforms. As a Kentucky superintendent remarked, reform success does not rely only on more dollars but rather on "a systemic change in how those dollars are used" (Adams, 1994, p. 383). Reformers need the answer to a related finance question: How do reform dollars support educational change?

Adequacy: A New Approach to School Finance

Providing more money to Kentucky's public schools was consistent with legislators' intent to improve the adequacy of education funding. However, as the Task Force on Public Education noted, adequate funding remains a challenge for Kentucky. Spending lags behind the national average, the base guarantee has not kept pace with inflation, and some reform strands are not fully funded. The task force's Finance and Management Issue Group recommended annual increases in the base guarantee to accommodate the costs of living.

Marginal increases in the base funding level will never be sufficient to address educational adequacy. By requiring an adequate education, the justices of the Kentucky Supreme Court created a new constitutional standard for school finance. They linked school funding with educational practices that produce specified types and levels of student achievement. They defined a constitutional responsibility to provide an adequate education to every youngster in the state and to provide an amount of funding sufficient to secure that adequate education. Since *Rose* nine states have included adequacy requirements in their school finance judgments.

This focus on achievement marks an evolution in courts' perceptions of the central issue in school finance law, from disparity in education funding to the productive use of those funds. The Kentucky justices ruled that the state must fund an adequate education for every student, not just an equal or uniform one. From a policy perspective the real contribution of *Rose* was the establishment of new funding criteria that blend financial and educational outcomes. Adequacy transforms school finance into a catalyst for student performance, linking school finance to the fundamental purposes of education.

There is no adequacy technology, however—no definitions, principles, measures, or policies to choose from—as there is with equity. To achieve adequacy policymakers must rethink the relationship between resources on the one hand and learning, productivity, incentives, and capacity on the other. They must redesign finance systems specifically to support high achievement, ensuring that the system can achieve specific results. Kentucky launched a national debate on educational adequacy. It has not followed through with policy designs capable of leading that debate.

The lesson here is that there is no way as yet to know whether the amount of resources available to Kentucky's public schools is adequate to support the efficient school system required by the state supreme court. The outcome measures themselves are new, and there is no production metric against which to assess the adequacy of funding. Only as these technologies become available will analysts be able to understand the extent to which Kentucky's new school finance policies satisfy the novel and rigorous demands of the supreme court—that education be not only equitable but also adequate. Until then, the true opportunity created by *Rose* will remain unrealized.

Conclusions

For policymakers, educators, parents, and others contemplating similar school finance reforms, these lessons offer some valuable advice.

Advice on seeking more equity and opportunity. Simply put, do it (or do more). It is possible. The technology exists. As a matter of fairness and constitutional duty, it is appropriate. Revisit the trade-offs embedded in existing policies and push them. Then monitor policy consequences so as to effect the desired result over time.

Advice on enhancing equity and productivity. Experiment with forms of school-based budgeting. As the "units of production," the places where teaching and learning occur, schools need more flexibility to control the use of educational resources. The Task Force on Education Reform (1989), which shaped the debates leading to KERA, asserted that "the school should be the primary unit of measurement" (p. 2). This advice stands as a useful guiding principle in structuring school finance reforms. Moreover, a focus on schools opens the heretofore unexamined question of resource distribution among schools, not just school districts.

Advice on blending finance and program reforms. Experiment with forms of program-based budgeting. Accounting systems that demonstrate specifically how educational revenues support instruction allow policymakers and educators to promote reform implementation and increase educational productivity. Reformers can increase the productivity of public investments.

Advice on pursuing adequacy. Begin now to develop the necessary infrastructure, which at minimum includes learning goals and performance standards, sufficient cost-adjusted funding to accomplish learning goals, an adequate physical school infrastructure, and enhanced mechanisms of educational productivity—such as student and teacher incentives, teacher skills and knowledge, and appropriate measures of success (see

Adams, in press). Harnessing education research to meet infrastructure demands would improve the knowledge base that states need to pursue adequacy. Adequacy represents a major new undertaking. It breaks new ground; it requires new funding goals, design concepts, leadership, knowledge, and public investment.

If school finance policy is going to make constitutional principle meaningful, it will have to explore these novel directions. States should begin now in order to position themselves to take full advantage of the educational opportunities that arise, remaining constantly mindful of their value to all citizens.

REFERENCES

Adams, J. E., Jr. (1994). Spending school reform dollars in Kentucky: Familiar patterns and new programs, but is this reform? *Educational Evaluation and Policy Analysis, 16,* 375–390.

Adams, J. E., Jr. (1997). School finance policy and students' opportunities to learn: Kentucky's experience. *The Future of Children, 7*(3), 79–95.

Adams, J. E., Jr. (in press). *Investing in adequacy: The challenges of linking finance to the purposes of education.* Washington, DC: National Academy Press.

Adams, J. E., Jr., & White, W. E., III. (1997). The equity consequence of school finance reform in Kentucky. *Educational Evaluation and Policy Analysis, 19,* 165–184.

Berne, R. (1988). Equity issues in school finance. *Journal of Education Finance, 14,* 159–180.

Brown, D. (Ed.). (1989). *The Corns ruling: An appeal* (video recording 10948C). Kentucky Educational Television (KET), The Kentucky Network.

Council for Better Education, Inc. v. Wilkinson, No. 85-CI-1759 [Findings of Fact, Conclusions of Law, and Judgment] (Franklin Cir. May 31, 1988).

Kentucky revised statutes, annotated, Vol. 7, Chapter 157, Section 316 (1996).

Minorini, P. A., & Sugarman, S. D. (1999). School finance litigation in the name of educational equity: Its evolution, impact, and future. In H. F. Ladd, R. Chalk, & J. S. Hansen (Eds.), *Equity and adequacy in education finance: Issues and perspectives* (pp. 34–71). Washington, DC: National Academy Press.

Odden, A. R., & Picus, L. O. (1992). *School finance: A policy perspective.* New York: McGraw-Hill.

Office of Education Accountability. (1999). *Annual report.* Frankfort, KY: Kentucky General Assembly.

Rose v. Council for Better Education, Inc., 790 S.W.2d 186 (Ky. 1989).

Task Force on Education Reform, Curriculum Committee. (1989). *Statement of principles*. Frankfort, KY: Author.

Task Force on Public Education, Finance and Management Issue Group: Legislative Research Commission. (1997). *Final report*. Frankfort, KY: Author.

3

A NEW VISION
FOR PUBLIC SCHOOLING

Jack D. Foster

ON JUNE 8, 1989, the Kentucky Supreme Court abolished every vestige of the previous system of public schools in the state and ordered the Kentucky legislature to enact a new system by the end of the next legislative session, which ended in April 1990. In response to this mandate, Governor Wallace G. Wilkinson and the legislative leaders of the House and Senate created a Task Force on Education Reform to write the necessary legislation.

After intensive work over nine months, the task force wrote what was known as House Bill 940 or the Kentucky Education Reform Act of 1990. I was one of six members appointed to the task force by Governor Wilkinson. As a member of the task force, I share in this chapter some of the vision we had for the new education system in Kentucky when we drafted the new legislation.

Given the task of creating a new system of public schools rather than improving an existing one, we started with a vision of what *should* be. The previous school system was gone in its entirety. Nothing that previously existed would continue unless we took the necessary step of re-creating it. But where do you start to build a new system of public education? In our case we adopted twelve principles that provided the philosophical framework for the new system. We then proceeded to build each element of the new system to fit with and reinforce every other element, using these twelve principles as our guide.

One thing that surely had to be different in the new school system was the expectations we placed on educators and the children they teach. Therefore the very first of the twelve principles that guided our work was a commitment to the belief that all children can learn and nearly all at high levels. With this principle as the cornerstone we set out to build a system of schools designed to make that belief a reality for *all* children in Kentucky.

Central to fulfilling this commitment to higher expectations were six performance goals we created for schools. The intent of these goals was twofold. The goals would define the system in terms of specific roles public education would be expected to play in society. It also would clearly state our expectations for the system, against which its performance would be measured in the future. These goals would be more than rhetoric because we intended to build a system of accountability for meeting these goals that would ensure that our expectations would be taken seriously.

What did we expect of the new system? We set the six goals for public schools as the first section of the Kentucky Education Reform Act (KERA). The first goal said that schools must expect a high level of achievement of all students. The second goal required schools to develop their students' ability to meet six specific learning subgoals that are discussed in more detail later. The remaining four goals required schools to reduce absenteeism, dropout and in-grade retention rates, and physical and mental barriers to learning as well as to improve the ability of students to make a successful transition to work, postsecondary education, or the military.

What Students Are Expected to Know and Do

Perhaps the most important of the six goals *for schools* were the six goals *for student learning*. These six goals for student learning would be the foundation for a new curriculum and a new statewide student assessment system. The six learning goals required schools to develop their students' ability to

1. Use basic communication and mathematics skills for purposes and situations they will encounter throughout their lives
2. Apply core concepts and principles from mathematics, the sciences, the arts, the humanities, social studies, and practical living studies to situations they will encounter throughout their lives
3. Become self-sufficient individuals

4. Become responsible members of a family, work group, or community, including demonstrating effectiveness in community service

5. Think and solve problems in school situations and in a variety of situations they will encounter in life

6. Connect and integrate experiences and new knowledge from all subject areas with what they have previously learned and build on past learning experiences to acquire new information through various media

These goals were originally created by the Council on School Performance Standards, then adopted by the Task Force on Education Reform, and finally approved by the Kentucky Board of Education.

Rationale for the Six Goals for Student Learning

The first learning goal was intended to endow students with the basic learning skills: reading, writing, speaking, listening, visualizing, basic mathematics, information gathering, and use of information technology. Obviously, these skills are the tools of learning in school and throughout life.

The second goal was intended to ensure that students learn the central ideas of the major academic disciplines. Because information is growing beyond the ability of any one person to master it, we thought that rather than concentrating solely on memorizing specific information academic disciplines had generated over time, students should learn to use the key ideas of the major academic disciplines to organize and interpret information.

The third and fourth goals were intended to help students develop life skills and moral sensitivity. Surveys of what citizens wanted from the public schools revealed that a majority of them expected schools to reinforce the common values of the community (such as honesty, respect for others, and respect for authority) and to help students become responsible adults. Although some of these values were often part of the school culture, they were not an official part of the school curriculum. These two goals required schools to formally address these values and behaviors as part of their regular curriculum.

Goals five and six focused on the so-called higher-order thinking skills such as analysis, synthesis, and evaluation of information. Previously students rarely were required to learn how to use information to evaluate the merits of an idea, to make decisions based on information, or to create new information. Kentucky business and industry leaders told us they wanted graduates who could reason, solve problems, and make sound judgments based on information. These two goals were intended to help students acquire a capacity to use information intelligently, to reason and form conclusions, and to solve problems.

A Curriculum to Support the Learning Goals

The research of the Council on School Performance Standards had documented that the public wanted more from the school curriculum than the simple acquisition of knowledge. The council had recommended that the new curriculum be designed to equip students with the tools of thought required to process information in a logical, meaningful manner. Students should be expected to learn how to connect and integrate their experiences and knowledge so they are able to create new knowledge, works of art, technology, and the like. Therefore we committed ourselves to the idea that the new curriculum must focus more on what students are able to do with what they learn than had been the case in the past. We wanted students to learn to properly employ a wide range of intellectual concepts and processes to understand, interpret, and use information. Although this was a major departure from a traditional curriculum, we believed this approach would better prepare students to live and work in an information-driven society.

There was a strong sentiment among members of the curriculum committee of the Task Force on Education Reform that the state should not continue to mandate specific courses or subject matter, as had been done in the past. Over the years there had been a steady increase in curriculum mandates that left teachers with little discretion as to what and how to teach. We wanted a curriculum that was more dynamic and flexible so teachers could keep current with the rapid growth in knowledge in almost every academic discipline. We also wanted a curriculum that could easily be adapted to the unique learning needs of children, based on the professional judgment of the classroom teachers.

In lieu of defining a curriculum by law, we took the position that the state should clearly define the expected *outcomes* of twelve years of formal education in terms of *performance* goals. The rationale for this shift in approach was the belief that the goals we set for the system were focused on student performance and not just acquisition of knowledge. Therefore, we reasoned, we should focus the system on achieving these performance goals and let educators at the classroom level determine the curriculum content and instructional methodology needed to ensure that all children could achieve these goals. Given the wide geographical, rural-urban, and cultural differences in the state, we thought teachers were in the best position to develop a curriculum that could take these differences into consideration. The specifics of what was taught could vary as long as students could demonstrate the outcomes determined by the state. The Kentucky Department of Education was commissioned to develop a "curriculum framework." Each school was then expected to develop its own curriculum, using the state curriculum framework as a guide.

The underlying policy of this approach to curriculum was to open up the education system to innovation in both curriculum and teaching strategies. We wanted teachers to use whatever information, materials, and strategies they thought were necessary and appropriate to achieve the learning objectives set by the state. Decisions about the best way to help every child attain the learning objectives were left to the faculty of each school. The content of the curriculum and the way it was taught were made a school-based decision; they could vary widely from school to school as long as they helped students meet the state performance standards.

Assessment of Learning

A central characteristic of this new approach to curriculum design was the expectation that students be able to demonstrate their ability to use what they learned in lifelike situations. This new focus obviously required new forms of assessment at both the state and local levels. We expected students to document their understanding of an academic concept or process by successfully performing tasks that required them to use the concept or process. The tasks were expected to simulate what students might find in the world outside of school.

We approached the assessment of learning from two perspectives. At the state level we required the Kentucky Department of Education to create a special assessment program to support the accountability system. The primary purpose of the state test was to determine the progress schools were making toward the improvement goals the state board of education set for them. It was not our intention to measure all students' progress on every outcome, which would have been a burden to students and schools. It would also have been financially prohibitive. Random sampling of items was considered an acceptable approach.

We knew there were very few testing instruments available at the time that could appropriately assess students on all the specific outcomes identified by the Council on School Performance Standards. Therefore we commissioned and funded the creation of our own assessment program.

The Kentucky Department of Education was required to hire assessment specialists to design the new system. Then the department of education was to employ an outside company to actually develop these tests. We expected local teachers to be used extensively to administer and score these tests, in whole or in part, as a way to help them develop expertise in this new method of assessment. We wanted the state tests to illustrate how classroom tests should be constructed and scored at the local level.

We realized we had to begin the assessment process at the earliest feasible time so the accountability program could begin within two years of enactment of KERA. Consequently, we decided to develop the state student assessment program on two parallel tracks. Our short-term strategy was to jump-start the accountability system before the new assessment instruments could be created, by developing an interim test consisting of existing test instruments that would at least be criterion based. We did not want teachers and students to focus on using the information they learned and then test them with instruments that only measured rote memorization. We expected the interim test would continue to be used at least until the more performance-based tests could be created, validated, and implemented.

The interim test had to be developed for use in the 1991–92 school year. The sole purpose of the interim test was to provide as quickly as possible a reliable and valid measurement of what students knew about science, communications, mathematics, and social studies. In an effort to provide guidance for development of the interim test, we used the National Assessment of Educational Progress (NAEP) as a model. Because of poor language in the law, this approach turned out to be more confusing than it would have been if we had just required the interim test to be criterion based. Many people thought we wanted a special NAEP for Kentucky.

The Kentucky Department of Education was required to create a "primarily performance-based" assessment over a period of six years or more. However, the interim test was expected to remain part of the full testing program as long as necessary to provide continuity and stability to the assessment program in its early years, even after the primarily performance-based tests were designed, pretested, and validated. We expected a gradual transition from the interim test to the new tests. The interim test component of the assessment system eventually would carry less weight in calculating the amount of progress schools were making toward meeting the performance goals set forth in the law.

Some members of the Task Force on Education Reform expressed concern that we might become an education "island" unless there was some correlation between what we were testing and what other states were testing. Therefore, we decided to require the Kentucky Department of Education to develop a way to compare Kentucky students with students in other states. Given that the test envisioned for interim use most likely would be based on national norms, it could be used to make the national comparisons required in the law. We did not expect these national comparisons to correlate perfectly with the performance-based tests that would be created later, but we did think they would be similar in nature.

At the local level teachers were expected to measure student progress during the school year through a continuous assessment process, using testing methods appropriate to the performance-based curriculum and similar to those used in the state annual accountability tests. Every school district was required to create and maintain a districtwide policy of continuous assessment to guide testing practices at the school level. Obviously, these school-based assessments were expected to address all the specific learning outcomes initially defined by the Council on School Performance Standards and adopted by the state board of education in December 1991.

We identified the fourth, eighth, and twelfth grades as the "accountability grades." All students in these three grades were to take the state accountability test each year. Local school assessment practices were supposed to measure student learning at all grade levels, not just the accountability grades. In effect, schools were given three years to bring their students up to the standards set by the state for the accountability grades. The intent was to spread out the time required to bring all students to the expected performance level and not to pressure teachers with annual improvement at every grade level. We thought an effective continuous assessment program at each school would enable teachers to anticipate how their students would perform on the state accountability test long before they had to take it. We expected all teachers to put forth a special effort to help poorer-performing students improve before they reached the accountability grades.

We wanted Kentucky teachers to be heavily involved in the state assessment program as a way to promote changes in local assessment practices. However, we did not require all teachers to be trained in assessment practices different from those they previously used. Every school's performance would be measured by the state's performance-based tests; we thought this would provide sufficient incentive for teachers at all grade levels to acquire the assessment skills necessary to ensure their students' success on the state test.

Accountability for Results

The six goals defined the objectives of the new system of schools. More important, they also indicated that results would be the criteria for success. We hoped to cultivate a school culture in which teachers expected to get increasingly better at their job regardless of their students or circumstances. But goals are often like New Year's resolutions: they are made and then quickly forgotten. If the new schools were to be significantly different from the old ones, we had to build powerful mechanisms for change into the new system. We firmly believed that some form of professional accountability would be necessary to provide an incentive to work toward these goals.

The belief that some children simply will not learn was (and perhaps still is) pervasive among educators. A certain level of failure was expected. Educators contended that the primary causes of academic failure lay outside the school. They believed that teachers could only do a limited amount to overcome these problems. They do what they can and let the chips fall where they may. At least that is what policymakers, parents, and the public had been told for years.

The consequences of such attitudes were obvious to us. Certain children were being written off very early. Their future failure was predicted and ultimately fulfilled. Kentucky had a high level of adult illiteracy, a history of persistent poverty, and a high dropout rate at the time. This was a clear testament to the social and economic price we were paying for an educational system that essentially absolved itself of the responsibility to educate all children regardless of background or preparedness to learn. We took the position that educators could no longer be allowed to take credit for educating "good students" while blaming their failures on everyone but themselves.

In almost every private enterprise, improvement is a matter of survival. Although public education had for many years experienced some competition from private schools, it had not been enough to be an incentive for change. The ideas of school choice and privatization were being advanced at the time as ways to stimulate change in public schools. However, we rejected these ideas in favor of a system where the incentive to improve did not have to come from competition. We wanted improvement to be driven from within the enterprise itself. We envisioned a system of consequences for the people most directly responsible for educating our children as the necessary engine to drive all the dramatic changes we wanted in public education in Kentucky. We understood that a law by itself could not change long-standing beliefs and practices. It was our view that change would only come when it was in the self-interest of the adults in the system to make these changes.

Other states had experimented with rewarding good teachers individually. Although we had no objection to rewarding the best teachers, we wanted to provide an incentive for successful teachers to help their poorer-performing colleagues improve. Therefore we elected to hold the entire school accountable for its effectiveness, with a range of rewards and sanctions to be applied to everyone, based on the performance of the school as a whole. The matter of how to do this was left to the faculty and staff at each school. We anticipated that the better teachers would complain that they were being punished because of the weaknesses in others, but these same teachers had previously shown no willingness to put pressure on their peers to improve. They shut their doors and ignored the poor education children were receiving in classes down the hall. We wanted that attitude to change. We hoped a collective approach to accountability would help achieve this objective.

We also wanted to engage every school in the task of improving itself. We acknowledged there were many good schools in Kentucky, but even these schools would not likely measure up very well against the new performance standards. Therefore we wanted measurable improvement to occur concurrently at *every* school in the state. Otherwise we could not hope to achieve the goals we had set for the system as a whole. That was the rationale for making individual schools the locus of accountability. It is at the school level that education occurs, so it was at the school level that improvement had to be stimulated and measured. Each school had to be held accountable for improving its own performance.

We knew that in the interest of fairness we could not expect historically poor-performing schools to be measured against better-situated schools. So we stipulated that the measure of success would be based on the previous performance of each school rather than on a fixed standard derived from what other schools were able to do. It was our belief that even schools that by objective measures were not very good should at least be rewarded for getting better and that these schools would eventually become good schools when measured against a fixed standard. We wanted an accountability system in which a school would not lose simply because its students performed less well than students in other schools. If the percentage of successful students steadily improved over time, a school could be declared an "improving school" and thus be eligible for financial recognition.

Measurement of School Improvement

Consistent with the accountability policy, we required every school to show improvement over two years regardless of its students or circumstances. Every school was to be given an improvement goal every two years. Schools that exceeded the goal would receive a cash award in recognition of their achievement. Schools that failed to meet their goal or fell below their previous level of performance would be subject to an array of consequences, including state intervention and assistance. In extreme cases the school would be declared "in crisis" and be taken over by the state. (This element of the law was changed significantly by the General Assembly in 1998. All references to a "school in crisis" were repealed, along with the original method and nature of state intervention.)

We expected standards to be created that defined successful performance for each academic concept and process. All students would be expected to attain them, "most at high levels." The percentage of students in a school whose performance met or exceeded these high standards would determine how successful a school was in meeting the second goal for schools. (Goal 2 required schools to develop their students' abilities to apply core concepts and principles in mathematics, the sciences, the arts, the humanities, social studies, and practical living studies to situations they will encounter throughout their lives.) The percentage of successful students was expected to increase with each biennial assessment cycle.

As previously mentioned, all students in the accountability grades were required to take the state accountability test annually. The results of these tests were to be used to measure school improvement in reaching the second goal for schools. The scores on the state test for two consecutive years were to be combined and averaged. One reason for combining the two years was to increase the statistical base for small schools. We also thought annual improvement scores might be less valid because they could be skewed somewhat by differences in classes from one year to the next. The averaged score was to be used as one element of a school improvement index.

Good performance on the state accountability test was considered only one element of school improvement. As discussed earlier, schools also had to reduce absenteeism, dropout and in-grade retention rates, and physical and mental barriers to learning as well as improve the ability of students to make a successful transition to work, postsecondary education, or the military. The department of education called these "noncognitive goals." We required the Kentucky Department of Education to create a school performance index that included measures of each of these goals and scores on the accountability tests. The department of education later named the school performance index the Kentucky Instructional Results Information System.

We allowed the various elements of the school performance index to be weighted to give greater importance to one or more components. However, each element was to be measured over a period of two years, and the scores for each element averaged just as was required for the test of student learning described earlier. The score for the noncognitive element of the index was to be based on all students in the school. The academic element of the index would be based on the students taking the accountability test. The scores for each element of the index were then to be added together to produce an overall accountability index score. The overall score was to be used to determine the amount of improvement a school had made over the two-year accountability cycle.

The law specified that a successful school was one in which the proportion of students failing to reach or exceed the state standard decreased by an amount the state board of education designated. It was expected that the performance index would be calibrated according to this definition of success. The actual index score was expressed inversely—as the proportion of students who met or exceeded the standard for the various elements of the index. Furthermore, the law specified that the amount of improvement required for an award be steadily decreased as the score grew closer to the best possible score. This was done to motivate poorer-performing schools to accelerate their improvement and to recognize that it gets increasingly difficult to improve as the proportion of students at or above state standards increases.

Consequences of School Performance

Exceeding the improvement goal brings the school financial rewards. Failure to meet the improvement goal could result in a variety of consequences such as an academic audit, possible state intervention, and technical assistance. A school that experienced a dramatic decline in performance over two years was declared to be in crisis and was to be taken over by the state. Parents could request that their children be transferred to other schools and the faculty placed on probation until evaluated by a "distinguished educator" assigned to the school by the state. Schools that met or exceeded their improvement goal were eligible for a financial award. The size of the cash award was to be commensurate with the amount of improvement made above the state-assigned goal. We left the design of this element of the program to the Kentucky Department of Education but stipulated certain features we wanted it to have.

We wanted the consequences to be based on demonstrated improvement as measured by the state accountability and assessment system. Each school was to be given an improvement goal to reach or exceed over a period of two academic years. Consequences were to be based on documented improvement (or a lack of it) as measured against the goal set for each school every two years by the state board of education. An improvement index score was to be developed to determine whether a school was eligible for a cash award or subject to one or more sanctions. No exceptions were provided. All schools were expected to make steady progress toward achievement of all the goals. Even the best schools as measured by current standards were expected to improve.

The actual amount of gain required for a school to qualify for a cash award was set by law to be at least 1 percent above the index goal set for the school. The intent of this provision was to ensure that a cash award would not be granted unless the amount of improvement was greater than might be obtained by chance. The 1 percent figure was originally used during a task force discussion as an example of how the system might work in practice. It was only intended to be an illustration but erroneously was written into the law. The Kentucky Department of Education later took the reference literally and required schools to exceed their improvement goal by at least one index point to qualify for a cash award. Although this decision was not necessarily inconsistent with the intent, it would have been better if the value had been research based rather than an arbitrary value based on a questionable interpretation of the law.

The cash award was considered a cash bonus to be distributed to the staff at the school as determined by the school council. (This element of the law was changed by the General Assembly in 1998. The award is now made to the school and not the faculty, but the school council still determines how it is to be used.) Involvement of the school council in this decision was not thoroughly discussed during the deliberations on the accountability program and became a controversial policy later on. The amount of the financial award earned by an eligible school was to be based on the average salary of the certified staff of the school. The actual amount awarded to schools with the same amount of improvement therefore could vary if the average salaries were different. An alternative proposal to make the amount equal everywhere and to be shared by all employees of the school was considered but not adopted.

A unique feature of the accountability program was the use of distinguished educators to mentor or even take over management of schools declared in crisis. A distinguished educator was to be a Kentucky teacher or administrator who had demonstrated the ability to effectively manage change. The Kentucky Department of Education was given responsibility for selecting, training, and deploying distinguished educators. Under the school-in-crisis provision of the law, a school that had shown a real decline in performance from the previous benchmark had to be interdicted by the Kentucky Department of Education. A distinguished educator was required to be assigned to the school to evaluate the situation and make recommendations for change, which could include recommending the dismissal or transfer of staff. This part of the law had some precedent. In the mid-1980s the legislature passed a school deficiency law that gave the Kentucky Department of Education authority to take over a school district. What was different here was the decision to directly intervene in individual schools.

The underlying philosophy for this dramatic provision was predicated on the concept of public safety. If the local public health department were to inspect a school and find unsanitary conditions, the school would be closed immediately and remain so until the conditions were remedied. We felt that public knowledge that a school was in serious decline warranted a similar action, stopping short of closing the school immediately. No parents should be required to send their child to a school that the state has determined to be potentially harmful to the students who attend it. Distinguished educators were not intended to be "storm troopers" who would be sent into a school to fire everyone. Rather, we wanted them to be rescuers armed with authority to do whatever was necessary to turn the school into an improving one. Our decision to suspend the tenure of every teacher in such schools was based on legal advice. By treating everyone as a member of a class, we felt the state could prevail against any legal action that might follow from dismissal of one or more teachers based on the recommendation of a distinguished educator.

School-Based Decision Making

Because we were going to hold schools accountable for improving student learning, we wanted the education professionals at the school level to have maximum feasible freedom to determine the best means by which to help children reach the outcomes expected by the state. The role of local schools in developing and delivering curriculum was noted earlier. But we extended this role to other aspects of the instructional process as well. As a sort of quid pro quo, the faculty and administrators at the school level were given total control over every aspect of the instructional process. The authority for this control was vested in something we called "school-based decision making."

School-based decision making gave teachers at the school level direct control of the key variables in the learning environment, such as the characteristics of the staff, the use of teacher and student time, classroom management techniques, assignment of students, curriculum and learning materials, and the use of equipment and space. The scope of authority granted to the school council was tightly circumscribed, and it was limited to matters that most directly affected the ability of teachers to create an effective learning environment for all the children in their care.

Employment decisions are generally regarded as solely a managerial prerogative and therefore beyond the authority of a school council. However, we wanted a local school to have a meaningful role in personnel decisions within the system through its school council, so we required the council to define the personnel needs of the school before staff positions were filled. The council then was given the right to refuse personnel assignments the members felt did not match their needs.

The rationale for giving school councils a role in personnel decisions was based on the reality that people are the most important resource in a school. On the one hand, we did not think teachers should be hiring each other. On the other hand, we did not think they should be subjected to the consequences of unilateral central office decisions to place people in certain schools for political or noninstructional reasons. Of special concern to us were the cases where individuals did not fit the personnel or instructional needs of the school as determined by the school council.

We also understood that granting control of decisions about instructional materials would be meaningless unless the school had financial resources with which to acquire them. So we appropriated funds for this specific purpose and required school districts to allocate a specific amount of this money to each school for the purchase of instructional materials and other nonpersonnel resources.

Fully aware that teachers had little previous experience with the authority given to them under school-based decision making, we felt that some kind of organizational structure was necessary to facilitate the decision-making process. Therefore we vested this decision-making authority in school councils that had to be created at each school within five years. The rationale for creating school councils was based on the idea that there had to be some group within a school that had the authority to finalize decisions about matters covered in the law.

A model configuration for council membership was written into the law to ensure certain characteristics would exist in the body we authorized to manage the school-based decision-making process. At a minimum a school council had to consist of three teachers, the principal, and two parents. This model was mandated primarily to ensure a somewhat uniform implementation of school councils across the state. The decision to limit the membership to six people in the model configuration was quite arbitrary. We knew there would be circumstances where a different configuration would be better, so we granted authority to the state board of education to approve other designs as long as the ratio of teachers to parents was maintained.

Our reason for involving parents in this process was to give them a formal position at the table when issues of importance to them were discussed. Very simply, we thought it was important for parents to have a meaningful way to participate in the decisions of school professionals. However, parent membership on the council was never intended to give parents control over the professional decisions of the faculty. The intent was to ensure that parents' perspectives could be considered before important instructional decisions affecting their children were implemented. We made the faculty, not parents or school councils, accountable for the effectiveness of the instructional process of the school. Therefore we never considered giving parents an equal voice in school councils.

Preschool and Primary School as Equalizers

In order to give every child a fair chance to succeed regardless of preparedness for school, we created a preschool program at every school for children from economically disadvantaged families and children with disabilities. The intent was to better prepare such children for entry into school at age five. The most dramatic change was the creation of the nongraded primary school, a school design that allows continuous progress from kindergarten through third grade without regard to age.

Our intent in creating the nongraded primary program was to permit children to progress as rapidly as their ability would permit, regardless of their age or the number of years they had been enrolled in school, until roughly ten years of age. Prior to the reform as many as 10 percent of all kindergartners were failed in their first year of school. It was our vision that the nongraded primary school program would give all children an equal opportunity to grow educationally without risk of failure so early in their school experience.

The idea of having children move through the early years of schooling based on their individual needs and progress seemed common sense. We were told that teachers could not appropriately deal with individual student learning needs in classrooms with children who function at different levels. We thought giving them the authority to group children according to ability and need rather than age would provide the flexibility they needed to overcome this constraint. Most of all, we wanted instruction to focus on the individual learning needs of children rather than on lessons that disregarded the obvious differences between children in the classroom. We thought this was especially important in the critical early years of schooling.

The Task Force on Education Reform did not discuss this element of the new school system. It seemed not to be controversial at the time. Therefore nothing was written about how we expected the primary school program to function in the new system. The details of implementing this requirement were left to the Kentucky Department of Education to work out. This uncharacteristic lack of direction in the law resulted in considerable confusion about just what we expected from this rather dramatic change in school structure.

Equitable Financial Resources

The lawsuit brought by the Council for Better Education, Inc., in 1986 asked the courts to require the state to equalize the distribution of existing funds among schools with different tax capacity and to increase the overall level of financial support for public education. Obviously, a new system of public schools had to include equity in resources as well as new organizational structures and processes. Financing public education was the issue that brought about the need to restructure.

We created a new funding system called Support Education Excellence in Kentucky (SEEK). A base level of funding for all children was to be set every two years by the Kentucky General Assembly at the regular biennial session. We also required each school district to levy a minimum school tax, which could be levied against property and various other economic assets and activities. We wanted the *level* of tax effort to be equal among the school districts, even though the same tax rate in a property-rich district would realize much more revenue than in a very property-poor district. The intent was to equalize the tax effort among taxpayers in Kentucky.

The SEEK formula credited the local revenue against the base level of funding set by the legislature; the state would make up the difference. The state contribution ensured that every school district had the same base amount of money available per student regardless of the wealth or poverty of the district. However, equity meant more to us than just equal funding for every child. We knew all children were not alike. We wanted to ensure equity for children with special needs. Equal funding per student would not mean equal opportunity for all children, so we provided state and federal money beyond the base amount in SEEK to help schools educate students with special needs.

We also believed that schools with a disproportionate number of students from economically disadvantaged families carried a larger educational burden than schools in affluent communities. Thus we added an additional amount of money to the base for each student who qualified for the federal free lunch program. We assumed the district would in turn allocate this extra money to the schools in less privileged areas of the district, based on the proportion of economically disadvantaged students being served by these schools.

Leadership Responsibilities

The decision to give local school professionals a primary role in transforming teaching and learning was a major policy change. The role of everyone from school board member to classroom teacher had to change. We made major organizational changes in the new system that we hoped would support a system of schools that is self-improving, efficient, and effective. This meant greater responsibility for some people and less for others.

Perhaps the most visible and dramatic organizational changes were the abolition and re-creation of the Kentucky Department of Education and the transition from an elected superintendent of public instruction to an appointed commissioner of education as the chief state school education officer. The existing Kentucky Department of Education was abolished, effective June 30, 1991. A new agency was to take its place the next day under the leadership of a newly selected commissioner of education.

Although we left the nature and shape of the new agency up to the new commissioner, we wanted a decentralized organization that could provide direct assistance to school districts and local schools as they implemented the many innovations and programs we created under KERA. Just as the supreme court had abolished all the laws, it also abolished all the attendant regulations. Some regulatory functions had to be assigned to this new agency; however, we wanted the Kentucky Department of Education to lead, rather than dictate, change and to promote innovation at the school level. The department of education would have major responsibility for helping districts and their schools implement the many new elements of the reformed educational system.

The roles of the superintendent, school board, and central office staff were changed; many decisions they had previously made were transferred to local school staff through school-based decision making. Changes in the responsibilities of local school personnel, such as the introduction of school-based decision making and school councils, were discussed earlier. These changes directly affected the roles of central office staff who previously had been responsible for many of the things now delegated to the local school. The role of the school principal also was dramatically changed, from that of administrator to that of collaborator and instructional leader.

Although many functions of central office professional staff were changed, the management functions and administrative authority of the central office were left essentially unchanged, except that school board members could no longer be involved in personnel decisions beyond hiring a superintendent. It was our expectation that central office staff would now see their role as supportive rather than directive in the areas of instruction covered by school-based decision making. Each school remained part of a local system of schools. The creation of local school councils did not make them independent entities. Furthermore, the responsibilities delegated to them were limited to instructional matters. Everything else remained the responsibility of both the district superintendent and board of education.

Professional Development

Although some things remained the same, there were many elements of the new system for which school personnel were not professionally prepared. Among these were the implementation of the nongraded primary school, continuous assessment, development and implementation of a school curriculum, performance-based instruction, and the local planning and collaboration required by school-based decision making. It was very clear that professional development opportunities would have to be an essential part of the reform. The immediate need was to provide training to the existing workforce, but how to do this efficiently was a major issue for us.

As we did with other elements of the new system, we took two approaches to professional development. On the one hand, we clearly recognized the immediate need to prepare educators to implement the various elements of the new school law. Time was of the essence because many elements had to be implemented with very short time lines. We gave the Kentucky Department of Education primary responsibility for all professional development directly related to implementing the new law. No specific resources were provided for this effort, but the expectation was that the department of education would use various available resources, such as the Kentucky Educational Television Network and the state computer network to fulfill this responsibility. We also asked the Kentucky Department of Education to create regional service centers to facilitate easy access to technical assistance by school personnel throughout the state. These centers were to be created as quickly as possible, although no specific timetable was mandated.

We saw the need to provide professional development for the purpose of aiding the implementation of the new law, but we also had a longer view of professional development that focused on improving the professional skills of the workforce on a continuing basis. This kind of professional development would continue long after the initial implementation of KERA. We wanted individual teachers to continuously upgrade their knowledge and skills. Professional development opportunities in the past were carefully controlled by the local school district central office and usually were dedicated to organizational needs or districtwide programs. We wanted a professional development program designed to meet the individual growth needs of the professionals in the system.

There was strong sentiment in the task force against creating a professional development bureaucracy. Many of us also did not want to assign this responsibility to either the Kentucky Department of Education or the university system. Rather than develop a centralized training program, we finally decided to appeal to the marketplace to provide the learning opportunities teachers and others would need. We gave every school its own professional development funds to be spent as it saw fit to meet the unique needs of its faculty and staff. We presumed that organizations with training capability would develop consumer-driven training programs and that such organizations would be more responsive to the professional needs of teachers in this scenario than they would be under a state-sponsored training program and delivery system.

Teacher Quality and Improvement

Complaints were numerous at the time about the poor performance of some teachers in the system. We had to address this issue directly yet respect the due process rights of educators. We took several steps to improve the quality of the workforce on whose efforts this whole reform would ultimately rest.

We created an independent organization, the Education Professional Standards Board, to deal with licensure, certification, and professional conduct standards. The standards board was given authority to approve teacher preparation programs, discipline teachers, issue and withdraw certification, and develop performance standards for the profession. We also authorized the creation of an alternative certification program for persons with unique qualifications to teach based on experience and education. It was our hope that the profession would police itself with aggressive action against educators whose incompetence or ineffectiveness was well documented.

We also streamlined the dismissal process by providing for a review of every dismissal by a panel of citizens and educators. This panel was authorized to review every aspect of the dismissal and could either uphold it or require the school district to rehire the person. It was our intention that this procedure would not only provide due process and fairness but also reduce litigation, which often followed dismissals. The court system was slow to resolve these issues, and litigation was a costly remedy for everyone involved.

We did nothing about the teacher preparation programs at the college and university level, mostly because we had already entrusted this responsibility to the Education Professional Standards Board. We heard a long litany of complaints about these programs from educators in the state. However, we had our plate full with just rebuilding the K–12 educational system. This challenge was daunting enough without trying to take on the higher education establishment as well. In effect, we gambled that the education profession, which higher education programs most directly affect, would take the initiative to demand change. If more authority was needed, the legislature would be ready to strengthen the hand of the Education Professional Standards Board at some future time.

Conclusion

As I watched the implementation of KERA unfold, I became aware of some important omissions in our legislation. In particular, we should have given more guidance as to the philosophy underlying the primary program and its design. Primary programs already existed in the United States and a few existed in Kentucky at the time. It did not seem necessary to explain to educators what they should be like. We particularly did not want to write the specific details into the legislation. Given the problems that arose when this element of KERA was implemented, we should have been more specific about the *characteristics* of a primary program we expected to see. Also we should have developed a working document that explained our rationale for the program and what we expected it to accomplish.

The accountability program was another element of KERA that quickly ran into implementation problems. We wrote into the law the elements needed to provide the legal basis for the actions we wanted taken. However, we entrusted the specific design of the program to a panel of national experts in testing and measurement. The design then was to be used by a testing contractor to create the necessary instruments, provide the scoring, and then implement the system. Most of the people involved in these tasks were not present for any of the task force discussions, so they had little to work from other than some of the working documents presented to the task force.

After KERA became law, I provided information to the panel of testing experts and the department of education on many technical issues. However, in the end the work had to be carried out by people with relatively little understanding of the basic philosophy of the system they were expected to design and implement. Misunderstandings about the nature and intent of the interim test and time lines that were confusing and unreasonably short were the sources of most of the problems that beset the accountability system. In spite of its difficulties, Kentucky successfully developed an innovative approach to holding educators accountable for results and has served as a model for other states.

In my opinion, we also erred in involving the school councils in the decision about who should receive the financial awards. In the early discussions of this program by the task force, the award money was considered a cash bonus to be paid directly to the teachers and administrators of the qualifying schools. The only decision was how the money could be spent. Again, initially the intent was to leave that decision to the person receiving the award. In the last weeks of deliberation by the task force, these elements were changed in ways that later proved to be unfortunate.

We grossly underestimated the amount of professional development needed to help educators implement some elements of KERA such as the primary program, the continuous assessment process, teaching to performance rather than rote memory, and creation of a school-based curriculum. The task force gave considerable thought to how to bring about the enormous changes we expected in the most efficient manner. The difficulties encountered in these areas clearly indicate that a better job could have been done in this regard.

We also failed to ensure that school districts worked to achieve equity among the schools for which they were responsible. Although KERA did achieve the major goal of equalizing the money available *to school districts* to educate children regardless of the wealth of their communities, we still have a significant number of schools in the state that are not much better situated now than they were in 1990. We should have done more to require local school officials to reach certain equity levels among schools under their jurisdiction.

These are obvious disappointments. However, we have seen enormous change in what children are taught and how it is taught. In spite of the controversies surrounding the accountability system, it has survived every challenge to abolish it. Kentucky has kept its focus resolutely on results. This in itself is a major achievement.

It is much too early to know how much better educated our children are because of what we did in 1990. Some elements of the law are still evolving and the measurements of academic achievement continue to be scrutinized by many experts. However, it is clear that we have achieved great gains in certain areas such as writing. The emphasis on critical thinking skills and the instructional focus on performance rather than rote learning are now institutionalized in most schools. These are just a few of the many indicators that the new system has achieved much of what we hoped it would do to improve academic performance. It remains a work in progress.

As will also be pointed out elsewhere in this book, although we did not anticipate every possible problem that might arise when our ideas and policies were implemented, and though the implementation did not always remain true to our intention, we made a serious attempt nonetheless to create a system that was equitable, effective, and efficient. Others will judge how well we succeeded.

4

A LEGISLATOR'S VIEWPOINT

"A ONCE-IN-A-LIFETIME OPPORTUNITY"

Holly Holland

IN JUNE 1989, when the Kentucky Supreme Court declared the state's school system unconstitutional and ordered the legislature to rebuild it within a year, Joe Wright knew he had a "once-in-a-lifetime opportunity" to improve the odds for Kentucky's children.

As the Senate majority leader and a former county school board chair, Wright was familiar with the way politicians traditionally regarded the state's schools.

"Generally, in sessions of the General Assembly there's a minimalist effort," he said. "You kind of do what you have to do until the next session to satisfy the constituents."

But something had changed in the years leading up to the court's decision. In the early 1980s, Wright and other legislative leaders had fought to make the General Assembly more independent of the governor. In addition, former governor Martha Layne Collins, a retired teacher, had proposed education reforms in 1985. Although she failed to persuade the legislature to fund her plan, Collins's efforts helped focus attention on Kentucky's neglected public schools.

So when the court's mandate was announced in June 1989, Wright and his colleagues in the House and Senate approached it with "a sense of urgency" and responsibility.

Wright had joined the General Assembly in 1976, thinking it would be a brief tour of public service. But after his Democratic colleagues elected him to a leadership position in his second term, he stayed on for another eleven years, eventually enjoying the longest tenure of any majority leader in Kentucky history.

In Kentucky the state legislature meets in regular sessions for sixty days every other year. Besides having to attend committee meetings and occasional special sessions called by the governor, lawmakers are free to pursue their regular occupations the rest of the time. Wright is a third-generation farmer who lives in the same house where he was born. Along with his brother, he raises corn, wheat, soybeans, hogs, cattle, and tobacco in Breckinridge County, which lies along the state's northwest border with Indiana, about halfway between Louisville and Owensboro. Wright, his wife Barbara, and all four of their children graduated from Kentucky public schools and state universities.

Before serving in the state Senate, Wright was elected to the county school board and served as its chair. He is particularly proud of having helped persuade voters to pass a special 5 percent tax on utilities, which paid for several new school buildings during his term in office.

From the time he entered the state Senate in 1976 until he retired in 1992, Wright held a position on the Senate Education Committee. He was well aware of the problems plaguing the state's public schools, but he also understood how the entrenched bureaucracies and lobbying groups representing teachers, administrators, and school board members would fight any effort to reduce their influence.

Immediately after the Kentucky Supreme Court issued its 1989 ruling, Wright and other House and Senate leaders set up three committees focusing on finance, curriculum, and governance. They relied on advice from a few nationally recognized consultants but tried to keep state education groups at a distance. Although the curriculum and governance groups quickly delved into a spate of controversial issues, the finance committee could do very little initially because the governor, Wallace Wilkinson, had publicly stated his opposition to raising state taxes.

"We weren't going to be able to improve education in a substantial way without more money," Wright explained. The Kentucky General Assembly and the governor's office arrived at an impasse. "We just hoped something would break [it]," Wright said.

Legislative leaders quickly determined that they had to hold their strategy sessions in private. Meeting once or twice a week through the summer and fall of 1989, Wright and other members of the governance committee often gathered outside Frankfort, the state capital, sometimes in the homes of legislative staff members.

"This thing was going to have to be so revolutionary that if we had public meetings and we allowed the various education interests to nit-pick every change to death, we would not have change," Wright said. "The only way we could do it successfully was to drop it as a bomb all at one time."

The governance committee tackled some of the toughest issues on the education reform agenda, he said, including efforts to stop the nepotism common among school board members and to give individual schools more authority for running their own affairs.

Wright recalled the debates that flared in those private committee meetings as among the most "intense" of his legislative career. At one point, he said, he and his longtime buddy, Kenny Rapier, a Democrat from Bardstown, argued so vociferously about various proposals that they wouldn't speak to each other for six weeks. "We were good friends," Wright said. "But [on certain issues] literally we would not yield."

But both men, along with other legislative leaders, agreed that they had to propose substantial changes to justify the requested increase in state taxes. "You can't put a billion dollars or half a billion dollars into the same old system," Wright said. "That just did not make sense. We all knew what the same old system had gotten us."

By the time the regular legislative session began in January 1990, committee members had agreed on many key components of the reform package. But the question of how to pay for the plan remained unanswered.

Then, late on a Friday evening in early March when most of the legislators were leaving Frankfort for the weekend, Wright received a call from the House leadership asking him to round up other Senate officials and meet at the governor's office. Wright soon discovered that House leaders had cut a deal with the governor about how to pay for the education reform package. If the Senate wouldn't agree to the new finance plan, they said, the reforms were dead.

Wright knew he had little choice but to agree to the terms. Nevertheless, he bought time that evening by tracking down several of his key Senate colleagues by telephone and explaining the plan. He said he didn't want them to hear about the deal first from reporters who might get wind of the story.

One of the other surprises of the evening, Wright said, was the governor's nonchalant attitude about the proposed tax increase. Despite his public posturing, Wilkinson knew that because they would cast the actual votes for higher taxes, legislators would be the ones to take the heat from their constituents. But before he would agree to throw his support behind the measure, the governor wanted assurances that some of the new revenues would be earmarked for state roads, which would send political pork back to his home district and to contractors who had contributed heavily to his campaign, Wright said.

"Out of that came the discussion that [the governor] wanted this in writing because of his fears that he'd end up without the political leverage he'd like to have later," Wright said. "Finally, they got a short statement together, and it started going around the room for everybody to sign."

Seven or eight lawmakers signed their names to the document, Wright said, but the process stopped when Charlie Berger took it in hand. Berger, a Democrat from Harlan County in eastern Kentucky, was the assistant president pro tempore of the Senate, whose unfashionable burr haircut and stocky build accentuated his bluntness.

Wright recounted the story as it then unfolded. "He took the paper. I was sitting right beside him. He said, 'Now, boys, I'm not going to sign this. If we can't look each other in the eye [and approve this agreement] the paper's no good.' He affirmed in speaking what everybody else was thinking. He embarrassed everyone. The governor said, 'Charlie's right.'"

As the meeting was breaking up, Berger handed the paper to Wright, who wadded it up and started to throw it in the trash can. "But as the magnitude of the moment began to sink in, I realized it and put it in my pocket," Wright said. Later, when he got home, his wife ironed the paper and placed it in a scrapbook for safekeeping. Wright figures that he'll donate the deal-making document to the state archives some day.

The decision about how to pay for the education reform plan might have been the most dramatic private interplay of the session, but the public posturing was still to come. The following week legislative leaders dropped the "bomb," House Bill 940—nine-hundred-plus pages of education reform legislation that proved too massive and complicated for any opponent to gut. The result would be the Kentucky Education Reform Act of 1990 (or "KERA," as it was dubbed). Through the end of the regular legislative session, KERA "took on a life of its own," Wright said. "We had to move that thing [out of legislative committees and through the House and Senate] by the end of the next week. There were changes made as we went along, but I think it is almost unbelievable that there were no more mistakes or changes than we had. . . . The intense focus, the time constraints that you have—I hardly know how to describe my feelings about that or the way it affected me."

The intensity didn't end with the passage of the bill. For the next two years, before Wright left the Senate, the questions and complaints from his friends in the education community nearly wore him down. "I think they were feeling about like I was feeling three weeks out when we were trying to pass [the bill]," he said. "It was just, 'How are we possibly going to do all this in the time frame we have?' I think in retrospect we might have forced the issue too hard and quick, but then, maybe not, because it all appears to have come out okay in the wash."

State media helped to cool heads by urging patience, Wright said, although he feared for a time that opposition groups might succeed in persuading the legislature to scale back the reforms when the evidence of progress was scarce. "But I don't have that fear now. I think KERA is proving to be too positive, too progressive. The results are too good."

Wright's youngest child graduated from high school in 1992, too late to experience many of the reform law's changes firsthand. But his daughter, a high school teacher who started working after the school reforms were in place, has shown him the impact of having higher expectations for learning in Kentucky.

"She's very positive about it," Wright said. "She feels there's a lot of flexibility [in the curriculum], and she can use her judgment, and teach kids to think. . . . I think schools are so much better than they were fifty years ago, it's not even comparable."

Wright, now fifty-nine, looks back on the legacy he left for the children of Kentucky and feels especially proud of his work as a legislator. He knows that students still have a long way to go before they reach academic excellence but that they have a much better chance of succeeding than the generations who came before them. Perhaps they'll also learn that change is not something they have to fear, he said.

"It's kind of like my brother," Wright said. "Recently, we had a problem in our business, and he was just fussing about it, and he looked up at me and said, 'I hate change.' I'll never forget the look on his face. I think that's what most of the administrators and teachers were feeling about KERA."

PART TWO

IMPROVING
STUDENT LEARNING

5

STATEWIDE PERFORMANCE ASSESSMENT AND SCHOOL ACCOUNTABILITY

John P. Poggio

IMAGINE TAKING UP the challenge of improving educational opportunities for all children in a state that has backed this decision with financial resources and political support. Changes are to occur in all content areas, and a hallmark of the reforms will be academic outcomes representing new, complex, and challenging content. Imagine contemplating this task and then deciding to judge success using one form of evidence—higher standardized test scores. Imagine also that the tests have not been designed yet and that when they are ready, they will lack sufficient scientific basis to be considered valid. It is like planning a road trip, getting everyone to agree on the destination, then mentioning that the vehicle you have selected to make the journey has some mechanical problems. No matter how much you might want to get there, the trip will be unpleasant. In many respects this was the Kentucky Instructional Results Information System (KIRIS), a supremely innovative assessment and accountability system that lacked a proven engine. (For a more detailed description of KIRIS, see Kingston & Reidy, 1997; and Redfield & Pankratz, 1997.)

An Overview of KIRIS

KIRIS, which changed to the Commonwealth Accountability Testing System (CATS) in 1998, was the department of education's response for the Kentucky Education Reform Act of 1990 (KERA) mandate to create a primarily performance-based system of student assessment and school accountability. In 1991, a test contractor was employed to design custom assessments that measured Kentucky's learning goals. Open-response, hands-on performance events and multiple-choice items were administered to all children in grades 4, 8, and 12 to assess learning goals in reading, mathematics, science, and social studies beginning in the spring of 1992. Writing portfolios also were developed over the 1991–92 school year and scored. Beginning in 1993, the content areas of arts and humanities and practical living and vocational studies were added to the assessment. Each student tested received a score in each content area. Their scores were used to place students in one of four categories: novice, apprentice, proficient, and distinguished. The level of "proficient" was established as the targeted achievement level for all students. What made KIRIS high stakes was an accountability system that required each school to show substantial progress over a two-year cycle toward the goal of proficient as the average for all students. Each year schools received an accountability index that was computed by weighting student test performance 85 percent and nonacademic measures (i.e., attendance, dropout rates, in-class retention rates, and transition to post–high school experiences) 15 percent. Multiple-choice items were not used in KIRIS to compute the accountability index because they were not considered true performance assessments. Hence, KIRIS test scores were derived from student responses to open-ended questions in content areas, on-demand writing prompts, and writing portfolios submitted near the end of each school year. The accountability index was computed on a scale of 0–140 with an index of 100 as the goal for all schools where the average level of all students would be "proficient." Schools that exceeded their two-year goal received cash rewards, and schools with declining scores received assistance and could be taken over by the state. In the mid-1990s, performance event items were eliminated due to lack of reliability and the administration of the tests was spread over grades 4 and 5, 7 and 8, and 11 and 12. KIRIS operated from 1992 to 1998 over three two-year cycles; more than $70 million was distributed to schools that exceeded their improvement goals.

In 1998, the Kentucky General Assembly passed legislation that required the department of education to end KIRIS and recreate a new assessment and accountability system, CATS, that should be built on the strengths of KIRIS but eliminate weaknesses and make improvements. Under CATS, students continue to be tested toward the end of each school year in seven content areas. Multiple-choice items and the Comprehensive Test of Basic Skills administered in grades 3, 6, and 9 have been added to the assessment battery. In addition, a new standard-setting process is being implemented for CATS. The School Curriculum Assessment and Accountability Council and the National Technical Advisory Panel on Assessment have also been created to advise the department on the continued development and implementation of CATS.

In creating KIRIS to measure student achievement under KERA, the designers envisioned a groundbreaking system that would use more qualitative items to evaluate student learning instead of simply pulling a commercial multiple-choice exam off the shelf. So, in addition to multiple-choice questions, Kentucky relied on portfolios of student writing, on-demand essays, and individual and group performance tasks as part of its annual assessment. The state set performance standards that ranged from "novice" to "distinguished" and held schools accountable for steadily increasing the percentage of students who could reach those goals until all children had attained the "proficiency" level within twenty years. Each school's scores in reading, mathematics, science, social studies, writing, arts and humanities, and practical living and vocational studies were used to develop an accountability index, but the state also factored in nonacademic indicators, such as attendance, dropout, and retention rates, to help level the playing field. Under KIRIS Kentucky expected each school to meet its improvement goal every two years, at which time the bar moved higher. Schools that exceeded their goals would receive financial rewards; those that fell short would receive direct assistance from the state or, in the most severe cases, risk state takeover.

Put in a straightforward manner, the assessment design Kentucky created had never been tried on such a scale, and the difficulties the state encountered were never anticipated. Testing, assessment evaluation theory, and accountability were not up to the job demands. KIRIS was, as so many have put it, "a work in progress." The discipline of psychometrics was learning what to do and how to do it better each day. Yet everyone expected the system to be perfect from the start. That is a standard that no test and no state can meet.

I am not suggesting that KIRIS should have embraced lesser goals or chosen not to go as far afield from the approaches or ideas of the past. Rather, today I would ask for reasonableness in the standards and expectations we apply when judging KIRIS. We have in the past decade moved toward a technology-based, quasi-scientific orientation for school evaluation that assumes we can build tests that have the unerring ability to inform us about schools' successes and failures. This form of critical study and evaluation has become the standard by which we evaluate our progress, and—in theory—they remain beyond reproach. Perhaps the weakness in education reforms of the past decade is rooted in part in these methods and in our all too frequent absolute reliance on them to discern and reveal the truth. In my opinion this is the major problem with KIRIS—not just the inability to create and adjust curricular and instructional reforms but the inability to create evaluative methodologies capable of detecting the contributions or shortcomings of reform. Finding fault that the tests were not "perfect," however, should not cause us to conclude that the reform was a failure.

What follows is a presentation of results to show what the Kentucky Department of Education (KDE), through its testing efforts, reported over the life span of KIRIS (1992–1998) as indicators of change in student performance. Following this, I present and discuss the arguments put forth by KIRIS critics. To complete the chapter, I offer a sense of how CATS, the new initiative that replaces KIRIS, is taking shape. I end by offering conclusions and recommendations.

Assessment Context, 1992–1998

Kentucky's *Core Content for Assessment* was developed to define more specifically what all students should know and be able to do in seven content areas: reading, writing, mathematics, science, social studies, arts and humanities, and practical living and vocational studies. Although the learning goals listed in KERA described basic skill areas, important ideas in content areas, and required thinking skills, these general goals did not define for teachers and students specifically what should be taught and what will be assessed at grades 4 and 5, 7 and 8, and 10 and 12. While the Council on School Performance Standards and KDE produced publications in the early 1990s that further defined the learning goals, teachers continued to express concern that what they were to teach and the content for which students would be assessed was not clear to them. Therefore in 1995, KDE produced and distributed a document entitled Kentucky's *Core Content for Assessment* that defined the skills and concepts (core content) in each of the seven areas that would be assessed in elementary, middle, and high school. Since then, KDE has continued to revise and clarify Kentucky's core content document to be more teacher friendly. In 1998, KDE published a new document entitled *Program of Studies for Kentucky Schools* that defines what should be taught at each grade level. Together, these two documents guide the development of curriculum and assessment statewide.

Establishing the core content was a vitally important step for KIRIS. The core content provided the outcomes that would lead to rewards or sanctions. What had been in place prior to 1990 was being changed in significant and meaningful ways. In one of the innovations of KERA, curricular expectations were set down with sufficient specificity to guide and form instructional decisions in the state's schools. Yet in the context of evaluating the impact of KERA and KIRIS, this significant achievement—providing a clear blueprint for the reform at the level of each individual student—is rarely mentioned or noted. By 1995–96 it was clear what the subject matter expectations were. Once the core content was defined and disseminated and, more important, with the core content in place, local instruction could be aligned and associated with these expectations.

We know that the KIRIS test makers based their creation on the core content. Their efforts are discussed further on in this chapter. What about instructors, local curriculum coordinators, department heads, and administrators? Did they realize the significance of the core content indicators? Survey data captured from school personnel referring to the early years of KIRIS clearly suggest that in excess of 50 percent of school-based personnel were poorly informed regarding the core content expectations and that support for curricular and instructional reform was not adequate in its focus or duration (Thacker, Hoffman, & Koger, 1998). In later years, 1995 to the present, this situation did change, and the community of Kentucky educators at all levels reported being well acquainted with the core content and having worked to align local curriculum and instructional practices (Stecher, Barron, Kaganoff, & Goodwin, 1998).

This then was the very real context of change in Kentucky's schools. What would we predict? Absent any deliberate and comprehensive attention to the elements of change, should we expect student performance to advance dramatically or consistently? Hardly. From 1998 through 1999, during the transition from KIRIS to CATS, the details of the core content were once again subjected to close scrutiny. In 1998 the Kentucky General Assembly passed a law mandating a new assessment and accountability system (CATS) that would address concerns about KIRIS. With input from more than 6,500 Kentucky citizens, the Kentucky Board of Education created a system with multiple measures of learning, including the Comprehensive Tests of Basic Skills, a national norm-referenced exam, and the Kentucky core content tests, which comprise multiple-choice and open-response questions in reading, math, science, social studies, arts and humanities, and practical living and vocational studies. In addition, students now must complete writing portfolios and on-demand writing tasks (Kentucky Department of Education, 2000). Although Kentucky set new accountability indices, the absolute performance standards remain the same. The statements of the original core content also remained largely unchanged from the documentation set out from 1994 through 1995.

This is further testament to KERA's success: following a period of use, only minor adjustments to the curricular goals were needed.

But what about the KIRIS tests that took shape from the core content? In the test-making business the seed of each test question is identifiable and traceable back to one, or sometimes two, specific core content skills. The developer sets out to create test questions for each skill. Content validation reports from the contractor and KDE have confirmed that test questions properly reflect the core content skills (Haladyna, 1994). But it must be noted that Kentucky made a bold move. Upon review of its core content and policy expectations, it called for all tests to be performance assessments, which require students to respond with information, not just select among listed answers. Thus, in 1992 and 1993, a generation of students whose sense of "important tests" was defined by multiple-choice exams sat for assessments whose format and expectations were unfamiliar to them. What would we predict about their performance on such assessments? Results from studies in other states confirm the obvious. Until students become familiar with the testing format and the expectations of the tests, scores will underestimate student achievement. Further, underestimations can be expected to be more severe for students who have historically performed lower on standardized tests.

Was this a failure of KIRIS? Decidedly not. Some critics have spurned the changes in performance during the early KIRIS years, suggesting that the gains resulted from increasing familiarity with the testing format. If students acquired communication skills that the Kentucky Board of Education called for, are we to conclude that the change was not real or important? In one sense we should understand that the baseline might not have been valid until 1994 or 1995 (and perhaps much later for low-performing students). In other words, KIRIS tests might have been flawed, but this does not negate the fact that students were learning more.

KIRIS Results, 1992–1998

Following are charts and data summaries to inform the reader as to the changes in KIRIS test scores from 1992 through 1998. Following 1998 assessment, the tests were sufficiently changed as to make direct comparisons between KIRIS and CATS inappropriate.

Progress in Core Content Areas

KDE invested considerable energy and resources to produce score scales that could compare performance directly over time and make the score scales for each content area comparable. Figures 5.1–5.3 present data summaries reflecting changes in KIRIS scores at the elementary, middle, and high school levels from 1992 through 1998, the last year before the Kentucky assessments changed so radically as to make comparison of scores from KIRIS to CATS inappropriate. Data are exclusively reported for four subject fields: reading, mathematics, science, and social studies. In Figures 5.1–5.3, 140 represents the maximum possible score, and 100 is the goal.

Figures 5.1–5.3 rather consistently reveal the same story: at all grades in the content areas there are indications of score increases.

The assessment scores show different changes over time by grade level and subject matter. At the elementary school level the growth appears to have accelerated faster than at the middle school or high school level in all subjects, earlier years being the time of greatest growth. Although high school scores do indeed show early growth, a pattern of greater continuing growth in later years is also seen, especially in mathematics. At the middle school level, although there is evidence of score improvement, it tends to be more systematic and does not achieve the same level of proficiency as the other grades.

In reading, the elementary grades started at a level between high school (lowest reading scores in 1992) and middle school (highest reading scores in 1992) levels, then grew at a greater rate and achieved the highest standing by 1998. Within this framework middle school–level scores improved, but not at the same rate as high school or elementary school scores. Curiously, high school students showed greater gains in science than in any other subject, a pattern that continued throughout the tenure of KIRIS. Although elementary students showed some progress in science, their gains did not reach the learning levels of the 1998 high school cohort. And middle school–level science scores did not advance at all. Greater growth occurred in mathematics. All grades advanced considerably through 1998. It may be that changes in the testing format concurrent with 1995 testing had the effect of compromising estimates of growth or change. (I will discuss the impact of test format on performance later in this chapter.) Social studies scores grew moderately across the KIRIS years in the elementary grades, rose considerably for high school students, and fell off in the middle grades in the last years of KIRIS. A general review of these scores finds notable strengths and advances as well as inconsistencies: declining middle school–level scores in the latter years of KIRIS and limited gains at the middle level in every subject but mathematics. In the other KIRIS-tested content areas (arts and humanities, writing, and practical living and vocational studies), the growth is not as obvious. We

Figure 5.1. Changes in KIRIS Scores: Elementary School Level, 1992–93 to 1997–98.

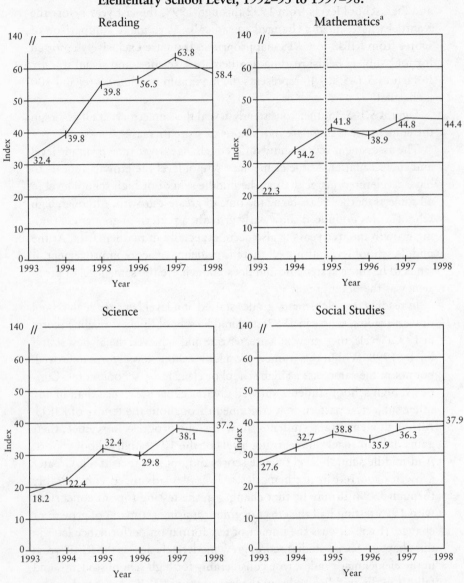

Note: *Elementary school includes results for grades 4 and 5.*

[a] *Mathematics index is based on the combination of on-demand and portfolio scores for 1993 and 1994 and on-demand scores only for 1995–1998.*

Source: Kentucky School and District Accountability Results. Accountability Cycle 3 (1994–95 to 1997–98). *Kentucky Department of Education, December, 1998, p. 18.*

Figure 5.2. Changes in KIRIS Scores: Middle School Level, 1992–93 to 1997–98.

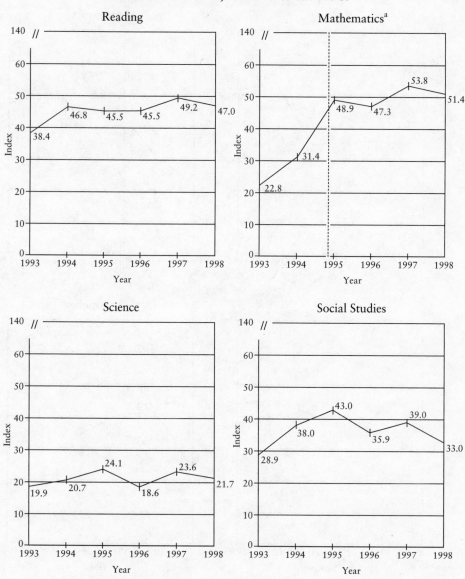

Note: *Middle school includes results for grades 7 and 8.*

[a] *Mathematics index is based on the combination of on-demand and portfolio scores for 1993 and 1994 and on-demand scores only for 1995–1998.*

Source: Kentucky School and District Accountability Results. Accountability Cycle 3 (1994–95 to 1997–98). *Kentucky Department of Education, December, 1998, p. 20.*

Figure 5.3. Changes in KIRIS Scores:
High School Level, 1992–93 to 1997–98.

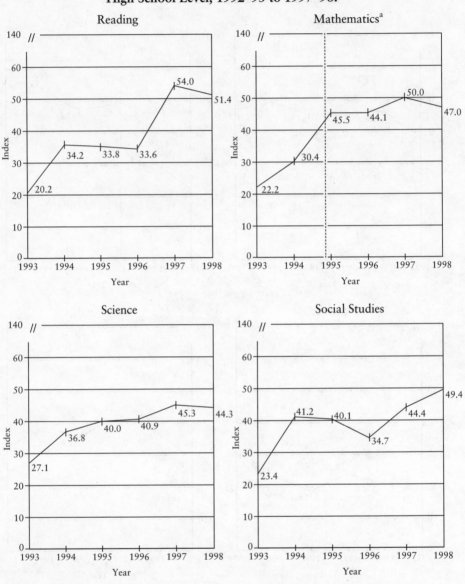

Note: *High school includes results for grades 11 and 12.*

[a] *Mathematics index is based on the combination of on-demand and portfolio scores for 1993 and 1994 and on-demand scores only for 1995–1998.*

Source: Kentucky School and District Accountability Results. Accountability Cycle 3 (1994–95 to 1997–98). *Kentucky Department of Education, December, 1998, p. 22.*

see some gains at the elementary school levels but no score changes in the middle school and high school levels.

Progress by Performance Classification

Another way to consider and evaluate the impact of KIRIS is to examine the classification of student performance on the assessments. Table 5.1 depicts such data for elementary, middle, and high schools in each of the four major subject areas (reading, mathematics, science, and social studies) from 1992–93 through 1997–98. Kentucky classifies a pupil's performance as novice, apprentice, proficient, or distinguished (abbreviated in Table 5.1 as "N," "A," "P," and "D," respectively). Much has been written about these categories, how they were established, and their properties. Two important features are worth noting. First, the range of scores is not the same for each category. In fact, the lower categories, novice and apprentice, span more of the score range than the proficient and distinguished categories. This is true for each content area and for each grade in which students take the tests. Thus we can and should expect to find at the outset of an academically challenging assessment program that most students score in the lowest categories. Kentucky did indeed challenge itself. (Whether the challenge was reasonable will be discussed later in this chapter.) Second, the distinguished category was to represent a performance that only the top 4 to 5 percent of all students could be expected to achieve. In other words, by the very design of the assessments, one end of the scale was anchored at a level that few would achieve. Conceivably, these two features could have created a scale that unwittingly suppressed the extent of growth that was likely, reasonable, and possible.

A review of the data is startling, to say the least. In all content areas and at all grade levels, scores advanced from majority novice to majority apprentice. From this perspective student performance did improve. In reading, at all levels, scores have moved into the proficient category and out of the novice category almost entirely. If we limited our review to these data alone (overlooking the results shown in Figures 5.1–5.3), it would seem that mathematics performance has not changed during the KIRIS initiative. However, we know from the results depicted in Figures 5.1–5.3 that the scores did increase. The frequency classification data in Table 5.1 with respect to mathematics appears to underestimate the extent of the growth. As previously noted, average scores increased, *but not enough to move groups of students into the higher classifications*. In science and social studies, patterns are similar to reading. Note the strong gains in high school science and social studies, with greater numbers of

Table 5.1. Percentage of Students Scoring at Each Performance Level, by Grade Level, 1992–93 to 1997–98.

	Reading				Mathematics (Open Response)[a]				Science				Social Studies			
	N	A	P	D	N	A	P	D	N	A	P	D	N	A	P	D
Elementary school																
1993	32	60	8	0	—	—	—	—	57	42	2	0	43	49	8	0
1994	18	71	11	0	—	—	—	—	47	51	2	0	38	50	12	1
1995	8	62	28	2	29	54	10	8	28	67	5	0	32	50	16	2
1996	7	62	30	1	30	56	9	5	31	65	3	0	30	58	12	1
1997	4	56	38	3	27	53	10	9	15	78	6	0	30	57	12	1
1998	5	63	31	2	28	53	11	9	20	71	8	0	29	55	14	1
Middle school																
1993	20	69	10	1	—	—	—	—	54	44	2	0	43	47	9	1
1994	12	69	18	1	—	—	—	—	50	49	1	0	31	53	14	2
1995	7	80	13	0	36	35	16	14	43	56	2	0	26	53	18	3
1996	6	81	13	0	36	36	16	12	54	45	1	0	30	57	12	1
1997	5	77	18	0	33	33	16	18	42	58	1	0	27	58	14	1
1998	6	78	15	0	34	34	16	15	47	52	1	0	35	54	11	1
High school																
1993	57	39	4	0	—	—	—	—	39	58	4	0	52	42	6	0
1994	33	55	11	1	—	—	—	—	22	69	8	1	28	53	17	2
1995	32	57	10	1	35	39	17	9	16	72	10	2	30	52	16	3
1996	31	59	9	0	33	44	16	7	14	76	9	1	34	53	12	1
1997	16	52	28	4	26	46	18	10	10	76	13	1	26	51	20	3
1998	16	56	26	2	32	42	17	10	8	80	12	1	24	47	25	4

Note: *Elementary school includes results for grades 4 and 5; middle school, for grades 7 and 8; and high school, for grades 11 and 12. Percentages may not total 100 due to rounding. Assessments are administered at the end of each school year.*

[a] *Mathematics includes results for 1995, 1996, 1997, and 1998. In 1993 and 1994, the test components were not equivalent and thus not comparable to later year assessments.*

Source: Kentucky School and District Accountability Results. Accountability Cycle 3 (1994–95 to 1997–98). *Kentucky Department of Education, December, 1998, p. 13.*

students moving into the proficient category. For the most part, these data offer very encouraging results that support the positive impact of KIRIS.

Progress as Measured by the School Accountability Index

One final perspective on evidence demonstrating changes in KIRIS performance between 1992 and 1998 merits attention. Table 5.2 reports data on the average school accountability index. Again, much has been written on this topic. In a nutshell, this approach computes the average accountability scores for a school by counting the assessment results as approximately 85 percent of the school's index, then placing into the index nonacademic factors, such as attendance and dropout rates contributing 15 percent. From this mixture comes a score that can range from 0 to 140.

A significant feature, indeed a hallmark, of the Kentucky reforms was the accountability model that rewarded schools when their accountability indices increased 1 percent beyond the biennial goals set by the state (and applied sanctions when recurring failures were observed). Table 5.2 shows the composite accountability index for the state at three grade levels. Elementary and high schools demonstrated progress and on average attained their goals. Results at the middle school level did not meet expectations. Overall, Kentucky's results support the finding of improved student performance, but not at all grades, not in all content areas, and not for all types of assessments.

In the preceding sections, I have offered evidence to suggest that the reforms did result in greater student learning, with some notable exceptions. Now I will turn to inspecting the decisions and data under the lens of critics. In the next section, I review the criticism and perceived failures of the assessment methodology adopted and followed by KIRIS.

Table 5.2. Average School Accountability Index Score by Grade Level, 1992–1998.

	1992–1994	1994–1996	1996–1998	Improvement Goal for 1998
Elementary school	38.3	46.2	48.9	51.0
Middle school	39.6	42.8	44.8	49.1
High school	39.0	44.0	50.8	50.0

Source: Kentucky School and District Accountability Results. Accountability Cycle 3 (1994–95 to 1997–98). *Kentucky Department of Education, December, 1998, pp. 15–17.*

KIRIS Results, 1992–1998: The Voice of Critics

Is it the case, as some would contend, that we cannot determine the impact of KIRIS because the monitoring and assessment methodologies were flawed? Or is it true, as others have posited, that the data suggest there has been no change in student learning? Based on my review of KIRIS findings, although the program made errors (such as not always being able to implement a best decision, create highly error-free tests, or ensure that all psychometric standards were met), it did inform Kentuckians of progress and more often than not was accurate in its appraisal.

Anyone who takes up the task of actually creating and putting in place a high-stakes assessment and accountability system can detail many points where theory would expect one course of action yet practice produces another. I mention this not to seek a waiver from deserved criticism but to acknowledge that if the system must be perfect, it will never be done. Politicians and the public insist on assessment and accountability measures and, try as we might to tell them about the fallibility of the processes and products, we have not decreased their appetite for perfection. The question must be how egregious the errors and shortcomings were. Enough to scuttle KIRIS? I do not believe so.

A handful of major reports have been written about KIRIS, each offering a critical analysis of what was done, what was intended, and what resulted. These include evaluations and audits by Catterall, Mehrens, Ryan, Flores, and Rubin (1998), Hambleton, Jaeger, Koretz, Linn, Millman, and Phillips (1995), Koretz and Barron (1998), Nitko, Amedahe, Al-Sarimi, Wang, and Wingert (1997), and Western Michigan University (1995). In the following paragraphs, I address some of the major deficiencies that KIRIS critics seem to rally around. My purpose is to provide a somewhat different interpretation. I also acknowledge that I do not always disagree with a criticism, but I may well conclude that the error nevertheless is not as severe as some might believe.

Cut Scores and Performance Classifications

Some authors have been critical of the way cut scores on the assorted KIRIS tests were determined (Hambleton et al., 1995). (A cut score is the score value used to separate students into categories; for example, the score value separating "novice" versus "apprentice" categories.) I would agree that the original methods would not have been my selection, especially as the procedures had limited exposure in practice and no fail-safe or backup methods were in place to verify the appropriateness of the results. However, following some initial criticism, the standard-setting procedures were reapplied following an approach that is growing in use and that largely affirms the original cut scores. Changes based on the reevaluation were not so great that they caused a loss of trend information, and score data were reequated to offset problems.

Other critics have challenged the reliability of the KIRIS scores, especially the performance classifications (Cunningham, 1996; Catterall et al., 1998). This critique would carry more weight if the KIRIS performance had been used to move a student to the next grade level or to attach a label to a diploma. My point is not to condone tests whose reliability is poor but to offer a comment about their purpose. Numerous reports are available from KDE to detail efforts to achieve greater reliability. A recent report by Miller (1999) demonstrated that the reliability of group means and school classification rates in Kentucky under KIRIS equaled or exceeded levels of observed reliability for comparable measures in other states.

Scoring Methodology

Some critics have faulted the unreliability of the scorers who graded the performance assessment questions (Cunningham, 1996; Hambleton et al., 1995). Although performance assessments tend to be less reliable than multiple-choice, machine-scored tests, the results also can give us broader and better information about students' ability to understand and use key concepts. Achieving reliability at the level of multiple-choice test items is not a realistic goal for performance assessments. But should we limit the measurement to achieve reliability? Or do we stay close to a gray line and work to improve the measurement while reflecting what we want students to know and be able to do? Today's composition of CATS scores is a blend of multiple-choice and constructed-response questions, which afford levels of reliability that are acceptable for the school and district accountability purposes of KERA.

KIRIS Versus Other Standardized Tests

A major critique of KIRIS is that the reported score gains were not observed on other standardized tests (Koretz & Barron, 1998). For some investigators the first sign of trouble occurred when KIRIS state averages were examined in relation to the state averages on the National Assessment of Educational Progress (NAEP) and the ACT Assessment over the same period of time. Because KIRIS scores at certain levels and in certain subjects improved considerably, the reasoning goes, we should expect to find similar gains on other measures of student achievement. Although no formal and deliberate studies were done to compare the content and questions of all the tests, this would have been instructive. In particular, I would suggest that a review of the ACT science questions finds little in common with the KIRIS and now the CATS test questions. The ACT moves into areas of reasoning and deductive and inductive inference, whereas KIRIS at the high school levels remains firmly associated with content knowledge.

From data assembled and reported by critics, the KIRIS gains seem to be considerably higher than growth shown on the NAEP (Koretz & Barron, 1998). Although Kentucky's average NAEP scores rose, up to 1996 the growth was as strong as KIRIS scores suggested. Two points are worth noting. First, NAEP has been criticized, indeed by many critics of KIRIS, for failing to adequately and appropriately measure the performance of the nation's schools. KIRIS has thus been subjected to criticism using the results of another test that has itself been criticized—a curious connection, to say the least (Linn, Koretz, & Baker, 1996; Sugrue, Novak, Burstein, Lewis, Koretz, and Linn, 1995). Second, Kentucky's NAEP results recently began to show increases on the order of those found in KIRIS. Moreover, after some debate, these growth indices were determined to be statistically significant.

Test Security and Professional Practice

A final area of criticisms concerns the allegation that scores on KIRIS increased because of undesirable teaching practices (Koretz & Barron, 1998). Of all the criticisms, I find this the most disturbing and unsupported, yet it continues to be a recurring theme. There is no evidence of widespread school breaches in security or professional practice. This hypothesis emerges in part because of the extreme pressure placed on school personnel to improve performance. I would note from experience that school personnel usually are the first to report infractions of professional practice. Indeed, this has been the case in Kentucky. Furthermore, the authors of studies that attribute score increases to items being overexposed or to security gaps in the testing system acknowledge that their own review of data failed to find a systematic effect. Scores on reused items are not consistently higher than on items used for the first time. Higher performance on reused questions appears more often, though not frequently, in mathematics as opposed to reading. With respect to this entire claim, I would suggest that if school personnel were indeed intentionally briefing students on test material prior to taking the exams, the effect would be most observable in reading, the area in which studies found little evidence of possible cheating. Reading is more susceptible to unethical practices because entire sections need to be exposed and read, and collections of questions answered. If a reading selection had been compromised, as is alleged, we would expect to see large gains because many related items would be exposed and thus be detectable. This did not occur, which suggests that unprofessional behavior was not rampant. Indeed, because different content areas produced different results, Kentucky's score increases almost surely did not result from any breach of the validity or security of the examinations.

In addition, scores progressively increased in KIRIS in both math and reading at most levels. For the allegation of deceitful practices to carry weight, not only would the majority of schools (and recall we are discussing the entire state showing sizable improvement) have to be in league on these practices, but the practices would need to occur annually. Each year, schools would need to artificially inflate scores *higher than* the preceding year's levels and continue this pattern of deception every year thereafter. This is a fallacious scenario. Thus the hypothesis that corrupt practices led to score increases must be rejected. Are there places where such unwelcome behavior occurred? Probably so. But I would venture to say that the frequency is negligible.

Validity of Criticisms and the Success of KIRIS

To return to a comment made at the beginning of this section, I do not reject or ignore all methodological criticism of KIRIS. Issues of equating error, form-content equivalence, reasonableness of cut scores, early score increases attributed to adjustment and growing familiarity with the test format, and the failure to engage in immediate impact and validation studies truly are weaknesses that were not controlled or investigated. But from the available results there is every reason to believe that from 1992 to 1998 KERA did result in progressively increasing higher learning in Kentucky's public schools. If we surveyed educators and asked them to identify the goals of their schools, higher achievement clearly would head the list for most. I recognize that the evidence of successful schooling goes beyond the extent of students' learning in school environments. Although the data are limited, in the next section I present findings to support claims that KERA resulted in change not only in the curriculum presented to students but in what and how it was taught.

KIRIS Gains and Staff Development

If, as I assert, the KERA changes were real and significant, then we should be able to identify activities in the schools that could explain or account for the higher KIRIS scores. Unfortunately, KIRIS did not go forward with a far-reaching plan to monitor test score change in relationship to documented school interventions. It was not until 1996 that the state actually began to invest in such studies and evaluations. As such, work of this type tends to be retrospective. In the future, CATS must be better served.

A handful of studies have reported the impact of KIRIS on schools and schooling practices. Work by Hoffman (1998), Hoffman, Harris, Koger, and Thacker (1997), Stecher and Barron (1999), Stecher, Barron, Kaganoff, and Goodwin (1998), and Wilkerson & Associates (1996, 1999) are especially informative, as are summaries of considerable detail by Petrosko and Lindle (1998, 1999). Surveys by Wilkerson & Associates (1996, 1999) signaled the early reactions to and subsequent impact of KIRIS. In the mid-1990s a survey of hundreds of Kentucky educators found that the reforms were having an impact: expectations were changing, improvements were recognized, and greater instructional opportunities for greater numbers of students were being realized (Wilkerson & Associates, 1996). On the downside, respondents indicated that there was a narrowing of the curriculum in some areas, that KIRIS goals were taking time from other efforts, and that the time spent on test preparation was increasing. Four years later, when Wilkerson resurveyed educators, attitudes were more positive, as were perceptions of the impact and value of the reforms (Wilkerson & Associates, 1999). In interviews with school personnel from rural schools, KIRIS was seen as the major instructional force guiding local reform efforts (Appalachia Educational Laboratory, 1994). Criticism of the reform tended to focus on excessive workloads and school staffs' inability to do what was required in the time available.

Koretz, Barron, Mitchell, and Stecher (1996) attempted to get a handle on specific issues and instructional practices. In a sample survey of teachers, these researchers found evidence of changes in instructional practice and curricular focus to align with the KERA goals. The KIRIS curriculum focus, although not overwhelming in its impact, was judged by these investigators to be having a small positive effect on instruction. Administrative personnel reported that they were emphasizing KIRIS goals. Among the "negative effects" noted were the perceived pressure to perform well and the need to restrict the curriculum to KIRIS outcomes. A couple of years later Stecher et al. (1998) pointed to significant changes, finding "ample evidence that teachers have changed instructional practice in response to KERA and that KIRIS, in particular, has had a major influence on instructional behavior" (p. 84). In a larger and more detailed survey study of Kentucky educators, Stecher and Barron (1999) reported with greater precision that the changes appear related to certain grade levels and content areas. Although there continued to be considerable evidence of the impact of KERA and KIRIS, Stecher and Barron's work underscored the finding that practices at the grade levels tested by KIRIS tended to follow the test expectations more closely.

Few studies have been able to link the extent of the interventions and reforms to KIRIS scores. Petrosko and Lindle (1998, 1999) found that, longitudinally, schools that showed the highest KIRIS scores also showed the greatest effort in implementing the recommended reforms. However, their study lacked sufficient controls, and the authors' findings are not causal. Studies by Hoffman (1998) and Hoffman et al. (1997) monitored KIRIS scores in select high- and low-performing schools. Part of their work confirms the findings of Stecher et al. (1998) that the tested grades receive greater attention than the nontested grades. As a result of monitoring schools for performance changes, Hoffman et al. replicated Petrosko and Lindle's finding that greater score increases are observed in schools that implement more of the reform initiatives. An investigation by Harris, Hoffman, Koger, and Thacker (1998) supports these findings.

In a related study involving interviews and classroom observations, Thacker, Hoffman, and Koger (1998) found that many teachers were unable to determine the level of detail or depth needed to prepare students for the KIRIS exams. An abundance of similar studies evaluate and digest key factors associated with the reform as it translated into local action and practice (Stecher et al., 1998; Wilkerson & Associates, 1999; Harris et al., 1998; Petrosko & Lindle, 1999). These studies make clear that over time teachers' understanding of the reforms grew. Subsequently, researchers found evidence of the impact of professional development sponsored by state agencies and local districts. In other words, test scores did not simply increase but resulted from state and local staff development initiatives.

Next Steps: Into the Twenty-First Century

In the early 1990s KERA was presented and justifiably discussed as a bold reform. In the years since, many other states have taken up the Kentucky challenge to improve education for all children and provide comprehensive curricular reforms. The importance of this leadership must not be undervalued. Kentucky offered large-scale performance testing, and the state made schools responsible for test results rather than holding students accountable for outcomes over which they had little control. The state devised an accountability system that, to this day, represents a model whose principles—which require schools to be held accountable for their own circumstances and progress—others desire to emulate. The state created an assessment program designed to shoulder and guide the reform while accepting responsibility for providing a large segment of the reform itself. In the early years writers and commentators on the outlook of the Kentucky reform initiative most often concluded that "others will be watching." Has the KERA-based, KIRIS-linked reform resulted in better and more diverse learning outcomes for Kentucky students? The answer is yes: more students have a higher capacity in the Kentucky core content areas than ever before. Data assembled from the Kentucky assessment efforts clearly support this conclusion. Do we know it unequivocally? Of course we do. KIRIS test scores have increased and instructional practices have changed. What we do not know is the exact extent of the changes. In Kentucky's effort to create sound and state-of-the-art assessments, it neglected to provide sufficient formal, comprehensive evaluations of the reforms to ensure the precise causal connection between the treatment and its result.

We need to see and understand the transition from KIRIS to CATS as an opportunity for improvement. The KIRIS assessments were not perfect at any time in their history. Likewise, CATS will be flawed in some respects. But that should not stop Kentucky from pressing on with school reform.

REFERENCES

Appalachia Educational Laboratory. (1994). Instruction and assessment
    in accountable and nonaccountable grades. *Notes from the Field:
    Education Reform in Rural Kentucky,* 4(1), 1–12. (Available from the
    Appalachia Educational Laboratory, P.O. Box 1348, Charleston, WV
    25325)
Catterall, J. A., Mehrens, W. A., Ryan, J. M., Flores, E. J., & Rubin, P. M.
    (1998). *Kentucky Instructional Results Information System: A technical
    review.* Frankfort: Commonwealth of Kentucky Legislative Research
    Commission.
Cunningham, G. K. (1996, April). *When performance assessment is not
    performance based.* Paper presented at the annual meeting of the
    American Educational Research Association, New York.
Haladyna, T. M. (1994). *Developing and validating multiple-choice test items.*
    Hillsdale, NJ: Lawrence Erlbaum.

Hambleton, R. K., Jaeger, R. M., Koretz, D., Linn, R. L., Millman, J., & Phillips, E. E. (1995). *Review of the measurement quality of the Kentucky Instructional Results Information Systems, 1991–1994.* Frankfort, KY: Office of Education Accountability.

Harris, C. D., Hoffman, R. G., Koger, L., & Thacker, A. (1998). *The relationship between school gains in 7th and 8th grade KIRIS scores and instructional practices in mathematics, science and social studies for 1997* (Report No. FR-WATSD-98–05). Radcliff, KY: Human Resources Research Organization.

Hoffman, R. G. (1998). *Relationships among KIRIS open-response assessment, ACT scores, and students' self-reported high school grades* (Report No. DFR-WATSD-98–27). Radcliff, KY: Human Resources Research Organization.

Hoffman, R. G., Harris, C. D., Koger, L., & Thacker, A. (1997). *The relationship between school gains in 8th grade KIRIS scores and instructional practices in mathematics, science and social studies.* Radcliff, KY: Human Resources Research Organization.

Kentucky Department of Education. (1998). *Kentucky school and district accountability results, accountability cycle 3 (1994–95 to 1997–98).* Frankfort: Author.

Kentucky Department of Education. (1998). *Program of studies for Kentucky schools: Grades primary–12.* Frankfort: Author.

Kentucky Department of Education. (2000). *Results matter: A decade of difference in Kentucky's public schools 1990–2000.* Frankfort: Author.

Kentucky Department of Education, Division of Curriculum Assessment Development. (1996). *Core content for assessment,* Vol. 1.0. Frankfurt: Author.

Kentucky Department of Education, Division of Curriculum Assessment Development. (1999). *Core content for assessment,* Vol. 3.0. Frankfurt: Author.

Kingston, N., & Reidy, E. (1997). Kentucky's accountability and assessment systems. In J. Millman (Ed.), *Grading teachers, grading schools* (pp. 191–209). Thousand Oaks, CA: Corwin Press.

Koretz, D. M., & Barron, S. I. (1998). *The validity of gains in scores on the Kentucky Instructional Results Information System (KIRIS)* (Education Report No. MR-1014-EDU). Santa Monica, CA: RAND.

Koretz, D. M., Barron, S. I., Mitchell, K. J., & Stecher, B. M. (1996). *Perceived effects of the Kentucky Instructional Results Information System (KIRIS)* (Report No. MR-792-PCT/FF). Santa Monica, CA: RAND.

Linn, R. L., Koretz, D., & Baker, E. L. (1996). *Assessing the validity of the National Assessment of Educational Progress: Final report of the NAEP technical review panel* (CSE Tech. Rep. No. 416). Los Angeles: University of California, Center for the Study of Evaluation, National Center for Research on Evaluation, Standards, and Student Testing.

Miller, M. D. (1999, April). *Generalizability of performance-based assessments at the school level.* Paper presented at the annual meeting of the American Educational Research Association, Montreal, Canada.

Nitko, A. J., Amedahe, F., Al-Sarimi, A., Wang, S., & Wingert, M. (1997). *How well are the Kentucky academic expectations matched to the KIRIS96 assessments, CTBS, and CATS?* Lexington: Kentucky Institute for Education Research.

Petrosko, J. M., & Lindle, J. C. (1998, April). *Standards-based school reform in Kentucky elementary schools: A longitudinal study.* Paper presented at the annual meeting of the American Educational Research Association, San Diego, CA.

Petrosko, J. M., & Lindle, J. C. (1999, April). *State-mandated school reform in Kentucky: Year three of a longitudinal study.* Paper presented at the annual meeting of the American Educational Research Association, Montreal, Canada.

Redfield D., & Pankratz, R. S. (1997). Historical background: The Kentucky school accountability index. In J. Millman (Ed.), *Grading teachers, grading schools* (pp. 185–190). Thousand Oaks, CA: Corwin Press.

Stecher, B. M., & Barron, S. (1999, April). *Test-based accountability: The perverse consequences of milepost testing.* Paper presented at the annual meeting of the American Educational Research Association, Montreal, Canada.

Stecher, B. M., Barron, S., Kaganoff, T., & Goodwin, J. (1998). *The effects of standards-based assessment on classroom practices: Results of the 1996–97 RAND survey of Kentucky teachers of mathematics and writing* (CSE Tech. Rep. No. 482). Los Angeles: University of California, Center for the Study of Evaluation, National Center for Research on Evaluation, Standards, and Student Testing.

Sugrue, B., Novak, J., Burstein, L., Lewis, E., Koretz, D., & Linn. R. (1995). *Mapping test items to the 1992 mathematics achievement levels descriptions: Mathematics educators' interpretations and their relationship to student performance* (CSE Tech. Rep. No. 393). Los Angeles: University of California, Center for the Study of Evaluation, National Center for Research on Evaluation, Standards, and Student Testing.

Thacker, A. A., Hoffman, R. G., & Koger, L. E. (1998). *Course contents and KIRIS: Approaches to instructional and curriculum design in middle school science and social studies* (Report No. FR-WATSD-98–07). Radcliff, KY: Human Resources Research Organization.

Western Michigan University, Evaluation Center. (1995). *An independent evaluation of the Kentucky Instructional Results Information System (KIRIS)*. Lexington: Kentucky Institute for Education Research.

Wilkerson & Associates. (1996). *The 1996 statewide education reform study: Final report*. Lexington: Kentucky Institute for Education Research.

Wilkerson & Associates. (1999). *The 1999 statewide education reform study: Final report*. Lexington: Kentucky Institute for Education Research.

6

LINKING CURRICULUM
AND INSTRUCTION TO
PERFORMANCE STANDARDS

Stephen K. Clements

ON A LATE SEPTEMBER SATURDAY in 1999, an extraordinary array of teachers, parents, principals, and superintendents from twenty-one schools around Kentucky—eighty individuals in all—assembled in Louisville for a daylong miniconference on school success. What made this group of school representatives extraordinary? Each individual was associated with a Kentucky school that had attained "reward" status in all three Kentucky Instructional Results Information System (KIRIS) accountability cycles (1994, 1996, and 1998). During each two-year cycle each school had improved its accountability score well beyond the state's expectations. Only thirty-eight of the approximately fourteen hundred schools in Kentucky achieved this status. Two state advocacy groups, the Prichard Committee for Academic Excellence and the Partnership for Kentucky Schools, had sponsored this gathering to learn why these schools had consistently succeeded. Most of the high achievers were elementary schools; only three high schools garnered this honor, and no middle schools were among the thirty-eight.

After several hours of discussion one theme loomed large. Namely, each school had made as its priority a well-articulated curriculum aligned with the state's evolving assessment, and the adults in those schools focused on ensuring that every child had an adequate opportunity to learn the curriculum. This was not simply a matter of deciding what would be taught and when. Rather, teachers in these schools collaborated constantly to determine "how best to teach different topics, and how better to diagnose student needs" (David, 1999, p. 2). They worried together about how to align curriculum across grade levels, when students should meet various performance standards, and how to adapt curriculum to suit individual student needs. They also sought ongoing, site-based professional development opportunities to strengthen their instructional efforts. And they received strong support from principals, superintendents, and other school leaders in these activities. In short, says Robert F. Sexton (1999) of the Prichard Committee for Academic Excellence, these schools developed a rich curriculum that makes sense, effective instructional leadership, and well-connected teachers who concentrate on the learning needs of each child as well as their own needs.

These actions represent perhaps the epitome of what Kentucky education policymakers had in mind when they created the Kentucky Education Reform Act of 1990 (KERA). That scarcely more than three dozen schools have managed so far to surpass the goals set by the state, however, suggests the difficulties involved in implementing the vision of a revolutionary new approach to curriculum, teaching, and learning. This is not to imply, of course, that positive curricular changes have not taken place in many other Kentucky schools during the past seven or eight years. But putting together all of the reform pieces in a manner that leads to consistent student achievement raises substantial challenges that relatively few schools so far have been able to meet.

The pages that follow recount Kentucky's experiences with a new approach to curriculum under systemic reform. This account shows how much easier it is to describe what the state is attempting to accomplish with curriculum reform than to actually carry through its implementation. It will also show how crucial to the success of systemic reform are the timing, clarity, and availability of new curricular materials, especially those linked to a high-stakes assessment system. Many of the difficulties Kentucky has faced in implementing reform indeed stem from serious underestimation of the amount of time necessary for the state to create a high-quality core curriculum and from an overestimation of the capacity of teachers to adapt state frameworks to their own classrooms.

The Roots of Curricular Reform

The origins of Kentucky's new approach to school curricula were in the national and state school reform policy debate that raged during the 1980s.

That debate was actually started in the late 1970s, a time of sagging standardized test scores and economic stagnation, but reached a feverish pitch in 1983 with the publication of *A Nation at Risk,* the report of the National Commission on Excellence in Education. In the wake of *A Nation at Risk* a host of additional public school reports and critiques appeared, most of which fingered a poor curriculum and low expectations as chief culprits in the underdevelopment of student knowledge and skill levels (for a synopsis see Toch, 1991). New players joined the education policy scene during this time, including governors, business executives, and professional organizations.

The initial response in most states was for the legislature to mandate more courses, more time in school, and more tests. By 1986, however, the National Governors' Association (NGA) had launched a new five-year policy initiative, Results in Education, that put the focus on a reform approach called "restructuring" (Murphy, 1990). The governors were ready, said NGA chair Governor Lamar Alexander of Tennessee, for some "horse trading." The states would take on the responsibility for identifying learning goals and stipulating the outcomes of schooling. And if educators would ensure that students made measurable progress toward those goals and outcomes, then state officials would be willing to reduce the regulation of what went on inside schools and classrooms (National Governors' Association [NGA], 1986). As the NGA sounded the call for an outcomes-based approach to reform, various professional organizations began publishing the skills they expected students to learn by certain grade school levels. These efforts meshed so that by 1989, for example, the NGA's major recommendations included building on the curriculum reforms suggested earlier that year by groups such as the American Association for the Advancement of Science and the National Research Council and setting learner outcome goals that emphasized higher-order thinking skills (NGA, 1989).

1980s-Style Education Reform

A smaller version of this same drama took place in Kentucky during the 1980s. The reform reports already mentioned helped catapult education to the top of the state's political agenda. In 1984 the newly elected governor, Martha Layne Collins, the superintendent of public instruction, Alice McDonald, and the House and Senate Education Committees all competed with one another to articulate a school reform approach for Kentucky. Also, elected leaders were nudged toward public school changes by newly formulated advocacy groups, such as the Prichard

Committee for Academic Excellence and Kentuckians for Excellence in Education (sponsored by the Kentucky Chamber of Commerce). The result of the education policy ferment during these years was the creation of new programs, most of which were mandated during the regular sessions of the General Assembly in 1984 and 1986, and in a special session in 1985 called specifically to promote education reform (see Clements, 1998).

Although much of this legislation focused on increased funding for teachers and more resources for poor school districts, some of it—in keeping with trends in other states—targeted assessment and classroom time spent on basic skills. In 1984, for example, the legislature required schools to teach and test "essential skills" in reading, writing, mathematics, spelling, and research and reference skills, a response to the perceived need for more accountability in education. At this time the state's curriculum was set informally and based on the textbooks approved by a state commission and the courses recommended in the *Program of Studies for Kentucky Schools.* Accordingly, for each grade and in each of these subjects, the Kentucky Department of Education (KDE) developed essential skills lists and contracted with a prominent testing company to develop the Kentucky Essential Skills Test (KEST) to assess student achievement. Eventually KDE also published manuals to help teachers develop lessons to introduce and reinforce those skills. The skills identified in these documents—some 640 in all—were basic and process oriented. Hence, a fifth-grade math student would be expected, among other things, to "read numbers through millions," "write (select) fractions in their simplest form," and "add fractions or mixed numbers with like denominators" (Kentucky Department of Education [KDE], 1984, p. 7). The activities manuals simply provided examples of problems or exercises that would demonstrate the skills described. But the skills lists were not an attempt to define what all the children should know and be able to do at different grade levels.

The experiment largely failed because of educators' dissatisfaction with the KEST examinations and with the rudimentary skills list. However, having the state stipulate learner outcomes and then give schools freedom to meet the outcomes—while holding schools accountable for progress—appealed to some politicians, most notably Governor Wallace Wilkinson, elected in 1987. Wilkinson, with the help of education consultant Jack Foster, developed his own restructuring plan but failed to secure its passage in the 1988 General Assembly. Unsure about how to sell his restructuring plan and cognizant that the *Rose v. Council for Better Education, Inc.* school-funding lawsuit was under consideration by the state supreme court, Wilkinson decided in early 1989 to move unilaterally to implement parts of his plan. He created the Council on School Performance Standards (CSPS), a group of citizens and educators that would collectively define what Kentucky students should know and be able to do when they graduated from high school and determine how to assess this learning. Concurrent with the work of CSPS, the chief justice of the Kentucky Supreme Court declared Kentucky's schools inequitable and inefficient and ordered the General Assembly to rewrite the education laws, re-creating Kentucky's public schools. The court order named seven capacities for all students, which CSPS translated into six learning goals.

Capacities, Goals, and Outcomes: The Formation of Learning Expectations

CSPS thus began the enormous task of identifying learner outcomes and assessment techniques under the assumption that its work would feed into some reform legislation upon which Wilkinson and the General Assembly might eventually agree. Five council task forces consisting of educators worked through the summer of 1989 to define six learning goals for all students and to propose a new statewide system of assessing student performance beyond paper-and-pencil tests. The six learning goals (Council on School Performance Standards [CSPS], 1989) included

1. Basic communication and mathematics skills
2. Knowledge and application of core concepts in six subject matter areas
3. Self-sufficiency
4. Responsible group membership
5. Thinking and problem-solving skills
6. Making connections across subject matter areas and between old and new knowledge

The six learning goals and recommendations of the CSPS were presented in September 1989 to the legislative Task Force on Education Reform, the group responsible for crafting a reform plan. In turn, the six learning goals were incorporated into House Bill 940, more commonly known as KERA. KERA charged CSPS to reconvene and define the six goals in measurable terms by December 1991.

The work of CSPS has been ably summarized elsewhere (CSPS, 1991; Foster, 1999; Steffy, 1993). A truncated version of this story is that approximately 450 educators—both classroom teachers and college and university faculty members—applied for membership on eleven designated task forces, and 125 of these individuals, along with KDE representatives, formally participated in these subcommittees. Task force deliberations were often arduous and contentious, given that each group sought not to identify basic or essential skills but rather the so-called big ideas in each subject area and to relate this crucial knowledge to real-life experiences. At the end of the eighteen-month process, eleven task forces described seventy-five concepts or processes that defined what all students should know and be able to do. These were presented in a 250-page document and called "valued outcomes" because they defined what was most valued to learn. The technical report written to inform educators about what students were to learn under KERA also contained examples of more than 400 student performance tasks and examples of 150 performance assessments. As one might expect, more than half of the outcomes concerned goal 2, which involved core concepts and principles from six broad disciplinary categories: science, mathematics, social studies, arts and humanities, practical living, and vocational studies. The remaining outcomes were dispersed among the other five goals.

As Foster (1999) and others have noted, difficulties surrounding the new curriculum blueprint developed not long after the CSPS report (1991) *Kentucky's Learner Goals and Valued Outcomes* became available. For one thing, although the seventy-five valued outcomes were widely discussed among educators and the media, neither the technical report itself nor a thirty-one-page summary (prepared by a marketing consultant and written in layperson's terms to communicate with parents and the public) was ever widely circulated. No one knows how many Kentucky teachers and administrators themselves spent much time with a copy of the technical report, but only several hundred documents were distributed to districts and schools. Most professionals associated with Kentucky curriculum development assume that only a small percentage of instructors ever examined or worked with this material.

Other problems arose as KDE officials tried to produce curriculum frameworks based on the report. According to KERA, KDE had eighteen months after release of the CSPS report to provide an initial framework. The document that was eventually introduced in July 1993, *Transformations: Kentucky's Curriculum Framework* (KDE, 1993), was lengthier than the CSPS report (more than five hundred pages spread across two volumes) and considerably more detailed. Similar to the CSPS technical report, *Transformations* was designed around the seventy-five valued outcomes and attempted to communicate in one or two pages how to approach each outcome in curricular terms.

Although *Transformations* cited a host of illustrations on how the many "processes and concepts" associated with the outcomes could be taught and assessed and used an array of specific facts in examples, it failed to specify which facts associated with each discipline or subject area were important and which were not (Foster, 1999). This helped fuel the notion among some educators that facts were not important and had simply been replaced by concepts and processes as the objects of instruction. Nor was it clear what the relationship would be between the curriculum framework and school textbooks that were (and still are) in use. KERA retained the pre-1990 state textbook selection process, wherein an appointed state commission approved lists of textbooks, texts that were not produced with Kentucky's curriculum specifically in mind.

In addition, many Kentucky teachers, trained for a more traditional "material coverage" approach to curriculum and course preparation, were simply unfamiliar with the terms, pedagogical styles, and assessment techniques presented in *Transformations*. The curricular framework document also suffered from the same limited exposure problem as the CSPS report. A notebook containing the volume was sent to the principal of each Kentucky school. There was no coherent plan for ensuring that educators in Kentucky schools adequately received, adapted, and implemented the performance-based curriculum.

Finally, and perhaps most important, *Transformations* had been preceded by the first two rounds of KIRIS tests. This problem grew out of KERA politics. KERA contained a curriculum development timetable that would yield a framework document during the middle of 1993, but it also obliged the state to move forward with creation of an assessment system that would be fielded and would establish baseline measures *before* completion of the curriculum. As a result, the first rounds of KIRIS were administered before most teachers had received any curricular guidance, much less incorporated the new materials and methods into their classrooms. According to Jack Foster (1999, p. 40), it would take local schools at least two years after publication of the curriculum framework to alter programs and practices.

Although the intent of school reform architects followed a logical sequence, KIRIS development operated on a different track than the curriculum. Of course, rewards or sanctions for school personnel would flow from KIRIS performance, and it was unclear for several years how strong the relationship was between KIRIS assessments and the curricular guidance offered by KDE. As a result, Kentucky teachers tended to devote much more time early in KERA implementation to analysis of released

KIRIS items, which were available, than to the CSPS report or *Transformations,* which seemed inscrutable and too vague to many teachers (Appalachia Educational Laboratory, 1995). Test results mattered, and the curricular materials were bulky, tending to be hard to understand and work with. Teachers also could not discern from *Transformations* what specific skills and knowledge would be assessed through KIRIS. Focus on the test therefore won out as the preferred method of pursuing early local curricular revisions.

As KERA implementation progressed through the middle and latter part of the 1990s, KDE attempted to address some of the confusion over curriculum. In response to the clamor from teachers for better guidance about the crucial facts students needed to know for the state assessments, KDE in 1996 produced *Core Content for Assessment,* which sought to present specific concepts and content in the subject areas that would be the basis for future KIRIS questions. This material was no panacea for teachers but did provide more guidance for direction-starved educators across the state. KDE released a revised version of *Transformations* in 1995 (KDE, 1995), but *Core Content for Assessment* seemed to get more attention from Kentucky educators.

Several matters of contention involving the curriculum were dealt with in part through formal and informal political processes. For example, some conservatives around the state, especially those sensitive to potential governmental encroachment upon religious and family prerogatives, charged that learning goals 3 and 4—which concerned self-sufficiency and effective group membership—amounted to a kind of state-imposed thought control. These allegations also were being made at a time when conservatives in other states were attacking the outcomes-in-education movement on the grounds that localities would lose control of education, politically correct educational philosophies would be imposed by state bureaucracies, and process would replace content in the curriculum. During the 1994 Kentucky General Assembly, these complaints were given serious attention by the legislature, which asked KDE to investigate the matter. In response Education Commissioner Thomas C. Boysen convened a group to review the seventy-five valued outcomes. The review committee ultimately reduced and streamlined the number of outcomes to fifty-seven, changing their appellation to "academic expectations." Boysen also pledged that goals 3 and 4 would not be assessed through KIRIS. These moves seemed to placate some KERA critics and deflated some of the support they had garnered. The 1995 revised version of *Transformations* was constructed around the fifty-seven academic expectations.

Evidence of Curricular Change

By the middle of the 1990s both qualitative and quantitative research studies began appearing to document the impact of curricular alterations over the years. The Appalachia Educational Laboratory (AEL) conducted a study, which included an analysis of documents and a series of focus group interviews with teachers, principals, and staff members of KDE. The AEL report (1995) substantiated the widespread complaints about curriculum confusion. Curriculum alignment with the academic expectations and KIRIS tests was really just beginning in many schools, owing to uncertainty about the alignment process itself, confusion about the expectations, and unfamiliarity with the curriculum-writing process. Teachers had not been trained to produce curriculum. Traditionally, they had used materials from textbooks or state agencies and adapted them for their own use. Nor was adequate time given for teachers to learn the new approach. Professional development on curriculum alignment was limited and uneven in quality. Based on Jack Foster's ideal two-year schedule for curriculum implementation mentioned earlier, this is about where teachers were expected to be at mid-decade, but it was insufficient given the phasing in of the accountability system. In addition, KDE's role in assisting schools and districts in continuous assessment strategies was never implemented to the extent that KERA architects intended.

As the mid-1990s passed, educators gained experience with KERA, with the curriculum alignment process, and with changes in Kentucky's testing system. But by the late 1990s the KIRIS-based assessment and accountability system had come under attack as well (Guskey, 1994; Petrosko, 1997). In brief, a host of Kentucky educators and school officials had an array of complaints against the system. In addition to expressing their concern that too little assessment-related curricular guidance had been made available to schools, they complained that the assessments, especially the writing portfolios, consumed too much time during the year. Educators also complained that KIRIS narrowed the curriculum and was not a valid and reliable measure of what they taught, especially if the results were used to issue rewards and sanctions. A Kentucky Institute for Education Research (KIER) survey (1997) captured educators' opinions about KIRIS: 69 percent of teachers polled thought KIRIS did a poor job of measuring student progress on the academic expectations, and 67 percent thought the accountability index unfairly measured schools' performance. In 1998 and 1999, in response to a General Assembly mandate, various external committees worked with KDE and state board of education officials to revise the assessment system. The revamped assessment, known as the

Commonwealth Accountability Testing System (CATS), was launched in 1999 and has so far alleviated many of the concerns about KIRIS.

In addition, KDE has continued to recast its curricular materials in terms that will be more understandable to teachers, principals, and parents. The department issued a new version of *Core Content for Assessment* in 1999, which reflected changes designed to reconcile Kentucky's curriculum with evolving performance standards from national professional organizations. Moreover, the latest edition of *Core Content for Assessment* was published on the Internet through KDE's Web site, which will presumably make it more available to a broader audience. KDE (1998) has also published a new version of *Program of Studies for Kentucky Schools*. Rather than provide a list of courses, the new edition of *Program of Studies for Kentucky Schools* relates the academic expectations to the content knowledge and process skills youngsters should possess at each grade level in primary and middle school, to high school courses, and to the subject areas that will be assessed through CATS. This version therefore provides a kind of K–12 continuum into which teachers can fit curricular materials they are developing for specific courses. Both of these changes are potentially significant to curriculum evolution, but it is still too early to measure their impact on Kentucky classrooms.

Since Matthews's research review appeared in 1997, several additional studies—most commissioned by KIER—have appeared that allow us to make additional inferences about the curriculum changes in Kentucky's fourteen hundred schools. One of these studies examined curriculum and other reform components at eighteen middle and high schools that participated in a five-year study. The report noted that "for all intents and purposes the curricula of middle and high schools have been aligned with the Core Content and, in many instances, district and/or national standards, perhaps with some being more carefully aligned than others" (Craig & Kacer, 1999, p. 1). The authors also noted, not surprisingly, that the schools that typically had students with higher KIRIS achievement scores (both in aggregate and in subject area assessments) continuously engaged in curriculum review and analysis, communicated effectively and openly about curriculum alignment, set high academic expectations, promoted the application of thinking skills to real-world situations, shared responsibility for their students' success, and provided a continued academic focus toward higher standards. Successful Kentucky schools, in other words, tend to be those that have gotten serious about what their students should know and be able to do.

Additional evidence supports the finding that many Kentucky schools are making progress in terms of curriculum alignment. During mid-1998, for example, teachers undergoing KDE training reviewed consolidated plans from a host of schools and districts around the state. Curriculum alignment activities loomed large among the plans of these districts; indeed, they almost dominated the work agenda for some locations (KDE, Office of Leadership and School Improvement, 1998; KDE, Office of Regional Assistance, 1998). Although curriculum alignment is an ongoing challenge, teachers, principals, superintendents, and school council members recognize that success on state assessments hinges in large measure on this activity.

Further evidence about curriculum implementation comes from annual classroom observations conducted by Kentucky's Office of Education Accountability (OEA) and from a recent survey of Kentuckians. OEA staff members have conducted annual classroom observations for several years in an effort to gather systematic information about KERA implementation. In 1997 they observed 129 classrooms—a mixture of elementary, middle, and high schools—and found that nearly all lessons directly related to Kentucky's learning goals and academic expectations. They also found that 67 percent of the lessons flowed from *Transformations* and that 77 percent used *Core Content for Assessment* (OEA, 1997). In 1998 observers visited 53 elementary school classrooms and found that 60 percent of the lessons reflected *Core Content for Assessment* and that 47 percent reflected *Transformations* (OEA, 1998). According to this evidence, then, between two-thirds and three-fourths of the state's classrooms contain curricular materials that are at least loosely aligned with the state's reform-oriented curriculum. These findings also agree with those of a survey of school board members, principals, teachers, parents, and members of the general public conducted by Wilkerson (1999). One goal of this survey was to determine changes in perception regarding what students are learning in Kentucky's public schools. Large percentages of those surveyed thought student performance in writing, thinking and problem solving, reading, and computer skills had improved some or a lot in the previous five years. Smaller percentages (though still over half) perceived improvement in basic subject matter knowledge and math computation skills. This study therefore links perceptions of improved student performance with the hard work of recasting curriculum along performance- and standards-based lines.

The assessment results from KIRIS, the National Assessment of Educational Progress (NAEP), and the new CATS tests suggest, too, that schools have been paying attention to curriculum improvement. In 1999 the Prichard Committee for Academic Excellence released the most comprehensive review to date of assessment results. This review (Prichard Committee for Academic Excellence, 1999) shows substantial improvements in the percentage of Kentucky students attaining the highest two achievement categories on the KIRIS tests, particularly in reading, math, and social studies—although middle school score improvements generally lag far behind those of elementary and high schools in all subjects but math. The improvements, which were substantial in several subjects, would have been unlikely without school officials' paying careful attention to curriculum, teaching, and assessment issues. Similarly, the analysis shows Kentucky NAEP scores moving up. Kentucky students have passed the national average in reading and are nearing the national average in math and science. As a result, Kentucky students have moved from the lowest-performing group of states on most NAEP measures to the middle-performing group. Again, such shifts indicate that curriculum changes have been made in Kentucky schools and that such changes are beginning to bear fruit in terms of academic performance.

The evidence from longitudinal studies of elementary, middle, and high schools across the state (Craig & Kacer, 1999; Petrosko, 1999) shows not only that ongoing curriculum alignment is related to student performance but also that considerable variations exist in the degree of curriculum change both within and between schools. The reality of this variation in schools' ability to align their curriculum with the new performance standards is evidenced by the wide variation in improved student performance across the state on statewide assessments. A University of Kentucky Appalachian Center analysis of KIRIS data reported by the Prichard Committee for Academic Excellence (1999, p. 14), for example, showed that schools in regions 6 (south central Kentucky), 8 (southeast Kentucky), and 3 (Jefferson County–Louisville)—not unexpectedly, the districts with the most impoverished students—have aggregate academic index scores below the state average and well below the districts in central, north central, and western Kentucky. Schools in all regions of the state, it should be noted, have improved under KERA. But the regions with the lowest baseline scores have not closed the gap in scores between themselves and the better-performing regions of the state.

In addition, schools across Kentucky have been facing the increasingly arduous task of moving large percentages of children from the "apprentice" to the "proficient" performance category on the state assessments. Kentucky's standards-based assessments have been built around four NAEP-like performance categories: novice, apprentice, proficient, and distinguished. A score of 100 is proficient, and in order for a Kentucky school to reach KERA's twenty-year goals, students will need to average 100—a feat that can only be accomplished if most children become proficient in all subject areas (a few scores of 140, in the distinguished category, can offset some of those who score at the apprentice level). The academic index scores achieved to this point are largely due to schools pulling large percentages of students from the novice to the apprentice category, although the proficient percentages have increased substantially at elementary and high school levels in reading, math, and social studies. Moving large percentages of students from the apprentice to the proficient level, however, may take more of a curriculum and instructional revolution than many Kentucky educators can now fathom, and this remains the most profound challenge facing the state's school communities.

It is noteworthy, of course, that no group or individual has yet undertaken a large-scale, broad-based study or survey of implemented curriculum across the state. Such a study would be revealing but would also be prohibitively expensive and time-consuming. Its results would not be comparable with a baseline study of curriculum in Kentucky in the prereform era because no such study was ever conducted. Until such an inquiry is made, however, determinations about the extent of implementation of Kentucky's new curriculum will have to be based on case studies and inferences from surveys, classroom observations, and school performance results.

In summary, there is evidence that the curriculum in Kentucky's schools has, to varying degrees, changed since the advent of KERA. The most recent KIER opinion survey (KIER, 1999) found that nearly four out of five teachers, parents on school councils, and local board members believe Kentucky's student achievement standards and the guidelines of *Core Content for Assessment* are working moderately or very well to improve teaching and learning; fully 90 percent of principals believe this to be the case (p. 24). (Interestingly, only 57 percent of parents of children in public schools and 52 percent of the general public agree that this is the case—findings possibly due to lack of knowledge about the core content or how it figures into the curriculum picture.) About 90 percent of parents on school councils and educators believe instructional decisions should be made at the school level. Perhaps ironically, however, a majority of principals (57 percent) and teachers (51 percent) in the sample also support the notion that the state should establish a statewide curriculum for each grade level (p. 40). This suggests that educators still struggle with the conflict between being responsible for deciding what to teach and being told exactly what to teach, between autonomy and prescription. They wish to have considerable autonomy with regard to curriculum content, yet at the same time they tend to prefer an established curriculum they would have great confidence in teaching, particularly if they are being held accountable for student learning based on statewide tests.

Hard Lessons from a Slow Revolution

What has Kentucky learned from its long and sometimes harsh experience with curriculum reform? First, it appears that the distance between the theory of a standards-based approach to schooling and effective practice continues to be substantial. Simply put, although the idea of defining what students should know and be able to do at different ages and grades, then measuring progress toward performance goals, is still attractive to many Kentuckians, it is nevertheless a daunting task to set standards in understandable terms and design a strong—but nonmandatory—curriculum. Although the learner outcomes (the fifty-seven academic expectations) emerged from an open and participatory process, too few teachers and principals understand how to translate them into practice. KDE's curriculum framework materials—the versions of *Transformations, Core Content for Assessment,* and *Program of Studies for Kentucky Schools*—have not provided the kind of help most teachers and principals have been seeking, at least as far as many Kentucky educators are concerned. Moreover, KDE has been unable to provide the training and other resources needed to help a majority of school practitioners make better use of these documents to improve instruction. Educators have been forced to cope as best they can under the circumstances, sometimes consulting KDE curriculum guides but often relying on their own intuition, approved textbooks, third-party materials, and published state assessment items to craft their own lessons.

It remains to be seen whether KDE will, in the future, be able to provide teachers with more helpful materials and resources, rather than unwieldy tomes, to guide improved instruction. Unfortunately, there seem to be no external companies or organizations devoted to producing core content pamphlets, booklets, or multimedia materials for Kentucky's teachers or to providing models that supplement those put forth by KDE's curriculum specialists. It is possible, of course, that such a capacity could emerge in coming years. Interestingly, one of the most popular curriculum tools is a large set of multicolored, three-inch-square cards on which key concepts from *Core Content for Assessment* are recorded—different colors corresponding to different subject areas. Created by the Kentucky Association of School Councils, this simple set of cards has been extremely popular with teachers and with parents on school councils, who can arrange and rearrange the cards as necessary to understand the "flow" of the core content. This suggests that other consumer-oriented items could find a market niche in Kentucky. Similarly, the Internet could provide new tools for more effective curriculum guidance in Kentucky, although the future of this technology, its availability, and its uses are hard to anticipate.

A second and perhaps more important lesson is that it is unrealistic, at best, to expect teachers and schools to design curriculum if they are given little direction and no significant resources to pay teachers to do so. In contrast, Kentucky has spent about $10 million a year creating its assessment and accountability system and has employed a great many individuals and outside contractors in the effort. Teachers have not been well trained to develop curriculum, and the state would need to invest heavily in professional training to create a cadre of skilled, sophisticated curriculum writers. If under KERA a de facto state curriculum could have been generated more quickly and disseminated well and if resources had been provided to extend contracts for one-quarter to one-half of the state's educators by a month or two each year, then it would have been more likely that the curricular expectations of the reform act could have been met. Under the circumstances, however, teachers were put in an impossible situation, being forced to respond to a strange new assessment without guidance and, later, with guidance but without the resources or training needed to meet the challenge. Only in the final years of the 1990s did many educators come to grasp the relationship among the curriculum frameworks promulgated by the state, the ever evolving state assessment, and the performance standards articulated early in reform implementation. In short, standards can have little meaning in a high-stakes testing environment unless and until teachers see these relationships and have the time and resources to respond appropriately.

Kentucky's experiences with failed attempts to provide educators with guidance for implementing instruction that meets reformers' expectations is not unique. Cohen (1995) reviewed the efforts of a number of states from the mid-1980s through 1994 to provide policy guidance for instruction. He notes that although there has been a broad movement toward more intellectually ambitious instruction, reform efforts have created more variety in curricular approaches and less coherence. Several factors are identified as root causes of increased variability in state and local guidance for instruction, including conflicts between state and local policymaking, the fragmented nature of school systems, and conflicting signals from different groups. Despite an increase in political and administrative efforts related to instructional guidance, little progress has been made in increasing the capacity for instruction. Cohen agrees that curriculum change cannot be driven merely by producing standards and assessments. Rather, teachers' knowledge, professional values, and commitments, as well as social resources that remove barriers to learning, are the primary systems that interact to produce instruction. Knowledge, professional values, and commitments are key ingredients that regulate practice.

Given this framework, Kentucky's advances in writing instruction may provide the experience base for a breakthrough in designing much more effective approaches to teaching and learning. Standards of performance in writing have been developed to the degree that teachers across the state now have access to student work that shows examples of high, mediocre, and poor performance at different stages of writing development. This tool has produced such positive reactions from writing teachers across the state that KDE has assembled a task force to explore how these benchmarking performances can be produced in other core content areas.

Thus, although curriculum changes in Kentucky over the past ten years have not matched the expectations of the designers of KERA, both the failures and successes in curriculum development need careful examination and analysis. Learning from the past is the key to ensuring all children will have the opportunity to learn in the future.

REFERENCES

Appalachia Educational Laboratory. (1995). *The needs of Kentucky teachers for designing curricula based on academic expectations.* Lexington: Kentucky Institute for Education Research.

Clements, S. K. (1998). The changing face of common schooling: The politics of the Kentucky Education Reform Act of 1990 (Doctoral dissertation, University of Chicago, 1998). *Dissertation Abstracts International,* 59(01a), 0302.

Cohen, D. K. (1995). What is the system in systemic reform? *Educational Researcher, 24*(9), 11–17, 31.

Council on School Performing Standards. (1989). *Preparing Kentucky youth for the next century: What students should know and be able to do and how learning should be assessed.* Frankfort, KY: Author.

Council on School Performing Standards. (1991). *Kentucky's learner goals and valued outcomes: Technical report.* Frankfort, KY: Author.

Craig, J. R., & Kacer, B. A. (1999). *A longitudinal study of eighteen selected middle and high schools in Kentucky.* Lexington: Kentucky Institute for Education Research.

David, J. (1999). *Creating successful schools: A continuous commitment.* Paper prepared for the Partnership for Kentucky Schools and the Prichard Committee for Academic Excellence, Lexington, KY.

Foster, J. D. (1999). *Redesigning public education: The Kentucky experience.* Lexington, KY: Diversified Services.

Guskey, T. R. (1994). *High stakes performance assessment: Perspectives on Kentucky's educational reform.* Thousand Oaks, CA: Corwin Press.

Kentucky Department of Education. (1984). *Essential skills: Mathematics.* Frankfort: Author.

Kentucky Department of Education. (1993). *Transformations: Kentucky's curriculum framework.* Frankfort: Author.

Kentucky Department of Education. (1995). *Transformations: Kentucky's curriculum framework* (2nd ed.). Frankfort: Author.

Kentucky Department of Education. (1998). *Program of studies for Kentucky schools: Grades primary–12.* Frankfort: Author.

Kentucky Department of Education, Division of Curriculum and Assessment Development. (1996). *Core content for assessment* (Vol. 1.0). Frankfort. Author.

Kentucky Department of Education, Division of Curriculum and Assessment Development. (1999). *Core content for assessment* (Vol. 3.0). Frankfort. Author.

Kentucky Department of Education, Office of Leadership and School Improvement. (1998, August 8). *Highly skilled educators summary of analysis of school consolidated plans.* Frankfort: Author.

Kentucky Department of Education, Office of Regional Assistance. (1998, July 20). *District CP report on indicated needs.* Frankfort: Author.

Kentucky Institute for Education Research. (1997). *1996 statewide education reform survey of teachers, principals, parents and general public.* Lexington: Author.

Kentucky Institute for Education Research. (1999). *1999 Statewide education reform survey.* Lexington: Author.

Matthews, B. (1997). Curriculum reform. In J. C. Lindle, J. Petrosko, & R. Pankratz (Eds.), *1996 review of research on the Kentucky Education Reform Act (KERA)* (pp. 51–77). Lexington: Kentucky Institute for Education Research.

Murphy, J. (1990). *The educational reform movement of the 1980s: Perspectives and cases.* Berkeley, CA: McCutchan.

National Commission on Excellence in Education. (1983). *A nation at risk: The imperative for educational reform.* Washington, DC: U.S. Government Printing Office.

National Governors' Association. (1986). *Time for results: The governors' 1991 report on education.* Washington, DC: Author.

National Governors' Association. (1989). *Results in education: The governors' 1991 report on education.* Washington, DC: Author.

Office of Education Accountability. (1997). *1997 annual report* (pp. 34–37). Frankfort: Kentucky General Assembly.

Office of Education Accountability. (1998). *1998 annual report* (p. 77). Frankfort: Kentucky General Assembly.

Petrosko, J. (1997). Assessment and accountability. In J. C. Lindle, J. Petrosko, & R. Pankratz (Eds.), *1996 review of research on the Kentucky Education Reform Act (KERA)* (pp. 3–50). Lexington: Kentucky Institute for Education Research.

Petrosko, J. M., & Lindle, J. C. (1999, April). *State mandated school reform in Kentucky: Year three of a longitudinal study.* Paper presented at the annual meeting of the American Educational Research Association, Montreal, Canada.

Prichard Committee for Academic Excellence. (1999). *Gaining ground: Hard work and high expectations for Kentucky schools.* Lexington, KY: Author.

Sexton, R. (1999). *Changes in our schools: Schools that work.* Lexington, KY: Prichard Committee for Academic Excellence.

Steffy, B. E. (1993). *The Kentucky education reform: Lessons for America.* Lancaster, PA: Technomic.

Toch, T. (1991). *In the name of excellence: The struggle to reform the nation's schools, why it's failing, and what should be done.* New York: Oxford University Press.

Wilkerson, T., & Associates. (1999). *1999 statewide education reform study: Final report.* Lexington: Kentucky Institute for Education Research.

7

CHALLENGES IN IMPLEMENTING KENTUCKY'S PRIMARY SCHOOL PROGRAM

James Raths

THE UNGRADED PRIMARY SCHOOL program that abolished grade level designations of children until the fourth grade was recommended by the designers of Kentucky's school reform to eliminate the possibility of failure in the very early years of children's formal education. Reformers acknowledged that children learn at different rates and in different ways, particularly at young ages, and believed that all children could be prepared through developmentally appropriate educational practices to enter the fourth grade with their peers. Given the reform mandate, state department of education professionals embraced the philosophy and learning framework published in 1998 by the National Association for the Education of Young Children (NAEYC) (1988). The NAEYC framework became the basis for the identification and definition of seven critical attributes of the program: developmentally appropriate practice, multiage/multiability grouping of children for instruction, continuous progress, use of authentic assessment, use of qualitative methods, professional team work, and positive parent involvement with the Kentucky Department of Education (KDE) (1991, pp. 30–41).

Kentucky's reform leaders saw the primary school mandate as a critical component of the revolutionary plan for restructuring the state's public schools. Before 1990 the status of education in Kentucky was shocking: high dropout rates, poor performance by Kentucky students on national achievement tests, and limited financial support for schools (Prichard

Committee for Academic Excellence, 1999, p. 4). To prepare Kentucky youth for the challenges and demands of the information age, changes had to be made early in the educational process, and the place to start was the early elementary grades. To this end, state leaders mandated change in the early elementary curriculum, teaching methods, and assessment practices, which challenged Kentucky's teachers to make significant changes in their practices. This chapter describes the impact of those mandates on both the primary school program (inputs) and the achievement results of primary students (outputs). It closes with some recommendations suggested by Kentucky's experiences with school reform.

Purposes of the Primary School Program

The ultimate goal of the Kentucky Education Reform Act of 1990 (KERA) was to ensure that all children in Kentucky had the same opportunity and access to an adequate education. To reach this goal schools in Kentucky were expected to help all students reach a high level of achievement (Foster, 1999, p. 68). As state leaders considered what was needed to meet these goals, they reached a consensus through positions enunciated by Governor Wilkinson. They decided that the very structure of schools ought to change to give teachers more flexibility in working with students of diverse abilities, learning styles, and interests (Foster, p. 70).

This sentiment led the curriculum committee of the Task Force on Education Reform, charged with spearheading implementation of KERA, to propose the following: "To abolish grade differentials up until entry into the 4th grade. That will eliminate the possibility of 'failing' kindergarten or the first grade. The basic school will, thus, extend from age 4 through roughly age 9, with the objective to have all youngsters ready to enter the 4th grade by age 8–10" (Legislative Research Commission, 1990, p. 65). This language, mandating an ungraded primary school in Kentucky, was incorporated into state law by KERA. Subsequent state law and regulation decreed that the curriculum of the primary school program would address the state goals of education and that instructional practices in the primary school program "shall motivate and nurture children in diverse cultures [and] address the social, emotional, physical, aesthetic, and cognitive needs of children" (Foster, 1999, p. 74).

A key assumption of this mandate was that by including children of different ages and abilities in the same classroom, teachers would be forced to abandon traditional practices of teacher-centered recitations. Instead, teachers would have no choice but to engage students in active, practical lessons that would lead to academic success. In a nongraded system children in the primary school would learn according to their own developmental schedules, not according to grade-level expectations. When children were ready for grade 4, they would be placed at that level. As there would be no grade designations (such as first grade, second grade, and so on) in the primary school, children could not be retained in the earlier grades; instead, each child would advance to fourth grade when the time was right. As a result, the stigma associated with retention in an early grade would be eliminated. Because of the strong correlation between early-grade retention and dropping out, the reform leaders hoped the nongraded primary school eventually would help reduce Kentucky's high dropout rate (KDE, 1991, p. 28).

But the switch to this new primary school model involved more than changing the school structure. A committee called the Primary School Matrix Team conducted a long-term study of the goals of primary school and the principles of learning that would help students meet those goals. The committee's inquiry included reviewing documents, consulting experts, and visiting sites where outstanding primary school programs were operational. After comparing what they had learned from these diverse sources, the committee developed a consensus about the characteristics of "good programming" for primary schools. As the committee explained, "we began to refer to those characteristics . . . as CRITICAL ATTRIBUTES and even though the list was eventually refined and shortened, the notion of what type of characteristics would be evident in a program which reflected current research and practice . . . helped us formulate a vision of how primary schools in Kentucky should look at some point in the future" (KDE, 1991, p. 37; emphasis in the original).

Implementation of the Critical Attributes

The critical attributes developed by the Primary School Matrix Team were soon formally approved by the Kentucky legislature, made into law, and put into action. Exhibit 7.1 lists the seven critical attributes, along with descriptions of each attribute that represent strategies a school might choose to incorporate into its action plan for implementing the primary school program.

This section addresses the effect of the primary school program mandates on Kentucky's elementary schools by reporting on the implementation of a selected number of the critical attributes. The critical attributes were not all implemented to the same degree. Some (such as professional teamwork) were fully implemented, some (such as authentic assessment) were partially implemented, and some (such as multiage classrooms) were

---

Exhibit 7.1. Critical Attributes of Kentucky's Primary School Program.

1. *Developmentally Appropriate Educational Practices*
   - Employs an integrated curriculum
   - Encourages active child involvement, interaction, and exploration
   - Uses manipulatives and multisensory activities
   - Balances teacher-directed and child-initiated activities
   - Applies varied instructional strategies, such as whole language, cooperative learning, peer coaching and tutoring, thematic instruction, projects, learning centers, independent learning activities, and so on
   - Creates flexible groupings and regroupings for instruction, based on interest, learning style, problem solving, short-term skill instruction, reinforcement, random, and so on

2. *Multiage and Multiability Classrooms*
   - Includes heterogeneous groupings
   - Uses flexible age ranges
   - Allows for family groupings

3. *Continuous Progress*
   - Permits students to progress at their own rate as determined by authentic assessment
   - Maintains an orientation toward success
   - Establishes non-competitive reward systems
   - Documents pupil progress through anecdotal records, observations, portfolios, journals, videotapes, computer disks, and so on
   - Implements practices of not retaining or promoting students

4. *Authentic Assessment*
   - Occurs continuously in a context of classroom involvement
   - Reflects actual learning experiences
   - Emphasizes conferencing, observing, examining multiple and varied work samples, and so on
   - Documents social, emotional, physical, aesthetic, and cognitive development

5. *Qualitative Reporting Methods*
   - Uses descriptive and narrative reports on an ongoing basis
   - Reflects a continuum of pupil progress
   - Includes varied formats, such as portfolios, journals, videotapes, narratives, and so on

6. *Professional Teamwork*
   - Secures regular time for planning and sharing
   - Employs varied instructional delivery systems, such as team teaching, collaborative teaching, peer coaching, and so on
   - Ensures regular communication among all professional staff

7. *Positive Parent Involvement*
   - Fosters home-school partnerships
   - Promotes school-community partnerships
   - Facilitates continuous exchange of information

Source: *KDE, 1991, p. 45.*

for all intents and purposes abandoned. This uneven implementation makes it very difficult to generalize about the impact of the attributes as a group.

I relied on two main sources for the evaluation presented in this section: research and writing from scholars studying Kentucky's school reforms; and my own observations of a sample of Kentucky schools over a seven-year period (Katz, Raths, and Fanning, 1992; Raths and Fanning, 1993, 1999). My observations focused on a small number of schools in eastern and central Kentucky, but these visits gave me the opportunity to talk with parents, teachers, and administrators and to observe actual teaching practices.

Grouping Practices

According to the reform agenda advanced by the KDE and enacted into law by the Kentucky legislature, elementary schools were expected to institute multiage classrooms, which included flexible age ranges and heterogeneous grouping. The designers of the primary school program intended for teachers to use the multiage and multiability classrooms flexibly, relying on decisions made at the level of the particular school building to determine how students should be grouped (KDE, 1991, p. 55). However, teachers I visited in Kentucky early in the reform period did not hear this message. Some suggested with confidence that the new policy meant than in every primary school classroom of twenty-four students, there should be six kindergarten students, six first-graders, six second-graders, and six third-graders. Or to be more correct in terms of the thinking behind the mandate and to ignore the grade designations, each classroom of twenty-four students should include six five-year-olds, six six-year-olds, six seven-year-olds, and six eight-year-olds. The mandate, as interpreted, was greeted with shock, derision, and anger by some of the teachers I interviewed.

Many teachers believed that instruction is most efficient when children within a group are addressing similar goals at similar rates. Teachers have always been suspicious of the reports of college professors that there is no difference in efficacy between teaching homogeneous and heterogeneous groupings. It seemed preposterous to many teachers that they could work effectively with such a wide range of reading abilities in one classroom.

Teachers recognized that even if every child progressed at his or her normal level of development, the result would be the equivalent of having four grade levels in the same classroom. Another concern on the part of teachers dealt with curriculum materials: many primary school teachers believed it would be difficult to use one set of materials for very young students and other sets of materials for older students simultaneously.

Teachers also received limited help in implementing the primary school model. As Gnadinger, McIntyre, Chitwood-Smith, and Kyle (n.d.) reported, "While professional development opportunities existed to help teachers understand developmentally appropriate practice and authentic assessment, few focused explicitly on multi-age groupings" (p. 1). On infrequent occasions when advocates of multiage grouping tried to coach teachers into using cooperative learning procedures and peer tutoring models, teachers, and some parents, argued that these approaches were handicapping the older and brighter students in the classrooms—by assigning them tutoring tasks instead of assignments that would advance their skills and understanding.

Schools made all sorts of modifications to comply with the mandate in minimalist ways in order to avoid state sanctions. Some of the ploys included

- ○ *Working with a full age range of students for thirty minutes at the beginning of the day.* This was often called "calendar time." Children from kindergarten through grade 3 would sit together in groups of twenty or so to discuss plans for the day or current events, do show-and-tell, and engage in other activities that involved sharing and group processes. Once calendar time was completed, however, students returned to "teachable" groups, based mostly on age or grade level, for the rest of the day.

- ○ *Ignoring kindergarten in implementing the primary school program.* This was especially true where kindergarten programs operated for only half a day. Half-day students might take part in some sort of calendar time program, but this was awkward because calendar time was not available for kindergarten students in the afternoon session. From the point of view of fairness, it did not seem right to engage the morning groups in calendar time when this activity was not available to the afternoon groups.

- ○ *Grouping students one way for homeroom but another way for actual instruction.* No matter how schools grouped students for homeroom—often in such a way as to demonstrate they were meeting the KERA mandate—they usually regrouped students for regular instruction.

- ○ *Using a partial grouping strategy.* Some schools implemented multiage grouping, but over a more narrow range—putting children in grades 2 and 3 together, for example.

A 1999 survey of primary school programs by KDE found that only about 5 percent of the 686 self-reporting elementary schools in the state were implementing the primary school model with classes of three or more age spans, 74 percent said they grouped children from two ages in one class, and 24 percent of the schools (N = 165) were organized traditionally, with single-age groupings (KDE, 1999). We do not know how many of these schools maintained single-age grouping from the beginning of KERA or how many reverted to single-age grouping after attempting multiage arrangements for a time.

Continuous Progress

Continuous progress, a key attribute in the primary school reform, was described thus: "students will progress through the primary school program at their own rate without comparison to the rates of others or consideration of the number of years in school" (KDE, 1993, p. 8). This definition was logically linked to multiage grouping; it was through the multiage grouping attribute that continuous progress could be implemented. In spite of enormous pressure exerted through state regulations, teachers resisted the multiage grouping mandate so fiercely that in 1996, almost five years after the mandate was supposedly operative, the state legislature voided the mandate and wrote that schools "may determine, based on individual student needs, that implementing multi-age and multiability classrooms need not apply for every grouping of students for every activity throughout the day. The school shall revise its action plan to reflect any changes in the Primary Program's design [based on this new language]" (Kentucky Education Reform Act, KRS ¶ 156.160, 1996).

Many teachers and administrators in the schools I visited interpreted this new law as giving them the authority to fail students who did not meet grade-level expectations. Children finishing kindergarten who were deemed not ready for first grade were held back in larger numbers with no complaints from the state board of education or its field agents. Now school principals estimate that as many as 10 percent of their students will take more than four years to complete primary school. This rough estimate is supported by data in the Office of Education Accountability (OEA) annual report (OEA, 1999), which indicated that 5,200 children were projected to complete a fifth year in primary school during the 1999–2000 school year. This number comprises approximately 3 percent of the cohort. If this figure is typical of all three years, the principals' 10 percent estimate is fairly well on target. If failure in the early grades is a predictor of dropping out of school, then the dropout problem that the primary school was expressly designed to address will remain a problem. Further, the practice of retaining students in kindergarten and first grade is clearly not in keeping with the spirit of continuous progress.

Developmentally Appropriate Educational Practices

A major concern addressed by those in charge of organizing the redesigned primary school program involved teaching methods. There was a feeling that schools were not only ineffective but boring—with teachers using lecture and drill sheets as primary instruments of instruction. The educational climate was reflecting increased interest in the ideas of "constructivism" and computer technologies. There was an increased focus on "developmentally appropriate" instruction and "active student learning," which included the use of a balance of teacher-directed and child-initiated activities, flexible groupings, and more modern strategies, such as learning centers, project learning, peer coaching, thematic instruction, cooperative learning, and whole-language instruction.

There can be little doubt that Kentucky primary education has changed a great deal with respect to this mandate since 1992. Teachers have altered significantly the ways they teach, as evidenced by a number of case studies and self-report surveys conducted over the past five or six years. An Appalachia Educational Laboratory study (1998) concluded that "primary teachers at all study schools made changes in their approaches to instruction, assessment, grouping practices, reporting methods, working with other teachers, and working with parents" (p. 4). Further, a comprehensive study of the effects of KERA on Kentucky's primary schools showed that, in general, primary school teachers were using more integrated instruction, more varied instructional strategies and group practices, and more authentic assessment since the primary school mandates had been advanced (Winograd, Petrosko, Compton-Hall, & Cantrell, 1996). Several factors accelerated the changes. First, the publishing industry made curriculum guides, materials, and visual aids available to Kentucky teachers for planning more appropriate practices. Teachers were given larger budgets, which allowed them to purchase the new materials, and time within the school day to work with colleagues in developing more appropriate lesson plans. In addition, staff development meetings gave emphasis to whole-language and project method teaching. The instruction offered in these meetings, often with classroom teachers serving in the role of instructor, were well received throughout the state.

In the schools I visited, KERA often was referred to in a jocular fashion as the "Kentucky Early Retirement Act." Older teachers were leaving the profession rather than adapt to the new primary school mandates. Their places were taken by new teacher education graduates who had been well prepared by Kentucky colleges and universities in whole-language instruction, ideas of curriculum integration, and other aspects of developmentally appropriate instruction. One of the often cited dilemmas of teacher education is whether candidates should be prepared for today's schools or tomorrow's. Teachers not prepared for today's schools may find current assignments difficult—and tomorrow may be a long way off. During the 1990s those teacher candidates who were trained to implement the KERA mandates were sought by principals and welcomed by colleagues for their knowledge and expertise in these new areas.

Authentic Assessment

As it was generally understood, an "authentic assessment" was one congruent with what students would be doing in real life. So, for example, using a traditional twenty-word spelling quiz to check for spelling accuracy is not authentic. Instead, a more authentic assessment would ask students to write a letter using the correct spellings of words under review. The extent to which teacher practices in this domain changed over time remains an open question. Although teachers respond to queries by attesting that they are using authentic assessment practices, Bridge (1994) found that most of the teachers who were keeping anecdotal records and using conferences and interviews instead of paper-and-pencil tests as the basis of evaluations were struggling with how to use the information they had collected. Most observers conceded that assessment practices changed very little and that authentic assessments were rarely seen. There may be some explanations for this mixed result.

There are at least two kinds of assessments: formative assessments and summative assessments. Formative assessments are used to coach students to do better work. They are characterized by informal, almost conversational, inputs from the teacher directed to students either as individuals or in groups. Summative assessments are used to assign grades and to determine whether a student should be promoted to the next grade. Because of the high-stakes nature of summative assessments, teachers may have been loath to experiment with them. If an adverse decision were based on authentic measures, the decision would need to be defended when parents objected. Almost everyone could understand a percentage score on a traditional test or quiz. To make judgments about spelling achievement by scoring the spelling of a paper written for a different purpose would be deemed authentic for evaluating spelling but perhaps problematic by someone looking for precise data for making decisions.

Qualitative Reporting Methods

The final attribute of the new primary school, qualitative reporting methods, called for new report cards. The new reporting methods were to describe children's progress through the primary school using methods that focused on the growth and development of the whole child, not simply using letter grades in various subjects. KDE developed a new reporting system, the Kentucky Elementary Learning Profile (KELP). Teachers reported that KELP took an enormous amount of effort, including record keeping and drafting of text to include in the report. Their complaints were so vociferous that KDE did not make its use mandatory (Appalachia Educational Laboratory, 1998, p. 5). Further, teachers generally felt that there was little payoff. Parents did not understand the KELP system and were disappointed that their questions (such as "How is my child doing?") were not addressed with sufficient clarity in the reporting system. Teachers reported that parents were interested in comparing their children's progress with that of classmates. It is not clear how widespread this concern was. Perhaps it was only among a select group of parents who were most influential in school policy.

Implementation of the Critical Attributes: Summary

It is important to remember that the original reform legislation did not mandate the critical attributes of the primary school aside from the general model of nongraded school organization. The foregoing discussion presents at best a mixed message about how successfully the primary school mandates have been implemented. Apparently, the most problematic and least implemented attribute of the primary school program has been multiage grouping. The most successfully implemented attribute has been increased professional teamwork. Other attributes, such as authentic assessment, have been somewhere in between. The issue, however, is how well the students in primary schools are being prepared. Only 36 percent of the teachers surveyed by OEA in 1999 agreed that "students exiting primary school are ready for fourth grade" (p. 63). This is the impression of a sample of teachers. The next section will examine the data.

Explanations for Uneven Implementation of the Mandates

The data seem to indicate that over the past nine years or so, the primary school program has not been fully implemented with respect to state mandates, nor has it met the goals set by state leaders as reflected in KERA. While acknowledging that there have been dramatic changes in primary school classrooms, the Appalachia Educational Laboratory (1998) says that "movement toward greater implementation of the primary schools has slowed considerably in our schools" (p. 6). What are some explanations for these disappointing results? Viewing the situation from the outside and with hindsight, it is possible to offer some credible explanations for the current situation, such as the following.

1. There was apparently very little communication between the members of the curriculum committee of the Task Force on Education Reform and the leaders in KDE who developed the essential attributes of the new primary school model. Two questions that may have been addressed if better and more effective communication had taken place are these: How are the critical attributes of primary school linked to the ultimate goals set by the task force (and subsequently by state law) in regard to the success and preparedness of all children by fourth grade? How will teachers, parents, citizens, and administrators know if a given child is ready for fourth grade?

With the possible exception of its work with the KELP instrument, KDE did not address the second question. The first question was also not answered in straightforward ways. The interventions conceptualized in the attributes represented what was taken to be good practice by the leadership of the National Association for the Education of Young Children (1988) at the time, but the link between those practices and achieving significantly higher learning outcomes in Kentucky schools was never firmly established. As the Appalachia Educational Laboratory report (1998) put it, "The program's overall goal quickly became lost in the single-minded focus on implementing the seven critical attributes. Rather than using the critical attributes as tools to help students progress at their own rate in preparation for fourth grade, many teachers in the study schools became pre-occupied with the multiaging component of the program" (pp. 6–7).

2. By issuing mandates for changes in practice, KDE focused teachers' attention on compliance. Some suspect that the focus on form rather than substance may have hindered Kentucky schools from addressing the goals set forth in KERA. Teachers may have been so concerned, for instance, about offering instruction that was "thematic" that they lost

sight of the goal of teaching to Kentucky standards as measured by the state assessments.

3. The focus on the primary school as a unit within each school building tended to isolate fourth-grade teachers from the planning process. If teachers are interested in preparing their students for fourth grade, it would seem important to engage fourth-grade teachers in the process. Fourth-grade teachers might negotiate expectations with primary school teachers and help them more accurately understand what it would take to become ready for fourth grade. Also, because the mandates were seen as directed solely to primary school teachers, fourth-grade teachers felt no need to change their traditional instructional methods. So, presumably, students leaving primary school classrooms that emphasized developmentally appropriate instruction, authentic assessment, and close school-parent ties might find themselves in a fourth-grade classroom where none of these attributes were operational. How these apparent schisms worked to hinder the effectiveness of KERA can only be estimated.

4. A fourth explanation has to do with the time line provided for implementing the primary school mandates. Originally, schools were given from 1992 through 1996 to implement them. However, shortly after this target was set, and after schools began writing action plans to demonstrate full compliance by 1996, the Kentucky legislature, evidently fearing that the original time line was too slow, moved the full implementation date to the 1993–94 school year. This new time line deprived state leaders of the opportunity to "sell" the primary school program to the public and to prepare teachers well to implement it. Neither the selling nor the preparation responsibilities were carried out well, in large part because of the abbreviated time line.

5. Finally, the mixed results might stem from the lack of steady leadership in implementing the program. In 1991, Abby Armstrong came to Kentucky to direct the program. She stayed less than three years and was followed by at least six different directors. Scattered and unpredictable leadership often makes it difficult to bring about major changes in school (or any other) systems.

The Primary School Program and Student Learning

Under KERA, achievement data on all fourth- and fifth-grade students were collected annually from 1992 to 1998 by the Kentucky Instructional Results Information System, Kentucky's statewide assessment and accountability program under KERA. Also, beginning in 1997, Kentucky tested all children in grades 3, 6, and 9 in reading, language arts, and mathematics with the McGraw-Hill Comprehensive Tests of Basic Skills (CTBS Edition 5). In addition, the National Assessment of Educational Progress (NAEP) test was administered to the fourth-graders in 1992, 1996, and 1998 to compare Kentucky students with their peers across the nation.

Although all three of these assessments show positive gains in student learning for third-, fourth-, and fifth-grade students, statewide achievement results from these testing programs will not be presented as direct measures of success of primary school program components. Attempting to link student gains with one or more attributes of the primary school program would be unwise because there is no objective measure of the degree of implementation of program components and no way to parcel out the effects on student learning of the primary program from other KERA initiatives on learning. While proponents of KERA have cited improvement in achievement scores as evidence of improved performance of elementary schools, at the writing of this chapter no data were available to link student gains to the implementation of the primary program attributes. (For a summary of KIRIS, CTBS 5, and NAEP scores, see KDE, 2000, pp. 71–87.)

Lessons Learned from the Kentucky Experience

Looking over the story of the primary school reform effort in Kentucky, we can extract some useful insights from which others might benefit.

There is evidence that the people who worked closely with the legislature to draft the language of KERA were not consulted closely over time by educational leaders in KDE who were charged with implementing the reforms. As a result, the rationale for some of the elements of the reform as reflected in KERA, such as multiage grouping, were advanced and advocated throughout the state for reasons other than those that suggested the innovation in the first place. Clearly, the innovative thinkers behind any reform movement must continue to participate and guide the implementation effort.

The legislature, under pressure from the public, modified the implementation dates that had been so carefully designed by the Primary School Matrix Team of KDE. This change by legislative fiat prompted a backlash on the part of teachers and parents who were already struggling to alter their practices in dramatic ways. Changes in announced plans must be made cautiously.

Finally, perhaps the most important point to note is that two fairly dramatic KERA initiatives were generated without a clear linkage between them. The two initiatives were KIRIS, which held schools accountable for the scores students earned on its tests, and the initiative for teachers to align their teaching with the seven critical attributes. It was not obvious early on, nor is it to this day, how student achievement on the high-stakes state assessment tests would be influenced by full implementation of the primary school attributes. In future efforts, two such important initiatives must be conceptually linked.

Future Directions for the Primary School Program

From the very start, the primary school reform carried with it the high hopes and ambitions of Kentucky's reformers. By getting all students off to a good start, in a school climate that recognized individual rates of development and different learning styles, the schools would overcome many of the obstacles that contributed to the state's education ills.

This chapter has summarized some of the difficulties the primary school reform has faced, including changing leadership, hurried deadlines, and modest gains on assessment measures. However, there are a number of signs that even the most pessimistic cannot overlook. First, the primary school reform idea may have represented the insights of a very small group of leaders, but it was maintained and propelled by the hard work of teachers in all corners of the state—primary school teachers who sacrificed time with their families to work on integrated units, grouping plans, and assessment procedures. According to recent surveys, teachers and principals are confident that schools are changing for the better as they strive to accommodate the mandates of KERA (Wilkerson & Associates, 1999). Further, as reported in this chapter, surveys of teacher practice suggest that instruction has changed dramatically in the primary school.

Also, the recent results of the Comprehensive Tests of Basic Skills have been encouraging. Beginning in 1997, Kentucky each spring administers the McGraw-Hill CTBS Edition 5 test to all third-, sixth-, and ninth-grade students as a measure of their basic skills in reading, language arts, and mathematics. Table 7.1 shows the test results for third-graders each year from 1997 to 2000. The CTBS scores are reported in percentiles. A score of 55, for example, means that the average student in Kentucky scored equal to or better than 55 percent of all students in the United States who took the test. The national average is at the fiftieth percentile.

Because there was some concern that the emphasis on thematic instruction, authentic assessment, and other primary school mandates might reduce the effectiveness of primary school instruction in the basic skills,

Kentucky leaders interpreted the statewide results of the administration of the CTBS Edition 5 as good news. In these results Kentucky third-graders are seen as maintaining a pattern of "no loss" in the basic skills area. In fact, the 2000 data suggest that third-graders are making excellent progress in basic skills. (See Table 7.1.)

Further, enormous efforts and resources have been invested in the primary school program. Educational leaders need to understand that change takes time and that the vision of the leaders who developed and implemented KERA was revolutionary and profound. Because research has demonstrated that for the most part Kentucky teachers and parents support the basic aims of KERA and its mandates and because the evidence from research is not negative about KERA's importance in raising the academic performance of children in the schools, the most important policy decision Kentucky leaders can make is to stay the course. It would be demoralizing—perhaps devastating—to educators if state leaders quit on KERA.

If the links between solid implementation of the critical attributes and performance on the state tests remain tentative over time, then it will be appropriate to consider major changes in the program. *But now is not that time.* Instead, it is important to take the following steps:

Persuade teachers that working harder is not the answer. Teachers are already working hard, but they must work "smarter." What this means is focusing on results. In a school outside Kentucky, teachers elected to assign social studies, music, art, and science instruction to one grade for one day of the week (Anderson & Pellicer, 1998). For example, special-

---

Table 7.1. Results of Statewide Testing of Third-Graders
with the McGraw-Hill Comprehensive Tests of Basic Skills,
Edition 5, 1997–2000.

	Percentile			
	1997	1998	1999	2000
Reading	49	50	51	55
Language	48	49	50	53
Mathematics	49	48	51	55
Total battery	50	50	52	55

Source: *R. Irwin, KDE, Office of Assessment and Accountability, personal communication, 2000.*

ists might work with the children in that grade on Monday while the teachers, freed from classroom responsibilities, met to evaluate individual student progress, review lesson plans, and seek help from consultants. On Tuesday the specialists would work with students from a different grade level while the teachers of that grade level had an opportunity to meet. On the four remaining days of the week, all instruction was devoted to literacy and mathematics teaching and learning. In sum, the focus of the teachers and the leadership was to do something to increase student performance in literacy and in mathematics, with less concern about school organization or other state mandates. During my visits to the state I saw another example of working smarter in an eastern Kentucky school where the principal dedicated ninety minutes every day to literacy instruction— with everyone in the school, including the principal, counselor, secretaries, and custodians, helping children learn to read better during that period. No interruptions were allowed during this time. The instruction was planned centrally in collaboration with teachers, and the children were grouped for instructional purposes—not according to state mandates. Neither of these examples offers a panacea, but each demonstrates efforts of creative thinking to help students become more effective learners.

Provide teachers an opportunity to learn about the practices of successful schools. The differences cannot be characterized in vague terms such as "teacher expectations" or "high-quality leadership." Those terms mean little to practicing teachers. Instead, if the methods of schools successful at grouping practices, assessment practices, and curriculum decisions were widely shared with teachers, perhaps some changes could be made.

Encourage schools to review what they do to help students learn in context. There is some evidence that quick fixes might have had some short-term and modest results on KIRIS scores. Practices such as holding pep rallies before the state assessment exam or teaching test-taking skills might help a bit, but they miss the point. KIRIS calls on students to demonstrate how they can use the knowledge they have acquired. Pep rallies will not suffice to address this challenge. What is needed is a rethinking of the curriculum and the goals of schooling. It is likely that highly successful schools have addressed the problem of inert knowledge by engaging faculty in curriculum reform efforts. Hong's study (1996) of an elementary school in Washington State that engaged teachers in curriculum reform illustrates this approach. The critical attributes advanced by the leaders in primary education in Kentucky suggested the directions that school faculties might take—from developmentally appropriate educational practices through authentic assessment practices. Teachers need to see the links between these attributes and performance on the state assessment exam.

Identify schools that are unusually successful in spite of significant demographic barriers to high achievement. The leaders of the school improvement movement in Kentucky, including the Prichard Committee for Academic Excellence, the Kentucky Institute for Education Research, and KDE, could spearhead such an effort. Researchers observing practices in those schools could identify factors that are present across different schools and attempt to link those factors to the more theoretical explanations for school success. This approach is modeled by Anderson and Pellicer's work (1998) and looks especially promising.

Recruit excellent teachers for low-achieving schools. Perhaps being designated "excellent" would motivate successful teachers to accept such a challenge. No other help should be provided to these teachers in their difficult context—no more aides, computers, or other resources than were there the previous year. Give these teachers three years to raise test scores. As low-achieving schools' scores are turned around, teachers across the state would become convinced that the effects demonstrated in KIRIS scores were not a reflection of sample group differences, parental support, or family poverty but in large measure the impact of effective teaching practices. Such a demonstration would be a boost to Kentucky teachers and policymakers and would provide evidence that the primary school program mandated by KERA and KDE was on the right track.

REFERENCES

Anderson, L. W., & Pellicer, L. O. (1998). Toward an understanding of unusually successful programs for economically disadvantaged students. *Journal of Education for Students Placed at Risk, 3,* 237–263.

Appalachia Educational Laboratory. (1998). Evolution of the primary program in six Kentucky schools. *Notes from the Field: Education reform in rural Kentucky, 6*(1), 1–12. (Available from the Appalachia Educational Laboratory, P.O. Box 1348, Charleston, WV 25325)

Bridge, C. (1994). *The implementation of Kentucky's primary program.* Lexington: Kentucky Institute for Education Research.

Foster, J. D. (1999). *Redesigning public schools: The Kentucky experience.* Lexington, KY: Diversified Services, Inc.

Gnadinger, C., McIntyre, E., Chitwood-Smith, T., & Kyle, D. (n.d.). *Primary program: A review of research.* Lexington: Kentucky Institute for Education Research.

Hong, L. (1996). *Surviving school reform.* New York: Teachers College Press.

Katz, L. G., Raths, J., & Fanning, J. (1992). *The status of the primary school reform in Kentucky and its implications.* Lexington, KY: Prichard Committee for Academic Excellence.

Kentucky Department of Education. (1991). *Kentucky's primary school: The wonder years* (Program Description No. 1). Frankfort: Author.

Kentucky Department of Education. (1993). *State regulations and best practices for Kentucky's primary program.* Frankfort: Author.

Kentucky Department of Education. (1994). *State regulations and best practices for Kentucky's primary program.* Frankfort: Author.

Kentucky Department of Education. (1999). *Demographic survey of primary programs 1999* (Data summary 10-16-99) [On-line]. Available: http://www.kde.state.ky.us/osle/extend/primary

Kentucky Department of Education. (2000). Data: Results. *Results matter* (pp. 71–87). Frankfort: Author.

Kentucky Education Reform Act, Kentucky school laws annotated. (1996). KRS ¶ 156.160.

Legislative Research Commission. (1990, February 23). Recommendations Related to Curriculum (adopted by the Task Force on Education Reform February 23, 1990).

National Association for the Education of Young Children. (1988). NAEYC position statement on developmentally appropriate practice in the primary grades, serving 5–8 year olds. *Young Children, 43,* 64–81.

Office of Education Accountability. (1999). *1999 annual report.* Frankfort: Kentucky General Assembly.

Petrosko, J. M., & Lindle, J. C. (1999, April). *State-mandated school reform in Kentucky: Year three of a longitudinal study.* Paper presented at the annual meeting of the American Educational Research Association, Montreal, Canada.

Prichard Committee for Academic Excellence. (1999). *Gaining ground: Hard work and high expectations for Kentucky schools.* Lexington, KY: Author.

Raths, J., & Fanning, J. (1993). *Primary school reform revisited.* Lexington, KY: Prichard Committee for Academic Excellence.

Raths, J., & Fanning, J. (1999). *Primary school reform in Kentucky: A third look.* Lexington: Kentucky Institute for Education Research.

Wilkerson, T., & Associates. (1999, August). *1999 statewide education reform study. Final report.* Lexington: Kentucky Institute for Education Research.

Winograd, P., Petrosko, J., Compton-Hall, M., & Cantrell, S. C. (1996). *The effects of KERA on Kentucky's elementary schools: Year one of a proposed five-year study: Vol. 1. Overview, findings, and conclusions.* Lexington: Kentucky Institute for Education Research.

8

A STUDENT'S VIEWPOINT

"YOU'VE GOT TO LEARN TO WORK WITH PEOPLE ABOVE YOU AND BELOW YOU"

Holly Holland

AS A THIRD-GRADER in 1990, Clinton Hackney wasn't aware of the political fallout that accompanied the passage of the Kentucky Education Reform Act of 1990 (KERA). While educators, parents, and politicians debated the merits of mixing five- through nine-year-olds in the same classroom and evaluating their progress through narrative rather than numerical report cards, Clinton tried to mind his manners and not let on how bored he was in his Johnson County elementary school.

But soon he began noticing some exciting changes. Although he missed out on the school's initial experiment with the nongraded primary school program—students were chosen randomly for participation the first year—Clinton benefited from other transitions occurring in his remote Appalachian school. For example, he no longer had to wait patiently while teachers endlessly repeated lessons for slower students. By grouping and regrouping children throughout the day, teachers allowed them to move at their own pace instead of marching to the same beat. Several times a week, Clinton said, he and a half dozen other students also met in the library for extended conversations with a gifted education specialist. And teachers started collaborating more often, which enabled them to specialize in certain subjects instead of trying to teach every topic well.

"I felt like I got a new individual attention from teachers," Clinton said.

The greater academic challenges kept him focused at a time when his home life was disrupted. Clinton grew up in Sitka, a rural community that abuts Paintsville, the county seat, and lies near Kentucky's border with West Virginia. The only child of parents who divorced when he was eight, Clinton eventually went to live with his grandparents. But he has had ongoing contact with and support from his mother and father.

"I didn't grow up on the side of a hill," he said, rebuffing the stereotype that all eastern Kentucky residents are poor, uneducated hillbillies. "I came from a good home."

When he entered middle school, Clinton noticed other instructional changes, which he later learned resulted from new resources and training made available through Kentucky's education reforms. For example, he said his teachers worked in teams and planned lessons that helped students to understand the connections between various academic subjects and to apply information they had gathered from lectures and textbooks. His teachers also gave students regular opportunities to work together on group projects, which showed Clinton that his classmates possessed special talents and skills. According to Clinton, instead of sitting in straight rows of desks, the students "had round tables in just about every class."

"We all worked on these problems and designs," Clinton said. "In history class we'd have to research a historical period and report about it. In science class we'd have two experiments a week and then tests. The teacher would assign us to groups, lecture to us, and then let us work together to solve a problem. I thought it was fun. You got to learn leadership, and you had to be part of a team. Everybody had to pull their weight to accomplish the goal."

At an early age, Clinton said, he discovered an important lesson about education that was reinforced through Kentucky's school reforms: the highest form of knowledge comes not from memorizing information but from being able to explain it well enough so others can learn. Defying the common belief that gifted students will be held back by working with their less able peers, he also fulfilled a fundamental premise of KERA— children might learn in different ways and at different speeds, but all of them bring important insights to the classroom.

"I think you can master a skill a lot quicker by helping teach it," Clinton said. "There were a lot of things that I didn't understand that [other students] would help me with, and I could help them on some, too. It felt good that we could work together. . . . I think it teaches good life skills. You've got to learn how to work with people above you and below you.

"As far as KERA, the biggest thing I learned was not academics, but motivational skills, people skills, rhetorical skills, how to talk and get your message across, how to be a leader, how to work with people around you. Whether I was in a room by myself or with other students, I probably would have accomplished things intellectually. I would have learned the facts. But I would have been a drag in the real world."

While he was becoming more comfortable solving problems with his classmates, Clinton also had opportunities to work independently in his strongest subjects. In eighth grade, for example, his math teacher helped him and several other high achievers move through the trigonometry text-book while their peers studied pre-algebra. The greater dimensions of learning didn't escape Clinton's attention and reflection. Even then, he said, he was aware of his generation's unique opportunity to expand the state's previously limited aspirations. Stereotypes aside, he acknowledged that the people of Appalachia, in particular, historically failed to appreciate the benefits of a strong education.

"KERA is slowly working to reform education in Kentucky," he said, "but I don't think it will come full swing until Kentucky changes its societal values."

Despite the area's high poverty rate, Johnson County's schools have made steady progress toward the performance goals set by the state. One of the county's schools, Central Elementary, is among only thirty-one schools in Kentucky that have improved their achievement test scores every year since the statewide assessment and accountability process started in 1991.

Expanded professional development opportunities for teachers obviously helped. As Stephen K. Clements noted in *Kentucky's Teachers: Charting a Course for KERA's Second Decade* (published by the Kentucky Long-Term Policy Research Center, Frankfort, 1999), after the state's reform law was enacted, teachers in Kentucky participated in specialized training at significantly higher rates than in the nation as a whole. Yet Clements also pointed out that although "several recent national studies of teacher quality [rated] Kentucky's teacher workforce system among the best in the nation," the studies hadn't really emphasized the outputs— "what teachers know and what they can do in the classroom" (p. 45).

Clinton said he had experienced the uneven results of Kentucky's teacher training efforts. He recalled some instructors who "didn't have a clue." Their limited subject knowledge and poor classroom management skills made learning difficult. The new demands of Kentucky's education reforms caused some teachers to stumble more than ever, he said. Clinton remembered having to race to finish essays that some teachers assigned at the last minute to fulfill the state's new requirement that students demonstrate proficiency in writing by submitting portfolios of their work. Over time, however, the greater emphasis on writing paid off. Clinton said he and his classmates learned how to critique their written work, revise it according to state standards, and gradually increase its length and complexity.

"I like writing, even though it's harder [than other subjects]," he said. "I'm writing a book. One of my goals is to have it written by the end of my senior year."

During his junior year in high school, Clinton earned an appointment to the Governor's Scholars program, which brings the state's top high school students together at college campuses each summer for six weeks of intensive study in their chosen fields. Clinton, a straight-A student who is captain of Johnson Central High School's academic team and its basketball squad, studied philosophy and technology at Centre College in Danville, Kentucky.

The Governor's Scholars award also earned him a full, four-year scholarship to the University of Louisville, where he plans to major in biology and chemistry in preparation for medical school. Although Clinton could have attended a top college out of state, he said he wanted to do his part to stanch the "brain drain" that continues to deprive Kentucky of some of its finest homegrown talent. He recalled one lecturer at the Governor's Scholars program who pointed out that Kentucky is one of the nation's largest exporters of educated young people, meaning that many move away for college and careers, never to return.

"If not for that scholarship, I'd be one of those who would go out of state, too," he said.

Instead, Clinton Hackney plans to put some of his knowledge to work in Appalachia, where Kentucky teachers showed him how an individual can become stronger through collaboration.

"I hope to better myself," he said. "Then I'll come back and better my community."

PART THREE

STRENGTHENING THE CAPACITY OF EDUCATORS

9

PROMOTING THE PROFESSIONAL
DEVELOPMENT OF TEACHERS

G. Williamson McDiarmid, Tom Corcoran

WHEN KENTUCKY POLICYMAKERS set out in 1990 to overhaul their public education system, they understood that teachers would need new
knowledge and skills to accomplish the ambitious goals that were being
set for them. Precisely what knowledge and which skills teachers would
need and how they would acquire them were unknown, not merely to the
policymakers but to virtually everyone involved. When the Kentucky Education Reform Act of 1990 (KERA) was signed into law, the state's policymakers, educators, and citizens embarked on a journey into terra
incognita. However, they had the foresight to invest in opportunities for
teachers to learn what they thought teachers might need to know to make
the journey successful.

In this chapter we will examine the professional development "system"
that emerged under KERA, how it evolved as the state's policymakers
learned from the experience of teachers across the state, and what was
known as of 1999 about its impact on classroom practice and performance.

The research presented in this chapter was supported by grants from the Pew
Charitable Trusts, the Spencer Foundation, the MacArthur Foundation, and the
Annie E. Casey Foundation. The authors would like to acknowledge the substantial contributions of the Partnership for Kentucky Schools, with special
thanks to Carolyn Witt-Jones and Ellen Skinner, and our colleagues on the Partnership for Kentucky Schools research team—Jane L. David, Pam Coe, Patricia
J. Kannapel, and Lois Adams-Rodgers.

The findings reported here come largely from several studies conducted by a team of researchers, including the authors, that has collaborated with the Partnership for Kentucky Schools (PKS) since 1994. This program of research is unusual because it evolved from collaboration between state policymakers and the PKS researchers on setting the agenda, interpreting the results, and determining the implications for state policy.

Professional Development Under KERA

Kentucky's policymakers reasoned that if they were to hold local educators primarily responsible for helping students reach the state's demanding learning goals, they should provide them with both the authority and the resources, including time, needed to do the job. As a consequence, the legislature shifted primary responsibility for planning professional development from school district administrators to the staffs and councils at each school. Concomitantly, the reform law dramatically increased funding for professional development—from less than $1 per student to $23 per student annually over several years. Control over 65 percent of these funds was vested in the school councils at each school, with the remaining 35 percent of the funds going to the district office. Finally, KERA permitted districts to request up to five additional days of professional development per year for all teachers, in addition to the four days required by law.

Teachers at each school elected a professional development committee both to plan activities for themselves and their colleagues and to oversee the use of the funds. These committees prepared professional development plans annually that were reviewed and adopted by their local school councils. Initially, the plans were submitted to the Kentucky Department of Education (KDE) and in some cases were reviewed by the staffs of the regional service centers (RSCs). Over time, to reduce paperwork and streamline the process, professional development plans were subsumed under a consolidated planning process, and professional development activities became part of each school's consolidated plan.

The role of the districts in professional development was defined largely in the negative. They did not control 65 percent of the funds. They did not set the priorities for the schools. However, they were expected to use their resources to support activities at the schools and to develop a districtwide professional development plan. If, as KERA ordained, the professional development committees at the school level were "sovereign," then districts had to learn to play supporting roles. Later amendments to the law required districts to employ professional development coordinators who were expected to assist the school committees by providing information about high-quality learning opportunities, to coordinate activities within the district, and to serve as liaisons between the district and KDE.

To assist schools with professional development and other aspects of the reform, KDE staffed eight RSCs around the state. Staffs at the RSCs were initially recruited to assist with implementation of the KERA "strands": technology, writing, portfolio assessment, family resource centers, extended school programs, school councils, and ungraded primary school programs. The RSCs were expected to "broker" opportunities for professional development by matching schools with potential providers of assistance. In addition, the RSC staff delivered professional development and helped schools create their professional development plans (and later their consolidated plans). In 1998, KDE shifted the focus of the RSCs from the KERA strands to the content of the core curriculum and required them to restructure their staffs to bring the requisite subject-matter expertise on board.

In addition to the RSCs, KDE has launched a number of other programs to support teacher development. Established prior to KERA, the Commonwealth Institute for Teachers (CIT) offers summer institutes with follow-ups during the academic year. CIT has served some fourteen hundred teachers to date. During the mid-1990s KDE worked collaboratively with the Kentucky Science and Technology Council and a number of universities to obtain support from the National Science Foundation for a statewide professional development initiative in math and science.

Through the RSCs, KDE also created networks of teachers in writing, mathematics, and technology. Adopting a "trainer-of-trainers" model, KDE expected teachers in these networks to disseminate what they learned from periodic KDE-sponsored workshops to their colleagues back at their schools. In the summer of 1999 KDE also began funding and organizing summer institutes focused on subject matter. To provide professional development for school leaders, KDE developed the Kentucky Leadership Academy (KLA) in 1997, drawing on the training that had evolved for distinguished educators (DEs). (The distinguished educator program, now known as the highly skilled educator program, was established under KERA to train experienced educators to go into Kentucky schools and help them meet reform goals.) DEs played a central role in designing and delivering the KLA training sessions that were staged both regionally and statewide (Coe & Adams-Rodgers, in press).

As is clear from this brief overview, the focus of professional development in Kentucky has evolved over the past decade. It has gone through three overlapping phases in which the emphases and modes of delivery have changed in response to demands from the field. The first phase focused on the implementation of the structural and programmatic components of KERA. This phase was characterized by workshops that helped teachers implement school-based councils, the ungraded primary school program, portfolio assessment, and other aspects of the reform. Although some attention was paid to test preparation and to curriculum, particularly in writing and mathematics, the primary focus was procedural. As schools felt the effects of the accountability system, the focus shifted. The second phase began in earnest with the development of the core content standards that led KDE, districts, and schools to shift their focus to curriculum alignment and preparation for the state assessment. In the unfolding third phase, policymakers and educators are paying greater attention to teachers' knowledge of content and curriculum.

Assumptions About Teacher Learning and Changing Classroom Practice

Underlying the actions of those who crafted the original KERA legislation were some critical assumptions about teacher learning and professional development. These assumptions have shaped policies, priorities, and professional development under KERA.

A key initial assumption was that identifying what students needed to know was also sufficient for identifying what teachers needed to know. That is, by identifying "valued outcomes" for students and producing curriculum outlines, policymakers appear to have believed that they had signaled to teachers what they needed to know as well as what they needed to teach in the core content areas (see KDE, *Transformations,* 1995, and *Core Content for Assessment,* 1996 and 1999).

This assumption has proved problematic for at least two reasons. First, teachers needed to know not only the information and ideas embedded in the learning outcomes and state curriculum guidelines but also how to transform what they know into opportunities for students to learn. Making these transformations was complicated by the fact that not all students learn in the same ways. For instance, although some students readily learn ideas and information from lectures, many do not. As KERA was designed to ensure that all students (not just those who had traditionally capitalized on formal schooling) learned at a high level, teachers needed to know multiple ways to help students learn.

Second, identifying student outcomes in specific subject-matter areas does not fully encompass what teachers need to know about the content itself. For instance, because students are expected to know operations with fractions, teachers must also know these operations. Yet, to address students' learning problems, teachers also need to know what they typically find puzzling or confusing about fractions. This knowledge is critical for teachers to diagnose the sources of student confusion and devise activities to help students overcome them. Over the past two decades we have learned a great deal about what both students and teachers find confusing in specific content areas. Much of this research was done after most Kentucky teachers finished their university preparation, so few have had the opportunity to examine it. Even recently certified teachers may be unfamiliar with this research, since typical preparation programs afford no obvious opportunities for acquiring such knowledge.

A further assumption appears to have been that additional time and money for professional development would generate sufficient demand to prompt growth in the supply of appropriate learning opportunities for teachers. Policymakers felt that they were creating a market to which existing providers would respond and for which new providers would appear.

Finally, policymakers, especially legislators, appear to have believed that the additional professional development days originally allotted for training teachers would be unnecessary after the first few years of the reforms. Teachers would learn—once and for all—what they needed to know to implement the reforms, rendering additional time for training unnecessary.

This last assumption reflects a widely held, linear view of how teachers learn in order to change their practice: that teachers encounter information about needed changes, master this information, and then "implement" the required changes in their classrooms. Studies of teachers' efforts to change their practice, however, paint quite a different picture (Featherstone, Smith, Beasley, Corbin, & Shank, 1995; Heaton, 1995; Jennings, 1996; Schwille, 1998). Before teachers can develop new ways of acting in their classroom, they often need to "unlearn" habituated ways of thinking about learners, content, and their own role that can interfere with their efforts to change their practice. This is particularly salient for teachers who have developed a limited view of themselves in relation to specific subjects (such as elementary school teachers when they teach mathematics). In addition, they must have a vision of how practice can be different—and more effective. They also need opportunities to try out new techniques. Finally, the responses of colleagues, parents, and students to teachers' attempts to change their practice strongly influence their persistence. In short, changes in practice appear to take place unevenly, over time, and piecemeal, and they are strongly conditioned by teachers' experiences and beliefs as well as the social context of schools. It is little wonder that recent research suggests that genuine changes in practice, even when supported with high-quality and sustained professional development, may take a minimum of three years (Consortium for Policy Research in Education, 1998).

Over time, all of these assumptions have proved problematic. It is, however, understandable that policymakers might underestimate or overlook the difficulties inherent in the changes in teaching practice required by the reforms. No one had had experience with standards-based instructional reform prior to that in Kentucky, and no one had set such ambitious performance goals. Furthermore, the knowledge base was weak. Research and theory about teacher learning were rudimentary a decade ago, and what was known was not widely disseminated to either policymakers or practitioners.

To attempt to understand what has happened in professional development since the enactment of KERA, we will consider what researchers have learned from teachers about their experiences under KERA. We will then attempt to explain the experiences teachers have (or have not) had. Finally, we will identify some of the issues that remain to be addressed and will suggest what other states might learn from Kentucky's experience.

Kentucky Teachers' Experiences with Professional Development Under KERA

Through both surveys and interviews, we have investigated the experiences of teachers in Kentucky with planning and participating in professional development activities (McDiarmid, David, Corcoran, Kannapel, & Coe, 1997; McDiarmid & Kelly, 1997). In addition, KDE and other researchers have studied teachers' experiences with professional development (Daniel & Stallion, 1995; Kentucky Department of Education, 1995, 1996; Thacker, Koger, & Koger, 1998). Data from these sources seem to support the following generalizations about teachers' professional development experiences under KERA.

> *In large part, because Kentucky teachers have been the primary planners of their professional development activities, they have found these activities more relevant and valuable than they did prior to the reforms.*

Teachers throughout the state attest to the improvement of professional development since the passage of KERA (Daniel & Stallion, 1995; McDiarmid et al., 1997; Thacker et al., 1998). Three-quarters of those polled in statewide surveys of randomly selected teachers conducted between 1994 and 1999 consistently agreed that their professional development activities were "working to improve teaching and learning" in their districts (Kentucky Institute for Education Research, 2000). Such high levels of approval derive largely from teachers' perceptions that current professional development activities are more relevant to the issues and challenges they face—particularly, preparing students for the test formats on the new assessments. Prior to KERA, many teachers expected little or nothing from their required time in professional development. For many it was simply time off, a respite from the demands of the classroom. Now many teachers view professional development as the primary means to help them improve their teaching and achieve school goals.

Teachers also believe that KERA has provided a focus for professional development. The reform legislation required teachers to learn new programs, practices, and procedures. Teachers have used professional development opportunities to do this. At the same time, in some schools, the way these opportunities are organized is also changing. Opportunities for professional development are now more likely to extend beyond a single day, and considerable numbers of teachers have participated in language arts, science, technology, and hands-on math programs that have been intensive and have sometimes extended over several years.

Teachers' perceptions that professional development activities are now more relevant than before KERA are due in large part to the fact that they are making the decisions. Prior to KERA, district administrators arranged professional development activities they hoped would address the needs of the majority of teachers. Teachers often felt that the resulting activities were too generic to address their specific grade-level or subject-matter needs. District staff often held low expectations for the effects of professional development on classroom practice and seldom did any follow-up to ensure that new knowledge and skills were being applied. Moreover, the incentives to improve practice were weak. Under KERA, teachers are far more involved in making decisions about their professional development activities, and the accountability system generates strong incentives for improving practice. As a result, teachers feel far better about the utility of professional development activities.

The high stakes associated with assessment results have led most Kentucky teachers to plan staff development activities largely focused on procedural knowledge and in particular on improving their students' test-taking skills and aligning their curriculum with the core content.

In many ways, KERA has been *too* successful in serving the purposes of its architects. These reformers wanted to direct educators' attention to improving student learning. To measure progress toward that goal, they created the state assessment system—the Kentucky Instructional Results Information System (KIRIS). Test scores, driven by a high-stakes accountability system, have subsequently become the dominant influence on teachers' decisions about professional development. In many ways this is consistent with the recommendations of national reform groups that student learning goals should drive teachers' professional development (National Commission on Teaching and America's Future, 1996).

Yet, as many critics have pointed out, teacher anxiety about improving student test scores may actually subvert the intent of the reforms, leading teachers to teach test-taking skills and rely on drill and practice to teach content out of context and in isolation from the larger curriculum. Preoccupation with short-term test scores has led teachers to avoid taking instructional risks and to focus on what they feel is most certain to produce the gains they need. Many have chosen to do more of what they have always done by changing time allocations in the school day or by adding time to the day or year. They also attempt to tighten the alignment between the test and their curriculum and instructional materials. These efficiency measures produce gains in the short run, but they also divert attention from teachers' content knowledge needs and deeper changes in practice—the real intent of the reforms.

The primary challenge that teachers faced in the early 1990s was how to interpret what state-level policymakers wanted. They were asked to institute mandated reforms (new student assessments, writing portfolios, site-based decision making, the ungraded primary school programs, and so on), raise student scores on the state assessment, and reinvent their classroom practice to achieve the deeper reforms in teaching and learning envisioned by KERA—often with few or no concrete examples of how reformed practice might look. Facing competing expectations and demands, teachers, not surprisingly, gave priority to satisfying the mandates and raising test scores.

Teachers' greatest initial need was for information about the reforms and the new expectations they entailed. To get this information, teachers relied heavily on "one-shot" workshops or presentations, the conventional format for communicating information to large groups. In one study, educators reported that nearly half of these workshops focused on procedural rather than substantive topics: restructuring, collaboration, discipline, classroom management, and so on (McDiarmid & Kelly, 1997).

The other half of the professional development activities in the early period of KERA focused on the curriculum or assessment. Three curricular areas predominated: literacy, technology, and mathematics. Teachers' lack of familiarity with assembling and evaluating the writing and mathematics portfolios that constituted major elements of the assessment explains why more professional development focused on portfolios than on any other curricular element. Another KERA strand, technology, was an area in which most teachers had little knowledge or skill at the beginning of the reform.

As the accountability system came into play, teachers collectively examined their scores on KIRIS to pinpoint "weaknesses" to be remedied. As a consequence, the focus of professional development shifted increasingly to curriculum alignment and test preparation in the areas of weakest performance. Mathematics scores were low in many schools, so strategies to raise mathematics scores became a major focus of staff development in many schools across the state.

In sum, under KERA most teachers in Kentucky have experienced more, and probably better, professional development than they had before the reform. However, the learning opportunities provided for teachers prior to 1998 were primarily geared toward implementing the components of the reforms, helping teachers align their curricula with the state test, and aiding teachers in preparing students for new testing formats. Teacher subject-matter knowledge and pedagogical content knowledge were largely neglected.

Kentucky teachers have adhered to familiar forms of professional development and have been reluctant to embrace unconventional but promising approaches, such as mentoring and coaching, study groups, collective review of student work, and teacher networks.

Central to understanding why professional development at so many schools in Kentucky has remained a set of separate activities focused on procedures rather than on substance is understanding the view that many teachers hold of professional development. Most educators, drawing on their experiences, equate professional development with stand-alone, short-term workshops with no follow-up. Few teachers in Kentucky (or elsewhere) have experienced activities that meet the standards established by the National Staff Development Council (1994) or the recommendations of the National Commission on Teaching and America's Future (1996). Few teachers have participated in study groups, action research, teacher networks, summer institutes with classroom follow-up, or other more innovative learning experiences. In planning, most teachers have selected formats that are comfortable, familiar, and acceptable to their colleagues and to others—administrators, parents, students, and the community overall. Deviating from the typical and expected is risky in the context of KERA and the accountability system. Despite the fact that KDE broadened the definition of acceptable professional development, conventional activities persist.

Until recently, more intensive forms of professional development, such as summer institutes, have been available to only a few teachers—for at least two reasons. First, the funding for professional development under KERA has been inadequate to support widespread teacher participation in such activities. The annual allotment of $23 per student generates $9,200 for a school with four hundred students, and many of the state's schools are smaller yet. For a faculty of thirty teachers this yields slightly over $300 per teacher. Consequently, more intensive opportunities for professional development in subject-matter knowledge and curriculum have been limited to externally funded projects such as the National Science Foundation's State Systemic Initiative in Kentucky and mathematics projects run by the University of Kentucky. Second, the universities have been slow to respond to teachers' needs for professional development, and until recently most had not invested their own resources to create such opportunities. Most of the response to the increased demand for professional development has come from small workshop providers and consultants.

Both supply and demand issues have impeded an increase in professional development activities that are integrated into teachers' daily work lives and focused on deepening their content knowledge.

Certainly, some schools have made professional development a more integral part of their operations. And some have adopted a continuous improvement approach. Yet, for many teachers, professional development still remains a set of separate and fragmented activities, disconnected from the overall effort to improve learning opportunities in the school. With KDE leading the way, more opportunities for teachers to develop an in-depth understanding of the subjects they teach are being made available today than at the beginning of the reforms, although this is still not the dominant emphasis across the state.

Teachers understandably bridle at the implication that they lack knowledge of their subject matter. Many pride themselves on what they know. Many teachers also equate subject-matter study with university arts and sciences courses (McDiarmid, 1999). Because many teachers experienced university courses that were neither well taught nor relevant to the K–12 curriculum, they are skeptical about the utility of taking additional courses to improve their students' test scores.

Yet KERA changed substantially what students are expected to know and be able to do. The knowledge imparted in the traditional school curriculum—the state capitals, the genus of shellfish, the elements of a short story, the causes of the Civil War, how to perform operations with fractions, and so on—may no longer be sufficient. Therefore what teachers are now expected to know and help students learn extends well beyond the circumscribed canon of information that has traditionally constituted the school curriculum. National and state standards have raised the subject-matter knowledge bar. KIRIS and the Commonwealth Accountability Testing System, which replaced KIRIS, include open-ended response items that require students to understand the complexities of issues such as slavery and sectional conflict in a depth not required by earlier forms of assessment. This has increased the cognitive and pedagogical demands on teachers.

But when and where would Kentucky's teachers have learned what they needed to know to help all students reach the new standards and expectations? Their own schooling likely consisted of mastering some aspects of the school canon of information. University arts and sciences courses for teachers, particularly for elementary school teachers, are unlikely to foster in-depth, conceptual understanding of topics and issues critical to the school curriculum. Few professional development opportunities in Kentucky have focused on teachers' content knowledge. In short, teachers—many of whom know a great deal about the traditional school curriculum—are being asked to help their students develop understanding that they themselves may lack and that requires learning experiences for students that teachers have not been trained to design or manage.

On the supply side, compared with conventional in-service fare such as pedagogical and management skills workshops or analysis of test scores and test items, high-quality opportunities for teachers to increase their knowledge of subject matter, and how to teach it, remain unevenly available and relatively rare. As already argued, few teachers (especially elementary school teachers) are likely to find conventional university arts and sciences courses appealing. When teachers do take university courses, these tend to be in the education department. When teachers in Kentucky pursue advanced degrees, they typically do so in education, not in a particular subject-matter area. Although the state compensation schedule offers teachers a salary incentive to earn a master's degree, many of them understandably pursue endorsements in additional content areas, administration, or counseling. And because most teachers take their graduate course work in education, arts and sciences departments have little incentive to develop courses with teachers in mind. Moreover, arts and sciences faculty members are not, at most universities, rewarded for developing and teaching courses for prospective teachers. On the contrary, investing time in such efforts detracts from high-reward activities such as teaching large numbers of undergraduates, mentoring graduate students, securing outside funding, and publishing journal articles and books.

Some colleges and universities, particularly in the summer, do offer arts and sciences courses they believe will appeal to teachers. Yet such courses rarely examine the curricular and pedagogical implications of the subject matter they cover. Instead, topics are typically examined solely from a disciplinary perspective. Teachers are, once again, left on their own to make the transition from the content knowledge gained in these courses to the school curriculum. Consequently, such courses seem to appeal only to those teachers with a deep and abiding interest in a subject area for its own sake.

Subject-matter associations also provide opportunities for teacher learning, but only a small proportion of Kentucky teachers, mostly at the secondary level, appear to be active in these associations. Those teachers who do participate in association activities typically appear to do so as individuals and, at most, attend the annual statewide or regional conferences (McDiarmid & Kelly, 1997).

Some schools are taking advantage of the training that accompanies "prepackaged" interdisciplinary programs produced by private vendors. For instance, a key feature of the widely used Different Ways of Knowing program is the in-service in which trainers model classroom activities. Again, however, the training appears to focus less on the curriculum content and more on the processes for engaging students with the curriculum materials. Many private vendors offer "off-the-rack" in-service programs or materials, but their products are likely to follow trends rather than to set them. Consequently, private vendors are rarely in the forefront of providing opportunities for teachers to deepen their content knowledge.

In short, content knowledge has until recently lacked a champion who would promote it. This is puzzling given that teachers statewide overwhelmingly support the idea that improving their content background should be a key factor in their professional development (Kentucky Institute for Education Research, 2000). There are some promising starting points for altering this situation. KDE, which for obvious reasons has previously championed training for portfolio assessment, technology, and curriculum alignment, is now designing subject-matter institutes. Kentucky Educational Television has offered courses in mathematics and science, taught by university subject-matter specialists and specifically designed for teachers. On the private side, vendors such as History Alive and the Galef Institute have promoted their programs. The NSF-funded Partnership for Reform Initiatives in Science and Math (PRISM) has provided training for mathematics and science teachers and has technical specialists who provide staff development to teachers in their regions. A critical question about all of these efforts is who is taking responsibility for ensuring that they become accessible to all teachers on a regular basis and fit their varying needs and circumstances.

Evolution of Staff Development Opportunities

As we have already suggested, the landscape of professional development has changed over time in Kentucky and continues to evolve. Recently, one of the most promising developments has been the reorientation of KDE's technical support and staff development activities. In 1999 KDE reorganized the staffs of its RSCs along subject-matter lines. As the RSCs represent one of the most important sources of professional development in the state, this should have a significant impact on both supply and demand.

In addition, as noted earlier, KDE launched subject-matter institutes in the summer of 1999. Meeting at the regional level, KDE, teachers, and university faculty jointly planned the institutes that were initially focused on middle school science and social studies teachers. To lead the institutes, KDE recruited university subject-matter experts who were expected to address the needs teachers had identified. These institutes will extend into the school year by providing follow-up sessions for participants.

Concomitant with the emergence of these new opportunities have been changes in the regulatory framework (Clements, 1999). School improvement activities that previously would not have qualified as legitimate professional development activities, such as work on the curriculum with colleagues, are now recognized as important learning opportunities. More innovative types of professional development—teacher networks, study groups, and so on—also now qualify.

Unsatisfied with the quality of initiatives undertaken by schools, several districts have figured out how to provide effective leadership for staff development. Because of teachers' authority to decide on their own staff development, the efficacy of the district's role largely depends on the quality of the central office staff, particularly the professional development coordinator. Effective coordinators are providing a districtwide staff development focus that affords sufficient latitude for individual schools to pursue their individual goals while ensuring quality, providing continuity over time, and making efficient use of available resources. These leaders help identify sources of quality training, raise resources to pay for them, and create on-the-job opportunities for teachers to learn new knowledge and skills (David, McDiarmid, & Corcoran, 2000). In short, rather than ceding the direction of professional development to the schools, some successful districts are working with school-level educators to identify districtwide needs and to muster the resources to meet those needs.

Finally, institutes of higher education (IHEs) in the state have also begun to find ways to support teacher development beyond conventional graduate courses and programs. As previously noted, IHE faculty members are providing leadership and instruction through the newly created summer institutes. Earlier, IHEs were instrumental in securing NSF funds for professional development in mathematics and science. Universities in the state have also collaborated with K–12 educators in a number of districts to establish professional development schools that offer teachers new site-based learning opportunities.

In sum, as we enter the second decade of KERA, teachers have available far more diverse and promising opportunities to learn more about the content their students are expected to learn and about how to teach that content. KDE has reorganized to help teachers deepen their content knowledge even as changes in the regulatory framework are affording them more options. Some district administrators are devising effective ways to provide leadership and direction for school-level professional development. And some IHEs are also finding ways to support teachers in learning to teach content more effectively.

Remaining Issues

At least two stories could be told about professional development during KERA's first decade. The first story highlights the faulty assumptions reformers initially made about the supply of, and demand for, high-quality professional development and about what was required for teachers to change their classroom practice. A subplot in this story is that teachers' lack of experience with innovative approaches undercut the demand for high-quality professional development. As a consequence, needed changes in teachers' opportunities to learn have been slow to develop. Many, if not most, Kentucky teachers continue to attend one-shot workshops focused on procedures rather than substance.

Another more comprehensive and more encouraging story can be told. This story is one of widespread and continuous learning. A growing number of practitioners and policymakers are learning about the opportunities teachers need to develop the knowledge and skills necessary to help their students reach higher standards. According to this story, over the past decade policymakers and practitioners have been paying close attention to the growing body of knowledge on professional development, particularly to research conducted in Kentucky. They have listened to teachers express their frustration in seeking better opportunities to acquire the knowledge and skills they need. Learning from research and experience, they have made adjustments in the original reform design.

The first chapter in this story was KDE's introduction of consolidated planning. This required schools to link professional development to overall school goals and plan activities that directly furthered those goals. In the next chapter, legislators, at the urging and with the assistance of KDE and others, broadened the range of activities that counted as professional development to include school improvement work, teacher networks, study groups, summer institutes, and other, noninstitutional opportunities (Clements, 1999). Recognizing the need for coordination and leadership at the district level, policymakers also required districts to appoint professional development coordinators. In the latest chapter, to enhance teachers' knowledge of teaching content, state policymakers have realigned the technical assistance offered by the RSCs along subject-matter lines and have created summer subject-matter institutes that include school year follow-ups.

A primary vehicle for this evolution of policy and priorities has been the PKS-sponsored Professional Development Policymakers' Roundtable. Convened semiannually by PKS, the roundtable has provided policymakers from KDE, the governor's office, the legislature, and professional associations, as well as university researchers and K–12 educators, with a forum in which they can examine data and discuss issues, concerns, and plans. For the PKS researchers these roundtables have been occasions to learn about the questions and issues policymakers face and to preview their research questions and designs. Over time, the researchers have brought back their data and findings to the roundtable. They have enlisted the participants to help them interpret the results and tease out their policy implications. KDE, the legislature's Office of Education Accountability, universities, and the Kentucky Institute for Education Research have also brought research findings and ideas to the roundtables for discussion. According to key policymakers, these roundtables have played a particularly critical role in the evolution of policy.

Although the second story suggests more progress and more optimism about the future state of professional development than the first, a number of issues remain. The most challenging—not just in Kentucky but elsewhere—is how to identify and "scale up" the most promising approaches and programs—that is, how to successfully expand such approaches to involve more teachers and more schools. The lack of good information on what schools are doing makes identifying promising approaches difficult. This lack of information inhibits examination of the effects of various approaches. Scaling up promising approaches is difficult given the lack of information. In the absence of compelling evidence of improved results, most teachers are reluctant to try new approaches. Clearly, the state needs to track the efficacy of different approaches and share the results of these studies with schools, districts, IHEs, and providers.

What else should the state be doing? The success of the newly created summer subject-matter institutes and similar professional development will depend on classroom support for teachers as they try to implement what they have learned. The Appalachian Regional Systemic Initiative is providing on-site classroom support in math and science and has developed a model for preparing coaches that appears effective and that other programs could emulate. Whatever the source—RSC staff, district coaches, or university faculty—classroom support is critical to the complex process of changing practice.

Getting teachers to participate in subject-matter institutes on a large scale will probably also require additional changes in the incentive structure. Participation in these institutes will attract more teachers if the experience counts for advancement on the salary scale. The content of the institutes also should be offered as university courses and weekend institutes for the many teachers who are unable to attend in the summer.

New incentives would also help overcome the "get in my required four days and be done with it" attitude that limits the genuine engagement of many teachers. These teachers do not value professional development and see no need for continuous learning—a view they share with those in the legislature who could not understand the need to continue funding the five additional professional development days each year. Altering the requirements for advancement on the salary scale and ensuring the availability of high-quality experiences will help persuade some of these reluctant learners to participate.

Finally, better data on teachers' experiences with professional development would allow KDE to examine the links between the type of learning opportunities provided for teachers and school performance. This will allow them to demonstrate to skeptical legislators that the investment is worthwhile.

In sum, professional development under KERA, while not an unalloyed success, is certainly a story of continuous learning and the concomitant evolution of policy. Whether subsequent chapters will continue this story line depends on a number of factors. Foremost among these are the willingness of policymakers and practitioners to continue critically examining the effects of their efforts and to make adjustments in policy as results dictate, the continued provision of the resources (including time and support) needed for teacher learning and change, and the development of incentives and mechanisms for dissemination of promising innovations and ideas.

REFERENCES

Clements, S. (1999). *Professional development and Kentucky's systemic education reform.* Lexington: University of Kentucky.

Coe, P., & Adams-Rodgers, L. (in press). *The Kentucky Leadership Academy: Training administrators to be instructional leaders.* Lexington: Partnership for Kentucky Schools.

Consortium for Policy Research in Education. (1998). *Expanding the breadth and effects of reform: A report on the fourth year of the Merck Institute for Science Education, 1996–97.* Philadelphia: Author.

Daniel, P., & Stallion, B. (1995). *The implementation of Kentucky's school-based professional development.* Lexington: Kentucky Institute for Education Research.

David, J., McDiarmid, G., & Corcoran, T. (2000). *The role of Kentucky districts in professional development: Exemplary cases.* Lexington: Partnership for Kentucky Schools.

Featherstone, H., Smith, S. P., Beasley, K., Corbin, D., & Shank, C. (1995). *Expanding the equation: Learning mathematics through teaching in new ways* (Research Report No. 95-1). East Lansing: Michigan State University, National Center for Research on Teacher Learning.

Heaton, R. (1995). *What is a pattern? An elementary teacher's early efforts to teach mathematics for understanding* (Craft Paper No. 95-1). East Lansing: Michigan State University, National Center for Research on Teacher Learning.

Jennings, N. (1996). *Interpreting policy in real classrooms: Case studies of state reform and teacher practice.* New York: Teachers College Press.

Kentucky Department of Education. (1995). *1995 teacher survey on professional development: Final report.* Frankfort: Author.

Kentucky Department of Education. (1995). *Transformations: Kentucky's curriculum framework.* Frankfort: Author.

Kentucky Department of Education (1996). *Core content for assessment.* Frankfort: Author.

Kentucky Department of Education. (1996). *Professional development support systems in Kentucky: A state and regional view.* Frankfort: Author.

Kentucky Department of Education (1999). *Core content for assessment.* Frankfort: Author.

Kentucky Institute for Education Research. (2000). *1999 statewide education reform study.* Lexington: Author.

McDiarmid, G. (1999). *Still missing after all these years: Understanding the paucity of subject-matter professional development in Kentucky.* Lexington: Partnership for Kentucky Schools.

McDiarmid, G., David, J., Corcoran, T., Kannapel, P., and Coe, P. (1997). *Professional development under KERA: Meeting the challenge.* Lexington: Partnership for Kentucky Schools.

McDiarmid, G., & Kelly, P. (1997, April). *Teachers planning professional development in a reform context: The case of Kentucky.* Paper presented at the annual meeting of the American Educational Research Association, Chicago.

National Commission on Teaching and America's Future. (1996). *What matters most: Teaching for America's future.* New York: Author.

National Staff Development Council. (1994). *Standards for staff development: Study guide* (Middle level edition). Oxford, OH: Author.

Schwille, S. (1998). *A biographical account of an experienced teacher struggling to change from traditional to reform-minded practice.* Unpublished dissertation. East Lansing: Michigan State University, College of Education.

Thacker, A., Koger, L., & Koger, M. (1998). *Professional development under the Kentucky Education Reform Act: A study of practices in 30 middle schools.* Radcliff, KY: Human Resources Research Organization.

10

IMPROVING SCHOOLS AND SCHOOL LEADERS

Patricia J. Kannapel, Pam Coe

AS ACCOUNTABILITY SYSTEMS SPREAD rapidly across the country, policymakers and educators alike are frustrated by the seemingly limited options available for improving low-performing schools. Creating rewards and sanctions proves to be the easy part. Figuring out what to do with schools that do not pass muster is much harder. Since 1990 Kentucky has worked to increase the capacity of schools to provide an efficient and equitable education. Kentucky's assessment-based accountability system is designed to motivate schools to continuously improve, to reward those that meet state-established goals every two years, and to sanction those that do not meet these goals. Unlike many accountability systems, however, the sanctions were coupled with substantial school-based assistance. In addition to a significant investment in professional development (described in Chapter Nine), the state offers (and formerly required) assistance to schools that have lost significant ground on the state assessment.

Data for this chapter were derived from a series of studies of professional development conducted by the Partnership for Kentucky Schools (an organization of the state's top business leaders) and funded by the Annie E. Casey Foundation and the Pew Charitable Trusts (Coe & Adams-Rodgers, in press; David, Kannapel, & McDiarmid, in press; Chapter Nine of this volume). In addition to the authors of this chapter, the research team included Lois Adams-Rodgers, Tom Corcoran, Jane L. David, and G. Williamson McDiarmid. We are also indebted to Jane L. David for assistance with this chapter.

Kentucky's intervention, known as the School Transformation and Renewal (STAR) program, is unusual in its focus on helping schools improve through intensive technical assistance. As part of the program, Kentucky assigns carefully selected and highly trained educators—initially called distinguished educators (DEs) and now called highly skilled educators (HSEs)—to assist eligible schools.

Early results of the STAR program, which began in 1994–95, indicated that the DE intervention was well received in most schools and successful in raising test scores. These positive results led to requests that the DE training model be made available to school leaders across the state. In 1997 the Kentucky Department of Education (KDE) developed the Kentucky Leadership Academy (KLA), a two-year training program for local administrators. This chapter reports on the structure and impact of both the DE and KLA programs. The goal of the DE and KLA studies was to learn how the programs were structured, what they focused on, how they were received by participants, and what effects they had. Data were gathered from 1997 through 1999, through a combination of interviews, observations, surveys, and document review.

The Distinguished Educator Program

Kentucky's assessment and accountability structure, described in Chapter Three, is undergoing revision by order of the 1998 legislature. Until 1998, DEs were assigned to all schools whose test scores declined over a two-year period, including high-performing schools. If the decline was less than 5 percent, the school was labeled "in decline," and the DEs were assigned a facilitative role. If the decline was 5 percent or more, the school was declared "in crisis," and DEs not only assisted schools in improving but evaluated certified personnel every six months and recommended their retention, dismissal, or transfer. In addition, students were permitted to transfer to a "successful" school. The "crisis" designation was in effect only during the 1996–98 biennium, then was eliminated when the 1998 General Assembly mandated revision of the entire assessment and accountability program. This chapter focuses on the DE program prior to the 1998 changes, which replaced DEs with HSEs.

During the 1994–96 biennium schools in decline received nearly one-on-one assistance, with forty-six DEs assigned to the 53 eligible schools (Office of Education Accountability, 1995). In the 1996–98 biennium forty-six DEs were funded to help 185 eligible schools, resulting in a dramatic reduction in the intensity of DE assistance except in the neediest schools. Each of the 9 crisis schools was served by two DEs: one to provide instructional support, the other to perform staff evaluations. Here DEs often spent as much as three days per week in the building. The remaining 176 schools were divided among the remaining DEs, assisted by staff from regional service centers (branches of KDE) who had received some training in the STAR program. STAR schools also received additional funding for school improvement.

The problem of having so few DEs assigned to so many schools was exacerbated by the requirement that DEs serve for only two years. The state board of education extended the terms of service for some DEs, but others rotated out of the program as new DEs rotated in. This rotation meant that some schools changed DEs—sometimes more than once—midway through the two-year accountability cycle, which disrupted continuity.

Rationale of the Program and Distinguished Educator Training

The STAR framework was based on the belief that all children can learn and all teachers can teach. The program also presumed that the best way to improve teaching and learning was to help educators understand the need for change and desire the benefits of change, to involve them in designing change, and to provide them with appropriate training. Thus the DE program was designed to be more facilitative than punitive in nature (Kentucky Department of Education [KDE], 1994).

To prepare DEs to lead schools in effecting change, KDE provided each cadre of DEs with intensive training, including a two-week summer retreat, and four to seven sessions of varying length (typically two to three days) that focused on such topics as personnel evaluation, school organization, school-based curriculum development, the state assessment, school finance, and school-based decision making (SBDM) (Office of Education Accountability, 1995, 1997). After this initial training, DEs assigned to schools continued meeting every four to six weeks in regional cadre meetings typically lasting two to three days (D. Allen, KDE, personal communication, December 1, 1999).

Activities of Distinguished Educators

Although DE activities varied somewhat from one school to the next, DEs followed the same basic process at all schools. Visiting their assigned schools anywhere from once every two weeks to three to four days per week, depending on the level of assistance required, DEs worked to focus schools on improving academic results as measured by the Kentucky Instructional Results Information System (KIRIS) test, the state assessment that was in place until 1998. They began by leading school staff through a needs assessment that included an analysis of KIRIS data and of survey data from school staff, parents, and teachers. Information from the needs assessment and surveys was used to identify school improvement goals, which typically targeted weak areas on KIRIS.

Once goals were identified, DEs led school faculty through development of a "transformation" plan that outlined how the goals would be achieved and identified needed professional development. These plans were developed by committees, often during after-school meetings. Committees were charged with overseeing implementation of their assigned components (for instance, a math component if math had been identified as an area of need). Component managers were designated to report regularly to the school council.

As the transformation plan was implemented, DEs helped schools determine how to spend the improvement funding allocated by the state and sometimes helped locate other resources to implement the plan. They also worked on building local capacity, through securing or providing professional development and sometimes through direct assistance or modeling in classrooms. Much of the professional development was focused on aligning curriculum with the KIRIS test and on developing teachers' ability to help students with producing writing portfolios and answering open-response questions. Many times faculty meetings were used for these types of professional development. Some DEs engaged in supportive activities such as helping students with portfolios, attending SBDM meetings, helping develop curriculum units, and helping teachers set up "evidence boxes" for gathering student data. A teacher in a "crisis" school described the work of the DEs this way:

> The DEs have helped us to align our curriculum so that we know what content is covered where and when it is supposed to be covered. They have observed us to teach us best-practice teaching techniques. They have helped us allocate funding to put together our curriculum and prepare for testing and helped with supplies for our classrooms as well.

General Reaction to Distinguished Educators' Presence

Initially resentful or embarrassed about the DE assignment, most educators came to appreciate the benefits of the extra technical support and funding—although there was some evidence of resistance in high-performing schools (Holland, 1997), and we visited a few schools where poor relations between teachers and the DE made improvements difficult. Overall, however, reactions were positive. A survey of schools involved in the STAR program in the first round of intervention (Davis, McDonald, & Lyons, 1997) found that over 80 percent of responding teachers, principals, superintendents, and DEs rated the program as effective. A separate survey of schools participating in the STAR program during the second cycle found that teachers rated highly the DEs' knowledge of the state assessment, their fairness in evaluating personnel, their emphasis on long-term improvement, and their leadership in improvement planning (Henry, Terry, & Lunney, 1998). An elementary teacher in our study remarked:

> I have had a very positive reaction to the DE program. . . . First of all they came in, we sat down, and we decided what areas on the KIRIS test were our lowest areas, [and] we targeted those. We set our goals and activities for each of the goals and began to carry those out immediately. We had meetings and meetings and meetings that first year. . . . As we went along, if the activity was not having a great impact, they suggested eliminating it and maybe adding another. They were always here for support; they would go into my classroom and demonstrate anything I wanted. They would go to different successful schools and pull information there. They were an endless resource. I think basically they were a shoulder to cry on, and someone to pat you on the back and say you are doing a good job.

A high school teacher in a crisis school commented:

> Our school needed a focus on curriculum. We have been bogged down by major discipline problems in the past. Students and teachers had a morale loss and needed to look ahead, not behind. The test gave us a focus, and the DEs gave our students added motivation. They were essentially cheerleaders for our school. I loved having them here. Although we worked very hard, it was a positive effort. I am thankful for the experience and more confident because of it.

Even though most teachers came to feel the DEs were helpful, they also found the intervention very labor intensive and stressful. When educators were asked generally about the results of having a DE, the three most common responses focused on increased stress or workload. Teachers reported that they spent more time on paperwork, felt more pressure on the job, and put in more hours on the job. One teacher wrote on the survey:

> There are not enough hours in the day to possibly do everything we are told we have to do now. . . . Too many added duties, paperwork, meetings prevent teachers from having any time to plan.

A perception on the part of educators that teachers had limited influence on student achievement may have added to the pressure. The vast majority of educators we surveyed blamed their school's declining test scores on factors difficult for the school to control, such as low student motivation or capability, lack of parental support, or the structure of the testing and accountability program, a finding also reported by Wakelyn (1999). And although teachers said the DEs helped the school focus more on student learning, most did not believe students had actually learned more as a result of DE presence. These findings suggest general resistance to schools' taking ownership of student learning, which could act as a barrier to bringing about long-term improvements.

Effectiveness of the Distinguished Educator Program

The effectiveness of the DE program can be judged by examining test score trends, impact on school culture and organization, and effects on staffing and student involvement. Each of these factors is discussed below.

IMPACT ON TEST SCORES. Available evidence suggests that DEs concentrated heavily on test-related activities as a first step to raising student achievement. When asked what had happened at their schools as a result of DE presence, many teachers reported improved preparation for the state assessment, including improved curriculum and instructional coordination at the school (which, in our experience, usually meant aligning the curriculum to what was tested and making sure teachers and departments knew who was teaching what), greater attention to test data, and increased information on how to prepare students to succeed on the state test.

Test score data indicate that these efforts paid off. As a group, schools that participated in the STAR program improved at a high rate on KIRIS. Results of the first two-year cycle of DE intervention showed significant gains on the state assessment in all fifty-three schools that received assistance from a DE; thirty-four schools actually met or exceeded their goals (KDE, 1996). At the end of the second cycle forty-six of these original fifty-three schools again improved their scores. In addition, 89 percent of schools participating in the STAR program during the second cycle improved their performance (D. Allen, KDE, personal communication, September 21, 1999). Whether improving test scores resulted from DE activities or from associated factors such as being labeled "in decline" or "in crisis" is impossible to determine. However, available data suggest that DE actions increased teachers' attention to the state assessment.

LONGER-TERM IMPACT. A critical indicator of the success of the DE program is whether DEs instituted changes beyond test preparation to improve student learning in the long run. Although it is a bit too early in the reform process to examine long-term trend data, certain evidence does point to potentially longer-lasting changes effected by DEs.

The first piece of evidence is a focus on student learning. In a study of DEs Wakelyn (1999) noted that the DEs he interviewed were adamant that every change in policy, school structure, and instructional practice must answer the question, How is this going to affect student learning? This focus apparently carried over into schools. A majority of teachers in our study reported that one result of DE presence was that their schools were more focused on student learning.

Second, roughly two-thirds of our respondents reported that improved instruction had resulted from the DE program. Teachers noted that DEs had helped them implement "best practices" in their classrooms.

A third effect, perceived by about half of the teachers in our survey, was improvement in leadership and collaboration. "Leadership" sometimes referred to improvements in the principal's leadership skills but equally often meant teachers were becoming better leaders. Similarly, collaboration often meant that teachers were spending more time analyzing data and planning with colleagues.

Fourth, educators at many schools reported that instructional planning and organization had improved at their schools. In particular, DEs strengthened the development and implementation of school improvement plans by organizing component committees and managers. Many schools retained this participatory strategy even after the DE departed.

Finally, many principals and teachers reported that professional development became more focused on curriculum, instruction, and the specific needs of the school as a result of DE presence. In addition, the format and types of professional development in schools participating in the STAR program showed some signs of movement beyond the workshop model. For instance, teachers reported that faculty meetings were often used for professional development and that professional development occurred over a period of time. In a few schools, teachers reported that the DEs had modeled instructional practices in their classrooms.

Although the DEs had an impact beyond improving test scores, it is not clear whether their two-year presence in schools will have a long-term effect on school culture. The reluctance of teachers to claim responsibility for declining test scores and to attribute improved test scores to DE presence suggests that changing entrenched attitudes and behaviors is a difficult and lengthy process. Some of the DEs we interviewed suggested that they would need more than two years to build school capacity. A teacher in a crisis school expressed uncertainty that teacher attitudes had changed enough to make a difference over the long term:

> I don't know [if the changes will continue when the DEs are gone]. . . . With myself, yes. As far as schoolwide, I don't know. . . . It does seem that we have a tough time for people to come together and unite and say this is what we are going to do as far as curriculum and discipline.

IMPACT ON SCHOOL PERSONNEL AND STUDENT TRANSFERS. Two of the most dreaded effects of the DE program in crisis schools never had a widespread impact: the dismissal of personnel and the transfer of students to "successful" schools. There was only one instance statewide of students transferring to another school. We did hear reports that principals or teachers had voluntarily retired or transferred, but statewide no administrators or teachers were terminated. This was because, at the end of the first six months of DE intervention during the 1996–98 biennium, the DE program adopted the position that six months was not enough time to identify weaknesses, develop improvement plans, mentor individuals, and observe growth. By the conclusion of the second six months, the Kentucky General Assembly was on course to revise the assessment and accountability program. KDE thought it best to not recommend terminations while this debate was occurring. A bill that eliminated the "crisis" designation was subsequently passed, so DE evaluation of personnel ceased (D. Allen, KDE, personal communication, September 22, 1999).

Although no personnel were dismissed by DEs, there is evidence that personnel evaluations had a positive impact on teachers. Of the teachers in our survey who said they had been evaluated by the DE, about two-thirds found the evaluation helpful. A teacher in a crisis school, comparing the DE evaluation with the annual evaluation by the building principal, came to this conclusion:

> I think the DE evaluation is more helpful. . . . [W]hen I sit down with the DE and he tells me what I am doing wrong, he's automatically telling me how I can do something to alter it. And then he's making sure in the next evaluation that I've done that, or he's trying to find things that I've done. When you sit down with your principal or these other administrators, they label things that maybe you have done wrong, but they don't come back and follow it up by saying, 'Maybe you could try teaching it this way or teaching that way.' The DEs do that.

IMPACT OF THE PROGRAM STATEWIDE. The DE program was available to a relatively small percentage of Kentucky schools. There is, however, evidence to suggest that the program has had at least a minimal impact on schools that were not served by DEs. The most obvious effect was the creation of KLA, based on the DE model, to develop leadership skills across the state. In addition, as DEs and HSEs are trained and then rotate out of the program, the state develops an ever larger cadre of highly skilled potential agents of change. Recent data from KDE indicate that of seventy-seven DEs who had exited the program, 22 percent used their skills in new positions in their home districts and another 35 percent accepted employment in a new district where they used their skills. About 17 percent retired, but some of these were working as consultants, helping districts that requested their services. Only 26 percent had returned to their home district in their original positions, where they may or may not have been using their DE skills (D. Allen, KDE, personal communication, January 31, 2000). A KDE staff member responsible for the DE program (D. Allen, KDE, personal communication, April 7, 2000) pointed out:

> The program has impacted schools other than those directly served by DEs/HSEs in several ways. DE/HSE tools and strategies for school improvement are now used in many non-STAR schools. Their adoption results from local district leadership, the KDE's own use of our web page for distribution of tools and strategies and teacher use of existing networks—formal and informal. The use of HSEs as trainers for the KLA also impacts non-STAR schools.

The Kentucky Leadership Academy

As the DE program proved successful at raising test scores and focusing attention on student achievement, KDE received requests from superintendents around Kentucky to train principals and district administrators in the STAR program. DEs were involved in the planning of the KLA program from its inception, and many DEs served as KLA coaches and trainers. Regional service center staff were also brought into the program during the planning period and remained highly involved.

Focus and Structure of Training

As with the DE program, all training focused on planning for continuous school improvement, effective instructional practices and curriculum development, accountability and assessment, and facilitating change. Participants were expected to achieve these outcomes by using the school transformation process (now expanded and called the "consolidated plan"); by developing curriculum based on national and state standards, the content to be assessed, and effective instructional practices; by designing an assessment process embedded in the curriculum, with student progress as the goal; and by demonstrating transformational leadership and support skills. The key question in each focus area was, Does this develop our capacity to improve student achievement? Particular attention was given to analyzing student work (KDE, 1997).

In 1997 districts across the state were invited to participate in KLA by sending teams to one of nine regional cadres. Of Kentucky's 176 school districts, 99 sent teams, for a total of 331 participants. District teams typically consisted of at least two administrators, representing both the central office and principals. Each cadre was led by a coach and several trainers, usually drawn from the ranks of DEs. Unlike the STAR program, which was imposed on schools but brought with it extra funding and assistance, KLA was voluntary, and the cost (about $1,000 per participant) was borne by the districts.

KLA participants met in cadre meetings during the school year and also in weeklong "retreats" held each summer for all the cadres together, for a total of eleven days of group instruction each year. Initially, a common script developed by the KLA design team (representing KDE staff, coaches, and trainers) was used in all cadres. District participants from each cadre were added to the design team during the second year. Cadre coaches visited each participating district about three times a year, assisting team members with problems or tasks they identified in leadership development plans. In the second year, cadres were organized into study-group networks that met between regular meetings.

Our research focused on five cadres, each of which developed its own character and feeling of family. Participating districts varied widely in their sophistication and reform-mindedness, and each cadre had a different mix of participants. Trainers and coaches were challenged to find content and activities that met the specific needs of the varied districts in a cadre. We heard some criticism of the relatively rigid content presented during the early months of training, but this criticism disappeared by the end of the training period, when participants reported satisfaction that the training had been tailored to their particular needs.

KLA training was geared to the school calendar, so that participants studied what they were currently being required to do. Thus they worked on analysis of test scores as soon as scores were released and on consolidated planning at the time of year when that was required. They focused on student work throughout. Participants brought student portfolios to

KLA meetings and analyzed them with the assistance of state and regional writing consultants. The focus of the training developed over time from short-term strategies for improving student test scores to longer-term strategies for developing district and school capacity for instructional leadership.

The trend for training to vary from cadre to cadre, depending on needs, also accelerated. However, the focus on continuous school improvement, effective instructional practices and curriculum development, accountability and assessment, and facilitating change continued throughout. Some common techniques and concepts explored in all cadres were the importance of looking closely at student work, often using a walk-through technique that involved visiting classrooms and asking students targeted questions about their work; exploration of leadership techniques that encouraged thoughtful reflection and faculty leadership development; and study-group networking among cadre members.

At the conclusion of the initial training period, an alumni group was organized to enable cadre members to stay in touch with one another and with the cutting-edge information disseminated through KLA. All of the districts we visited continued their participation in KLA, through the alumni group, through sending additional administrators for training, or both.

Impact of the Program

Unlike the case of the DE program, no data are yet available about whether participation in the KLA program is associated with gains in student achievement. This is because KLA, launched in 1997, is relatively new. No impact on scores can be expected until administrators have time to absorb what they learn from KLA and then learn—at least partly through trial and error—how to help teachers implement new practices. Some quick fixes learned through KLA that DEs found effective in bringing about quick test score improvements can certainly be expected to raise test scores quickly. But these initial results cannot throw much light on the question of whether KLA training enables participants to provide leadership that improves student learning continuously over time. A second problem in using test score data to judge the impact of KLA is that a new state test that cannot be equated to the previous one was administered halfway through the initial training period. It will be possible to ascertain whether and how KLA has influenced student learning only after the new test has been administered for several testing cycles.

We did, however, gather some evidence on the impact of KLA. Many participants told us they felt that KLA training made them more effective leaders, both by changing their conception of leadership and by giving them additional tools for leadership. They reported a wide variety of specific changes in practice, apparently depending on the school's or district's existing capacity. The most courageous action was that of a principal who began the arduous process of trying to help teachers improve their practice and documenting whether they did so. After this process had been in place for a year, five teachers resigned or transferred out of the school rather than continue to the point at which they might be terminated. The principal explained how KLA had been instrumental in this process:

> Having five teachers leave last year is a result of KLA. There was a section in there about our moral responsibility to make sure our teachers are meeting their standards. I began to look really closely at . . . teacher plan books, grade books, and classroom observation; and work[ed] with teachers trying to improve instruction. . . . Before, I would not have done that. One of those teachers had been here for four years, and I just ignored what was going on there.

In another district with a long history of implementing reform, administrators said that KLA had inspired them to give time for reflection at the end of each faculty meeting as well as to engage administrators and teachers in walk-throughs to look at student work. At the opposite extreme, in a district whose superintendent and central office administrators had enthusiastically adopted KLA-suggested strategies unfamiliar to most principals and teachers, the main change appeared to be more focused countywide professional development and a general edict that schools would be scrutinized and held accountable for improvement in student achievement. Teachers in the six schools we visited were aware of improvements in school planning and professional development, and most were aware of specific changes over the two years when their administrators received KLA training. Consolidated planning was an ongoing process in these schools, and most teachers could describe the process and its effects on their professional development, which was usually tied closely to analysis of test results.

Potential of the Program

KLA was sufficiently costly that participants would be tempted to drop out if they felt they were not receiving value for their money, but only two of the ninety-nine districts did so. By the end of the first two years, many participants we interviewed suggested that all Kentucky administrators should have the opportunity to participate in KLA. The apparent reason for this degree of satisfaction was that the KLA design team, as well as the coaches and trainers, were responsive to complaints and made improvements as they were demanded. For instance, the KDE program administrator reported that early in the program, participants were having difficulty perceiving how the various strands and offerings were connected. The planners subsequently made sure the connections were explicitly stated and then gave time for reflection on the connections (N. Privett, personal communication, November 19, 1999). Members of one cadre complained that the KLA training on consolidated planning was not timely for them, although it was timely for most cadres, so the trainers substituted more relevant topics.

It remains to be seen if the districts, under these administrators' leadership, will be able to sustain continuous improvement in student achievement. Nevertheless, it is clear that KLA represents a major advance in professional development for administrators. If training administrators to do what DEs do accomplishes the kind of school improvement seen in schools served by DEs, the benefits of the approach will be greatly extended.

Lessons and Challenges

Kentucky has made great strides in creating strategies for professional development and technical assistance to improve schools and those who lead them. Central to the DE and KLA programs is a focus on curriculum, instruction, and student results, coupled with a strategy of providing training and assistance over an extended period of time. The STAR program has been effective in improving student test scores and in organizing the school around a common set of curricular goals, particularly when the DEs are a regular presence in schools. This does not confirm that DEs caused the increase in test scores, but increases are associated with their presence. Although it is too early to know if KLA training will result in improved student achievement, our data suggest that this program, too, has helped schools begin to organize and focus their efforts toward improved student learning. Both programs modeled forms of intensive professional development (discussed in Chapter Nine) that are needed to bring about real change. Examples include on-site training and technical assistance, networking, and study groups.

Kentucky's experience with intervention in schools with declining scores raises several issues for Kentucky policymakers and others around the nation who are concerned with building school capacity. We focus here on five key issues: HSE placement and terms of service, which schools to serve, limits of this type of intervention, use of sanctions, and cost.

Highly Skilled Educator Placement and Terms of Service

Placing DEs and structuring their time proved to be a controversial issue in Kentucky. Many schools and DEs were well matched, but where they were not (or where DEs kept changing), the benefits of the program were not realized; in a few places serious problems developed. KDE continues to try to carefully match HSEs to schools, but an ongoing problem is the switching of HSEs midway through the accountability cycle. This situation is associated with the current policy of limiting HSEs' terms of service to two years. Because KDE wants to maintain a mix of experienced and new HSEs rather than have a complete turnover every two years, they are forced to change some HSEs in midcycle (D. Allen, KDE, personal communication, November 24, 1999). This problem might be corrected by exercising the option provided in the statutes for the state board of education to extend the term of service if deemed necessary—an option used in the early years.

A related problem is whether it is possible to effect long-term change in only two years (sometimes less when test scores that identify eligible schools are not available until midway through the school year). Given that the effectiveness of the HSE and the school is judged on the basis of test scores, an initial focus on test preparation represents a rational and responsible choice for HSEs. With two years or less to bring about change, it is difficult to move more than superficially beyond test preparation into long-term instructional improvement. It is not clear how much intervention is enough, but the level and length of intervention needed likely varies with the needs of each school. Thus policymakers should consider ways to extend the time HSEs are on the job in schools that need more than two years to make long-term changes.

Schools to Be Served

Most states and localities focus intervention efforts on their lowest-performing schools. Those who crafted Kentucky's intervention program argued that high-performing schools that had declined actually had problems, particularly in serving their lowest-performing students well, and that if the goal is continuous improvement for *all* students, the same standard must be applied across the continuum. Yet in the eyes of the public and educators, the notion that high-performing schools would be given a negative label and assigned a DE made little sense and was viewed by some as squandering a scarce resource on schools with far fewer needs than low-performing schools. This pressure, coupled with the scarcity of resources, has led to a refocusing on the lowest-performing schools as the assessment and accountability program has been restructured. This seems a prudent approach, especially if accompanied by some requirement that high-performing schools continue to increase the proportion of successful students—and perhaps if a less intensive level of assistance is provided to help them do so.

Limits of This Intervention

Policymakers must recognize that although external agents of change can help schools organize themselves around specific student learning targets, some problems may be beyond the influence of an HSE—particularly when the HSE is only in place for two years. We visited schools where the educational program had suffered years of neglect and schools that were experiencing serious problems, such as community and school factionalism resulting from school mergers, severe budget deficits, and frequent staff turnover. Schools in urban districts struggled to reach high levels of achievement with less advantaged students who were "left over" when high-achieving students departed to attend two or three magnet schools. A DE working in urban schools reported that the large bureaucracy was difficult to penetrate:

> A DE can make more ground in a smaller district than they can in this large district. The STAR program is just one little speck in this district.

These cases do not suggest that the state should give up on such schools and districts. Rather, school- or district-specific adaptations to the intervention program may be needed, such as lengthening the HSE's stay, increasing the level of improvement funds, or building community support for schools and school change. Building local capacity through the KLA program and similar strategies is another approach to helping schools and districts deal with local barriers to school improvement.

Use of Sanctions

A perplexing issue in Kentucky and elsewhere is whether sanctions are needed to get schools moving in a new direction. Kentucky teachers have reported that sanctions are stronger motivators (albeit negative ones) than are rewards (Kannapel, Coe, Aagaard, Moore, & Reeves, 2000). Yet sanctions based on test scores can result in superficial changes aimed at raising scores rather than long-term changes in teaching and learning. In addition, we found no major differences between DE activities or school responses in declining schools, where DEs were facilitators, and crisis schools, where DEs also evaluated teachers. The STAR program's emphasis on assistance rather than sanctions helped establish positive relationships that could be channeled toward improved school performance. It is not clear, however, whether the threat of sanctions kept schools motivated to work with DEs; it may have, because even schools in decline wanted to avoid a downward spiral that might eventually result in the "crisis" designation, which would have given DEs evaluative power. The KLA program illustrates that school improvement can be fostered without heavy-handed sanctions. It remains to be seen if schools led by KLA alumni will be successful in improving student achievement and if test score gains at schools where DEs or HSEs have been assigned will be maintained over time.

Cost

The kinds of targeted, long-term training and assistance to schools and their leaders that the DE and KLA programs have exemplified can get schools moving in a positive direction if the program receives adequate resources and time. But interventions of this type are a strain on state education budgets. David Allen (personal communication, April 7, 2000) reported that the average salary of HSEs in 1999 was approximately $81,100 and that, in addition, each HSE received reimbursement for travel and lodging expenses and accounted for a share of all costs associated with training. When 185 schools became eligible for the DE program in the second accountability cycle, the state was unable to provide the level of assistance that had proved so effective in the first cycle. A logical step was to offer the most intensive assistance to schools whose scores had declined the most, but this left other needy schools without intensive support.

Possible Solutions

KDE is attempting to address the problems in the design of the HSE program. HSEs are assigned to only one school unless two schools are small and geographically close. But this policy necessarily forces assignment of HSEs to only the lowest-performing schools. Schools at the intermediate level are assisted by regional service centers, and high-performing schools with declining scores rely primarily on local district resources to solve their problems. One solution to the resource problem is the KLA program.

If KLA is successful in arming district and school administrators with the skills and knowledge of HSEs, the program will be a cost-effective way of influencing student achievement more directly.

Conclusion

Kentucky is working to create a robust system for building school capacity to educate all students equitably. All districts and schools in the state receive substantial funding for professional development, access to regional service centers, and the opportunity for leadership development through KLA. In addition, schools with the greatest need receive supplemental funds and intensive assistance through the STAR program and the work of HSEs. Clearly, helping all students in all schools achieve a high level of learning is a challenge that has not yet been met in Kentucky or anywhere else in the nation. Kentucky has taken a prudent approach given the scarcity of resources. If the issues outlined in this chapter can be addressed effectively, Kentucky's model might be well worth emulating.

REFERENCES

Coe, P., & Adams-Rodgers, L. (in press). *The Kentucky Leadership Academy: Training administrators to be instructional leaders.* Lexington: Partnership for Kentucky Schools.

David, J. L., Kannapel, P. J., & McDiarmid, G. W. (forthcoming). *The influence of distinguished educators on school improvement: A study of Kentucky's school intervention program.* Lexington: Partnership for Kentucky Schools.

Davis, M. M., McDonald, D. H., & Lyons, B. (1997). *A preliminary analysis of the Kentucky distinguished educator initiative: A new approach to educational change.* Frankfort: Kentucky Department of Education.

Henry, K. J., Terry, D., & Lunney, J. (1998). *A study of perceptions of the Kentucky distinguished educator program.* Frankfort, KY: Office of Education Accountability.

Holland, H. (1997, October). Brown vs. the Department of Education. *Louisville Magazine, 48,* 38–48, 74–79.

Kannapel, P. J., Coe, P., Aagaard, L., Moore, B. D., & Reeves, C. A. (2000). Teacher responses to rewards and sanctions: Kentucky's high-stakes accountability program. In B. L. Whitford and K. Jones (Eds.), *Accountability, assessment, and teacher commitment: Lessons from the Kentucky reform effort* (pp. 127–146). Albany: State University of New York Press.

Kentucky Department of Education. (1994). *The Kentucky STAR project, school transformation, assistance, and renewal: A proposed framework for assisting "schools in decline."* Frankfort: Author.

Kentucky Department of Education. (1996). *Kentucky school and district accountability results, accountability cycle 2 (1992–93 to 1995–96): Briefing packet.* Frankfort: Author.

Kentucky Department of Education. (1997). *Kentucky Leadership Academy prospectus* [Brochure]. Frankfort: Author.

Office of Education Accountability. (1995). *Kentucky General Assembly, Office of Education Accountability annual report.* Frankfort, KY: Author.

Office of Education Accountability. (1997). *Kentucky General Assembly, Office of Education Accountability annual report.* Frankfort, KY: Author.

Wakelyn, D. (1999, April). *The role of external assistance in improving low-performing schools: Kentucky's distinguished educators.* Paper presented at the annual meeting of the American Educational Research Association, Montreal, Canada.

11

SETTING STANDARDS
FOR TEACHERS AND
TEACHER EDUCATION

Roger S. Pankratz, Bonnie J. Banker

ON APRIL 11, 2000, about 250 Kentuckians gathered in the state capital to celebrate the tenth anniversary of the signing of the Kentucky Education Reform Act of 1990 (KERA). The Kentucky Department of Education (KDE) brought fifty ten-year-olds from a nearby elementary school to the event, making the point that these children shared their birthday with the country's longest-running school reform movement. Governor Paul Patton (2000) commended key people from the courts and the General Assembly who had produced what he termed "Kentucky's most significant action of our government in my lifetime." Patton praised legislators in the audience for "standing alone ten years earlier to do what was right." "While our challenge is not complete," he went on to say, "we must continue the difficult course of excellence and not take the easy path of mediocrity."

As the governor continued his speech, the legislative leaders whom he praised for having the courage to pass taxes for this bold new initiative left the celebration to continue their debate over the 2000 budget. The General Assembly was nearing the end of its session, deadlocked over spending priorities, and had appointed a Free Conference Committee on Senate Bill 77 to reach some type of compromise. One of the major points of contention was a proposal to upgrade and support the way Kentucky's teachers were trained and certified.

The irony was not lost on those of us who had been active in both battles to improve the state's public schools. Here was another crossroads in Kentucky's education history where the state's future direction hinged on the ability of legislative leaders to break the impasse of politics as usual. On both occasions, just when all hope seemed lost, state leaders found the courage to do what was right for Kentucky's children.

The most recent drama featured the continuing saga of Kentucky's effort to raise teaching standards and improve teacher preparation. Through KERA Kentucky had created the Education Professional Standards Board to monitor the training and certification of the state's elementary and secondary school teachers, but supporters of the reform law were not satisfied with the board's progress in preparing teachers to help all children meet higher standards of learning. Proposals in House Bill 437 to raise teacher quality standards and include higher education professionals as members of the board passed in the House Education Committee but were weakened in the full House after intensive lobbying by organized teacher groups. The weakened bill passed the Senate Education Committee but was never called for action in the full Senate.

Selected provisions from House Bill 437 were attached to Senate Bill 77 and eventually passed both houses after a free conference committee worked out acceptable language. The official status of Senate Bill 77 on the morning of April 11 was forty-six pages of original language with eight amendments and no appropriations to fund any new initiatives. By the end of the day a budget free conference committee presented a budget of $17.2 million over two years to support professional preparation and the work of the Education Professional Standards Board (Free Conference Committee, 2000). Before the close of business on the tenth anniversary of the signing of KERA, both legislative chambers adopted the free conference report on Senate Bill 77 with only one dissenting vote. They could not have acted quickly enough. For, as previous chapters of this book have shown, Kentucky's ability to improve the quality of its teaching force may be the ultimate test of KERA's effectiveness, if not the key to its survival.

The fierce debates about issues of teacher quality and support that raged in Kentucky's 2000 General Assembly represent a shortened version of the ten-year old story of Kentucky's struggle to improve teacher quality. This chapter will analyze the state's effort to ensure that all teachers receive adequate preparation and meet sufficient standards of quality to enable them to properly facilitate student learning.

Kentucky's Shift to the Education Professional Standards Board

Prior to 1990 the State Board of Elementary and Secondary Education relied on the Council for Teacher Education and Certification to recommend policies that governed teacher preparation and licensure. Members of the council included the deans of education from Kentucky's eight state universities, three representatives from private colleges, fourteen representatives from the Kentucky Education Association (KEA), and nine representatives from other education stakeholder groups. Although an elected member of the council led the meetings, the director of teacher education and certification at KDE prepared the meeting's agenda. Issues related to teacher preparation were discussed and recommendations forwarded to the State Board for Elementary and Secondary Education. Because the deans of education of all state universities and selected representatives of KEA were members of the council, their interests dominated the deliberations. Representatives of these two groups sometimes disagreed about specific issues, but the quarterly council meetings generally consisted of productive communications between teachers and teacher educators.

In the late 1980s policymakers and educators raised concerns about the discussions at council meetings being dominated by deans of the colleges of education. At the same time there was a move by professional teacher organizations nationwide to have majority positions on state standards boards to control licensure and certification procedures. In 1988 Representative Roger Noe sponsored House Bill 384 to create a licensing board controlled by teachers, but the legislation never made it out of committee.

When it became clear that school and collective teacher accountability would be part of the proposed education reform law, KEA lent its support. Those close to the situation acknowledge that the proposal to include majority teacher membership on the standards board was a most important consideration in the Kentucky Education Association's decision to back the entire package of school restructuring initiatives (J. Foster, personal communication, September 1, 1999).

KERA moved the authority to license school personnel and approve teacher education programs from KDE to the new fifteen-member Education Professional Standards Board (House Bill 940, 1990, pp. 129–130). The board's membership included eight teachers, two school administrators, two deans of colleges of education, one representative of local schools, the commissioner of education, and the executive director of the Council on Higher Education. KERA designated six areas of authority and responsibility for the board (House Bill 940, 1990, 129–130), including the power to

o Establish the standards and requirements for teacher certification
o Set standards for, approve, and evaluate teacher education programs
o Issue, renew, suspend, and revoke teaching certificates
o Maintain data, submit reports to the governor and Legislative Research Commission, and make recommendations for the recruitment of minority teacher candidates
o Reduce and streamline the credentialing process
o Develop a professional code of ethics

Despite transferring the authority for approving teacher preparation programs and certifying school personnel, KERA gave little direction about the role teacher preparation and certification should play in the overall restructuring plan—a serious and surprising omission.

On October 11, 1990, Governor Wallace Wilkinson appointed the first thirteen members of the new Education Professional Standards Board. Kentucky's new commissioner of education and the executive director of Kentucky's Council on Higher Education, included by law, completed the fifteen voting members. The first meeting was held on November 26. Janice Weaver, education dean from Murray State University, served as the board's first elected chair.

The newly formed Education Professional Standards Board differed markedly from the former Council for Teacher Education and Certification in several respects. First, the representation from the teacher education community was reduced from eight to two members. Second, the role of KDE was changed but remained unclear. Although the standards board was expected to operate independently of the department, the executive secretary of the board also was the associate commissioner of teacher education and certification. She was employed by the appointed commissioner of education, who served as an ex officio voting member. A third difference was the teacher membership. The eight classroom teachers appointed to the new standards board constituted a majority of the members, but they were appointed by a governor who did not solicit the support of KEA members and did not consult them when making his appointments. Hence, although all eight board members were very able and competent classroom teachers, they were new to issues related to teacher preparation and certification. Previous representatives to the Council for Teacher Education and Certification had been well prepared for their role by KEA.

The Struggle to Become Operational Under KERA

The early history of the standards board was characterized by difficulty and slow progress. Because all day-to-day operations remained the fiscal responsibility of KDE and staff members were employees of the department, conflicts frequently surfaced between the agenda of the commissioner of education and other members. It soon became obvious that whoever controlled the fiscal resources also had a great influence on policy and operations. In addition, when differences arose between the department and other members of the standards board, the executive secretary was put in an untenable position because she was expected to serve two bosses simultaneously.

KERA also precipitated a turnover of key staff members in the Office of Teacher Education and Certification. The first executive secretary, who also headed the Office of Teacher Education and Certification, was new to the job, as were many department employees. Under KERA all employees had to reapply for their jobs when KDE was reconfigured in 1991. New staff members became responsible for issuing and monitoring more than eighty thousand school personnel certifications, managing about twenty-five hundred first-year internship and teacher evaluations, and approving all school personnel preparation programs in twenty-six public and private institutions.

In addition, the new standards board was charged with the added responsibility of hearing and making judgments about complaints of professional misconduct for all certified school personnel. The first major accomplishment was the development and approval of a professional code of ethics (Education Professional Standards Board, 1997). This was extremely important in guiding their work on hearing and judging cases of professional misconduct. When the board was first formed in 1990, there was already a backlog of more than forty cases. In the first three years, the board processed more than two hundred cases of professional misconduct (Education Professional Standards Board, 1995). This took up an inordinate amount of board members' time and minimized the opportunity for reforming teacher education.

Based on the language of KERA, the standards board agreed to focus its efforts on seven program components: oversight of the profession; streamlining certification; teachers' standards and assessment; accreditation of preparation programs for teachers and school administrators; the Kentucky Internship Program; alternative certification; and minority recruitment and retention. KERA neither directly nor indirectly required significant new developments in any of these seven areas. KERA also did not specify how the board's work should mesh with the law's other components. Further, the legislature did not earmark funding for expanded operations or the development of new programs.

To address the need for developmental funds, the standards board applied for and received a three-year grant from the U.S. Department of Education in 1992 to develop and implement new teacher standards aligned with KERA. With the resources of this grant, a twenty-two-member committee was appointed to assist the board in creating a "results-oriented, primarily performance-based" teacher preparation and licensing system and the program accreditation system by 1996. In addition, the committee developed eight new standards by which to judge the performance of teacher candidates applying for initial licensure in Kentucky (Education Professional Standards Board, 1994).

The 1993 Governor's Task Force on Teacher Preparation

With a belief that Kentucky was now ready to reform higher education in much the same manner as it had K–12 education, Governor Brereton Jones on July 13, 1993, created the sixteen-member Governor's Task Force on Teacher Preparation (Legislative Research Commission, 1993). His charge to the task force was to "review current practices in preparing Kentucky teachers, review related national and international trends, and with the assistance of expert educational consultants as the Task Force deems necessary, to develop policy recommendations which will promote and support a model teacher preparation program which is in keeping with the learning goals and outcomes delineated in KERA" (Legislative Research Commission, 1993, p. 1).

The task force included five legislators and one representative each from the Education Professional Standards board, the State Board for Elementary and Secondary Education, the governor's cabinet, the Kentucky Council on Higher Education, the Office of Education Accountability, the Prichard Committee for Academic Excellence, superintendents, and teachers. The absence of teacher educators or any university representatives sent a clear message that they were part of the problem that needed to be fixed.

In December the Governor's Task Force on Teacher Preparation presented its report to the governor and members of the General Assembly. The report contained four broad goals, eight priority areas, and twenty-two specific recommendations. Key recommendations aimed at significantly reforming teacher education and certification included

○ Requiring all teacher preparation institutions to demonstrate a commitment to the goals of KERA and to comply with expectations of the school reform law

○ Instituting a process and time line to evaluate all teacher preparation programs, public and private, and revoking the approval of programs that do not comply with the expectations of KERA

○ Establishing education certification centers across the state to measure the proficiency of beginning and experienced teachers applying for licensure and certification

○ Constructing a plan that ties teacher compensation to performance and phases out the master's degree requirement for certification

○ Developing valid and reliable measures to ensure subject matter expertise and teaching performance for certification (Legislative Research Commission, 1993, pp. 2–11)

(It is instructive to note the similarity of recommendations between the 1993 Governor's Task Force on Teacher Preparation and the 1999 Commonwealth Task Force on Teacher Quality, discussed later in this chapter.)

The report of the 1993 Governor's Task Force on Teacher Preparation addressed the major issues of performance-based teacher preparation and certification—where KERA was silent—and assigned clear responsibilities to the Kentucky Education Professional Standards Board, the State Board for Elementary and Secondary Education, and the Council on Higher Education. However, as soon as the report was released, KEA objected to the retesting of experienced teachers and to the recommendation to tie teacher pay to performance. KEA had worked for many years to achieve a salary schedule based on a ranking system tied to education levels and years of experience. The threat to job security and tenure for more than thirty thousand teachers brought on an organized reaction by KEA and its members.

Although the twenty-two recommendations proposed important reforms for teacher preparation and certification that were aligned with KERA, many of the recommendations carried high price tags. Earlier experience with assessment centers for principals showed that the process was expensive and labor intensive. Also, by 1993 Kentuckians were questioning the value of spending millions of dollars to develop a valid and reliable K–12 student performance system and were not ready to take on what looked like another very expensive venture.

The Struggle for Leadership and Resources

With no additional resources, the standards board put on hold any major initiatives that required significant funding and scaled back plans for a performance-based teacher preparation and certification system. Nevertheless, the board, assisted by teacher educators across the state, moved forward. Task force groups in twelve content areas developed on-demand performance tasks that could be used at assessment centers for beginning teachers. The board also adopted an action plan for streamlining certification and developed new standards for experienced teachers and administrators.

Because there were no existing performance-based models available, the board was unsure about the best way to proceed. Both the standards board and the teacher preparation institutions struggled to prepare new teachers for all the new K–12 reform mandates in KERA. Despite these obstacles, from 1994 through mid-1998 the standards board accomplished a number of important tasks (Education Professional Standards Board, 1999), including

- Approval of a revised teacher certificate suspension or revocation policy for processing hearings related to criminal proceedings

- Approval of a partnership between the state and National Council for Accreditation of Teacher Education for accreditation visits based on performance

- Adoption of a new interdisciplinary early childhood education certification

- Approval of a master plan for institutions reporting continuous progress of candidates

- Adoption of a school-based alternative certification program

- Adoption of new certification standards for school counselors

- Replacement of the previously approved standards for Kentucky school administrators with Interstate School Leaders Licensure Consortium standards

- Replacement of the classroom observation instrument for Kentucky teacher internship with an assessment form that addressed Kentucky's new teacher standards and required portfolio exhibits

A Look Toward the Twenty-First Century

In 1997 the board received funding from the National Commission on Teaching and America's Future to join a twelve-state consortium for the purpose of finding ways to implement new policies based on recommendations from the commission's report (1996) *What Matters Most: Teaching for America's Future*. An initial step was to bring all stakeholders to the table to discuss the current status of the profession and determine the next phase. A thirty-six-member oversight committee for Kentucky's partnership with the National Commission on Teaching and America's Future was formed. As a beginning activity of the oversight committee, an inventory of Kentucky standards and performance data was compiled for students (K–12), beginning teachers, experienced teachers, teacher preparation programs, and professional development.

Two months later the Southern Regional Education Board (1998) released its status report on how its fifteen-member states were faring on a variety of education indicators, including teacher preparation. The data showed that in Kentucky 25 to 45 percent of middle school teachers did not have a major in the subject they were teaching. Passing scores for some praxis tests (assessments used in most states to qualify teacher candidates for initial teaching licensure) that measured the content knowledge of Kentucky teachers were found to be lower than in several surrounding states. These data clearly supported those of the earlier report, *Kentucky's Teachers: Charting a Course for the Second Decade* (Clements, 1999, p. 16). Preparation and professional development needed to focus more on subject matter content and how to teach it.

At its summer 1998 retreat the standards board reviewed the research and used it to develop long-term goals and specific actions for improving teacher preparation and instructional quality. The six goals the board hoped to achieve by the end of 2000 (Education Professional Standards Board, 1998) included ensuring that

- Every teacher educator program in Kentucky had met all the accreditation standards established by the board

- All school personnel had obtained proper licenses and credentials

- Every beginning teacher and administrator had successfully completed a guided transition into the profession

○ Every teacher and administrator had maintained the standards of the profession through effective professional development programs

○ Research and development activities were undertaken to help the board meet its goals and responsibilities

○ The board would operate efficiently and effectively through adequate staffing, technological support, facilities, and financial resources

Gearing Up for Kentucky's 2000 General Assembly

Both the standards board and stakeholder groups with an interest in improving teacher quality and preparation realized that 1999 was the year to develop legislative support. In January the Kentucky Partnership Oversight Committee (1999), in cooperation with the National Commission on Teaching and America's Future, issued *The Status of Teaching in Kentucky: A Synopsis of Recent Report Findings and Recommendations*. This report was developed by teachers, school administrators, parents, business and industry leaders, higher education leaders, and community members across the state to serve as a foundation for reforming teacher preparation, induction, and professional development throughout Kentucky. It summarized the progress of the board, data and findings of recent studies related to teacher preparation, and projected goals for the year 2000.

With growing public demand for improved teacher quality, it was time for the executive branch to show leadership. In January 1999 Governor Paul Patton appointed the Commonwealth Task Force on Teacher Quality. The task force, cochaired by leaders of the Senate and House Education Committees (Senator David Karem and Representative Harry Moberly), had broad representation from stakeholder groups. The task force met monthly for a year and conducted extensive study, receiving input from national experts, special interest groups, and education groups. Early on, the task force agreed to address issues related to teacher supply and demand, teacher education, alternative certification, teacher compensation and benefits, and linking teacher performance to student learning.

A third factor that worked to reform teacher education was the involvement of the Prichard Committee for Academic Excellence. In a project funded by Philip Morris Inc., the Prichard Committee engaged the Task Force on Teaching for Kentucky's Future, which included nineteen citizens from across the state and was supported by a resource group with special expertise—teachers, school administrators, and university professors. The major purpose of the Prichard Committee group was to bring a citizen's perspective to the teacher quality discussions. Although this citizens' group would work in parallel to and advise the Commonwealth Task Force on Teacher Quality, it was to be an independent voice of the people.

On October 18 the Prichard Committee for Academic Excellence (1999) presented its report *Teaching for Kentucky's Future,* which included sixty-eight specific recommendations. Less than a month later the Commonwealth Task Force on Teacher Quality adopted its own report (Legislative Research Commission, 1999), which contained forty-four specific recommendations.

The House of Representatives was the first legislative group to take up their challenge. House Bill 437 (An Act Relating to Education and Declaring an Emergency) addressed the main issues of teacher quality debated earlier in the task forces and the recommendations that followed. Included in House Bill 437 were mandates to

o Establish statewide standards of evaluation and support for improving the performance of all certified school personnel

o Develop state and local teacher recruitment programs to address personnel shortages in middle and high schools

o Re-create the Education Professional Standards Board as an agency independent of KDE and increase the board's membership to include higher education professionals

o Establish teacher academies to upgrade the academic preparation of teachers, especially middle school teachers

o Provide extra compensation for teachers in critical shortage areas, including subject matter, geographical location, or diversity

o Provide more support for mentors who supervise student teachers and interns

Revisiting 1993—with a Different Outcome

Two provisions of the proposed teacher quality legislation raised immediate opposition from teacher groups. The first was a requirement that middle school teachers who lacked a major or minor degree in the subjects they taught demonstrate their expertise in some other way. This provision, coupled with new opportunities for professional development, aimed primarily to boost Kentucky's stagnant test scores in the middle grades. About one-third of the state's middle school teachers hold elementary certification, which does not require specialized study in content areas. The Louisville contingent of the state's largest teacher's union, KEA, viewed the provision as "an insult to duly licensed teachers" (Harp, 2000, p. A4). This local chapter of KEA soon organized a campaign to flood powerful legislators with negative feedback on the provision.

A second provision of House Bill 437 that drew opposition from teachers was the membership of the reconstituted standards board. Whereas the existing board had fifteen members, eight of whom were supposed to be classroom teachers, the new legislation proposed setting aside only eight of the nineteen board seats for teachers. Even though there would still be a plurality of practicing teachers on the board, KEA believed this was an affront that defied the original purpose of the standards board. As one legislator said, "[T]he bill's plan to do away with the teacher majority on the current standards board would send a message to teachers that they don't count" (Harp, 2000, p. A4]).

On the floor of the House of Representatives, legislators attached an amendment to the bill to increase the size of the standards board to twenty-three, with twelve seats designated for teachers. As amended, House Bill 437 passed with a vote of eighty-eight to nine. Supporters of the original bill were disappointed. As Robert F. Sexton, executive director of the Prichard Committee, put it, "This vote was not about how to improve teaching for kids, it was about how to protect jobs for teachers" (Harp, 2000, p. A1).

On March 15, still bleeding from surgery, House Bill 437 moved to the Senate Education Committee. With the controversial provisions eliminated, it won approval in less than five minutes, but the original sponsors of the bill did not support it in its weakened version. Thus the Senate Budget Committee decided not to fund any of the teacher quality provisions, and with only five days left in the legislative session, the sweeping bill to improve teacher quality was declared dead.

In a last-ditch effort Representative Harry Moberly salvaged some of the teacher quality provisions of his original bill—excluding the controversial middle school and standards board provisions—and added these to existing Senate Bill 77, an act relating to professional development for middle school mathematics teachers. This move breathed new life into legislation originally designed to support major professional development initiatives over the next biennium. On the final day that the 2000 Kentucky General Assembly was allowed to take action, legislators reached an agreement on the new teacher quality bill and provided $17.2 million in funding. Thus, on the tenth anniversary of KERA's signing, the teacher quality movement ended on higher ground. However, supporters of House

Bill 437 felt the omission of key provisions from Senate Bill 77 weakened the potential for real teacher quality reform.

Lessons Learned Along the Rocky Road to Improved Teacher Quality

Few Kentuckians have been pleased with the progress of the Education Professional Standards Board, KDE, or any of the institutions that have acted over the past decade to improve teacher quality. Yet over the past several years there has been a growing consensus in Kentucky and nationwide that increasing teacher quality is essential to raising student achievement. Although this was equally true in 1990, we now have the benefit of our past experiences to help us plan the future. We offer three important insights based on Kentucky's collective knowledge of what it takes to improve public education and teacher quality.

> States should keep improved teaching and learning for all children a highly visible focus of policies and actions aimed at raising standards of teaching, teacher quality, and teacher preparation.

KERA created a new standards board for education professionals and named six tasks it should address but failed to link its purpose and function to the central purpose of the reform—to enhance all children's learning opportunities and school performance. The standards board struggled for nearly eight years before developing its first published mission statement and set of goals explicitly related to improving teacher quality. The 1993 Governor's Task Force on Teacher Preparation developed key recommendations for teacher education and certification related to the goals of KERA; it also proposed linking teacher compensation to performance. However, the focus of these recommendations—improved student learning—was lost in the debate in the legislature as teacher security and welfare took center stage. A very similar scenario developed in 1999–2000. Again, recommendations and proposed legislation were clearly aimed at more aggressive teacher quality measures to ensure all children in Kentucky had an opportunity to learn, but too little effort was made to put improved student learning on the forefront of all debates on the issues. Certainly, the concerns of different groups needed to be considered, but they should have been considered without losing sight of the goal of improved learning for all children. The authors of this chapter firmly believe that if the main purpose of policies and actions related to the improvement of teaching and teacher quality had been more clearly articulated by the designers of KERA and maintained as a central focus of the standards board, the results would have been different. More progress would have been made to improve teaching and teacher quality, and concerns of teachers, school managers, and teacher educators would have been approached from a more positive perspective.

> States should invest in research and development to make the
> connection between teacher quality, teacher performance, and
> teacher preparation on the one hand and improved student
> learning on the other.

Based on ten years of experience with KERA and school performance results across the state, educators and policymakers are convinced that teachers make a difference. We have a long list of qualities and performance indicators we believe are important but very little hard data about what specific factors of teacher quality and performance lead to higher student learning—and why. During the 1990s William L. Sanders and his colleagues gained a national reputation by processing student learning data in several states and showing the tremendous variation in effectiveness among individual teachers (Sanders & Rivers, 1996; Sanders & Horn, 1998). But neither these researchers nor anyone else has a clear understanding of what factors make the difference—only that a difference exists.

Kentucky has at least eight years of student performance data. Other states, including Tennessee and Texas, now have student performance data linked to individual classrooms and teachers, and the database is growing in other states. It is time for states individually and collectively to invest in the research to answer important questions about what specific qualities in a classroom lead to higher student learning. Answers to these questions will have direct implications for how we recruit, train, certify, and provide professional development for teachers.

> States should find ways to counter the aggressive—and ultimately
> regressive—lobbying efforts of special interest groups whose
> goal is to water down teacher quality provisions in school reform
> legislation.

In 1993–94 and again in 1999–2000, Kentucky's efforts to raise teaching standards and institute measures of teacher quality resulted in a fierce battle. In both attempts the children of Kentucky ended up the losers. In 1993 and again in 1999, Kentucky governors created statewide task forces to overhaul and improve teacher preparation. Both times, legislation was developed to address what policymakers considered key initiatives that would raise teaching standards and improve teacher performance. The designers of new policies believed that because their plan logically fit what was best for students, it would gain broad support. Yet opposition from organized teacher groups rebuffed those initiatives because they threatened to dilute the power of the organized profession and to dictate standards. There is plenty of blame to go around for what is considered a watered-down attempt to improve teacher quality. Different groups have very different perceptions about what happened.

Proponents of higher quality standards for teachers should anticipate opposition from special interest groups, keeping several points in mind. First, leaders of state reforms to improve teacher quality should recognize that what they propose will likely be threatening to teachers, school managers, and teacher educators who must implement the changes and should therefore identify specific strategies to counter organized opposition. Second, a focus on improved student learning should frame the debate on all issues. Also, being able to show clear relationships between proposed policies and student learning would garner the support of decision makers. Third, leaders should make more deliberate efforts to address the concerns of special interests and design policies that produce more of a win-win scenario, instead of one with clear winners and losers. Reform leaders should look for incentives, programs, and practices that would minimize threats and hardships to those potentially most affected by proposed changes. We should not back away from policies we believe will improve teaching and learning, but we need to work smarter to develop strategies that will minimize opposition to our efforts and achieve the most important outcome—improved learning for all children.

Conclusion: Kentucky at the Crossroads of Teacher Quality

As already mentioned, Senate Bill 77 was signed into law. This new legislation mandates the development of a statewide performance evaluation for all certified teachers and administrators, raises the standards for teacher preparation, sets in motion a process to identify people who are teaching out of field, and takes steps to improve the odds that all students will find a qualified teacher in every classroom. The law also creates the Teacher Professional Growth Fund to improve the training of teachers in core content areas (with priority for middle school teachers through 2004), establishes a center for middle school achievement, and institutes a statewide recruitment system to identify and attract teacher candidates for high-need areas.

In addition, Kentucky has set aside $17.2 million for the next biennium to pay for expanded professional development opportunities and to provide extra compensation for supervisory and mentoring services as well as for teaching in difficult and high-need areas. The budget provides $2.3 million to improve the operations of the standards board and $2.9 million to develop a data collection and management system (Free Conference Committee, 2000).

The most recent development has been an executive order by Governor Patton effective July 1, 2000, to separate the standards board from KDE and have it answer directly to the office of the governor. However, the composition of the board has not changed, and most of the recommendations proposed by the Commonwealth Task Force on Teacher Quality have not been adopted as policy.

We could project two radically different scenarios for the standards board and issues of teacher quality over the next decade. On the one hand, we could project that not much will change. Supporters of the more radical reforms could argue that little will change because key policies they proposed for addressing teacher quality were rebuffed. On the other hand, we see reasons for hope.

First, although the new law is not what supporters of the original bill wanted, they found a way to enact and fund important provisions of the teacher quality initiatives recommended by the governor's and citizens' task forces. Second, the additional support for operations and data management systems provided in the 2000–01 budget, coupled with the long-term goals and strategies for the standards board, suggest greater potential for progress now than at any time over the past decade. Third, there are grassroots developments throughout the state and within the standards board. The new initiatives in professional development that McDiarmid and Corcoran describe in Chapter Nine, as well as the leadership for school and professional development that Kannapel and Coe project in Chapter Ten, seem promising. More exciting still are the grassroots initiatives by educators across the state to measure and report teacher candidate performance and to link teacher performance to student learning. Two years ago the standards board created a statewide committee to develop a structure for teacher preparation programs that would report on their effectiveness. Continuous assessment plans would be developed by all teacher preparation institutions in Kentucky that include identified checkpoints, along with qualitative and quantitative measures, to assess the progress of preservice teachers. By 1998 all public institutions had submitted plans to the standards board.

In 1999 the standards board created a benchmark committee to design levels and measures of teacher candidate performance that can be used to evaluate the programs from which teacher candidates matriculate. The benchmark committee is composed of national board–certified teachers, university faculty, and school leaders. To date, the benchmark committee has identified four levels where common performance standards and assessments will be applied on a continuum from the point of exiting a teacher preparation program to the point of national board certification or the equivalent. The benchmark committee also has proposed using portfolio exhibits that demonstrate a preservice teacher's competence in planning, implementing, and evaluating a four-week unit of instruction during the internship year. In addition, teacher candidates will be required to account for the learning results of all the students they teach. The standards board expects to test the recommendations of its benchmark committee in the 2000–01 school year.

Perhaps more important, the supporters of teacher quality did not go away after the 2000 legislative session. For example, the Prichard Committee for Academic Excellence has made improving teaching standards a continuing priority. In "Changes in Our Schools," a column sent to all weekly and daily newspapers in Kentucky, Robert F. Sexton (2000), executive director of the Prichard Committee, wrote, "It's time to get more serious about demanding and supporting excellence—in every school and every classroom. It's time to get serious about good teaching for every student." We believe recent developments give hope for a departure from business as usual in Kentucky.

REFERENCES

Clements, J. (1999). *Kentucky teachers: Charting a course for KERA's second decade.* Frankfort: Kentucky Long-Term Policy Research Center.

Education Professional Standards Board. (1994). *New teacher standards for preparation and certification.* Frankfort, KY: Author.

Education Professional Standards Board. (1995). *Five-year status report.* Frankfort, KY: Author.

Education Professional Standards Board. (1997). *Professional code of ethics for Kentucky school personnel.* Frankfort, KY: Author.

Education Professional Standards Board. (1998). *Mission statement, goals and 1998–2000 initiatives.* Frankfort, KY: Author.

Education Professional Standards Board. (1999). *Ten years of education reform, 1990–1999.* Frankfort, KY: Author.

Free Conference Committee for Senate Bill 77, Kentucky General Assembly. (2000). *Conference budget report analysis* (Report No. FB 2000–2002). Frankfort: Author.

Harp, L. (2000, March 15). KEA gets two provisions of teacher-quality bill killed. *The (Louisville) Courier-Journal.*

House Bill 940, Kentucky General Assembly, Regular Session. (1990), pp. 129–132.

Kentucky Partnership Oversight Committee. (1999). *The status of teaching in Kentucky: A synopsis of recent report findings and recommendations.* Frankfort: Author.

Legislative Research Commission. (1993). *Report of the Governor's Task Force on Teacher Preparation.* Frankfort, KY: Author.

Legislative Research Commission. (1999). *Report of the Task Force on Teacher Quality.* Frankfort, KY: Author.

National Commission on Teaching and America's Future. (1996). *What matters most: Teaching for America's future.* New York: Author.

Office of Teacher Education and Certification (1999). *The status of teaching in Kentucky: A synopsis of recent report findings and recommendations.* Frankfort, KY: Author.

Patton, P. E. (2000, April). *Results matter: A decade of difference in Kentucky's public schools 1990–2000.* Speech given at the tenth anniversary celebration of education reform in Kentucky, Frankfort, KY. [www.kde.state.ky.us/comm/commrel/10th_anniversary/]

Prichard Committee for Academic Excellence, Task Force on Teaching for Kentucky's Future. (1999). *Teaching for Kentucky's future.* Lexington, KY: Author.

Sanders, W. L., & Horn, S. P. (1998). Research findings from the Tennessee Value-Added Assessment System (TVASS) database: Implications for educational evaluation and research. *Journal of Personnel Evaluation in Education, 12* (3), 247–256.

Sanders, W. L., & Rivers, J. C. (1996). *Cumulative and residual effects of teachers on future student academic achievement.* Knoxville: University of Tennessee Value-Added Research and Assessment Center.

Sexton, R. F. (2000). *Changes in our schools, more ground to cover: A commentary.* Lexington, KY: Prichard Committee for Academic Excellence.

Southern Regional Education Board. (1998). *Southern Regional Education Board educational benchmarks.* Atlanta, GA: Author.

I2

A TEACHER'S VIEWPOINT

"WE DON'T HAVE ANY ANSWERS"

Holly Holland

ELEMENTARY SCHOOL TEACHER SUE CLIFTON was so upset about the changes recommended by the Kentucky Education Reform Act of 1990 (KERA) that she made sure everyone around her knew it.

She wrote all the state legislators on the House and Senate Education Committees. She confronted Education Commissioner Thomas C. Boysen. She spoke out during a public meeting in her Hickman County community. She shared her concerns with her husband, her children, and other families. And after attending an informational session sponsored by the Prichard Committee for Academic Excellence, she told the group she didn't appreciate being encouraged to support Kentucky's reforms.

"I told them, 'I *will not* be a cheerleader for KERA. I don't believe in it.'"

Five years later, no less passionate in her views about the state's reforms, Clifton spoke up again in a public setting. As a special resource teacher serving schools in three Western Kentucky counties, she was invited to talk to the Fulton Rotary Club about the classroom changes she had noticed. This time, however, Clifton pleaded not for outrage, but for absolution.

"I told them that it was kind of like being in church," she said, "that I had seen the light, and that any time you can watch students achieve . . . and moving into those academic areas that we had kind of just brushed off before . . . then you had to say, 'Amen.'"

Now, as director of state and federal programs for the Hickman County Public Schools, Clifton looks back on the past ten years and recognizes the fear and arrogance that kept her and many of her colleagues from embracing Kentucky's radical plan to improve education.

"I'm one of those people that . . . like to win," she said. "I like to be right, but if I realize it's going to work, then I'll just step back and say, 'Yeah, I was wrong.'"

Clifton admitted that her experiences with school reform altered her perspective. "I changed," she said. "I grew. And you know, I was really glad. I kind of look back at myself and laugh because I think, 'You were really pompous to think you had all the answers.'"

Teachers' self-confidence was one of the first casualties of Kentucky's education reforms, and Clifton was no exception. Because educators tended to teach the way they were taught in school, the pattern of instruction in most classrooms varied little from year to year. Teachers and students followed defined schedules, worked from standard textbooks, and generally stayed within the protected universe of a single classroom. Previous directives from the state had emphasized "time on task" requirements, which directed teachers to spend a certain number of minutes—no more, no less—on each subject each day. For a self-described rule follower like Clifton, the script was simple. It gave her both structure and a sense of purpose.

Kentucky's education reforms threatened the security of that certainty. The reforms urged teachers to collaborate, to connect their lessons to real-life experiences, to aim for subject mastery instead of superficial coverage, and to push students ahead according to their developmental needs instead of their age. Teachers also had to make more professional judgments about learning and testing, and none of the answers appeared in the guides that accompanied their textbooks. To move beyond mediocrity, teachers had to expect more from their students—and from each other.

The first challenges occurred in kindergarten through third grade, where the new state model required teachers to work with children of different ages and abilities and help them learn to read, write, and calculate faster and at deeper levels. Schools were not supposed to refer to the traditional first-grade or second-grade configurations but to consider primary school a continuum where children advanced—no matter their age—as soon as they had learned certain academic concepts.

In 1990, after sixteen years as a special education teacher, Clifton became a kindergarten teacher at Hickman County Elementary School. In the next few years, as schools adopted the primary school model, she taught a range of children in the primary grades. Up to that point, she said, her work in kindergarten had focused on developing the social skills of five-year-olds—"story time, play time, finger paint, nap time"—not on the more rigorous academic challenges specified in Kentucky's school reforms.

"We were moving to something that was totally strange to me, and strange to students and strange to parents, and I just didn't see how it could work," Clifton said. "I wanted the lines. I wanted to know how to accomplish this. The research may show us that it's appropriate, but show me how to work with a five-year-old and an eight-year-old and to move them both forward at the same time in the same classroom on the same day and the same hour."

She remembers parents and other teachers asking for her opinion of the recommended changes. She told them that what Kentucky had proposed wouldn't work—it couldn't work. She recalls, during one informational meeting in Paducah, sitting next to a woman from another state who spoke enthusiastically about Kentucky's revolutionary model of school reform, saying she had traveled there to learn more.

"And I said, 'Well, we don't have any answers.'"

Another time, Clifton attended a meeting with Education Commissioner Boysen and shared her concerns about a plan that "sounds great on paper" but contains many practical liabilities. She explained that she had tried to comply with the recommendations yet felt frustrated that the process was so difficult and so messy.

"He said, 'Well, you know, you have a lot of spunk,' which just really angered me," Clifton said. "I don't want to be known as a spunky person. I want to be known as an educator who addresses the needs of students. . . . I'm six feet [tall] with my heels on, so nobody has ever called me spunky before. I wanted answers, and I didn't feel like I got any."

Despite her reservations, Clifton kept trying to adapt to the changes. She was elected to serve on Hickman Elementary's first school council, a governing model state reformers created to give local communities more control over budget and curriculum decisions. Each council must include two parents, three teachers, and a principal—or adopt the same ratio in each category if the school decides to have a larger group. The first thing Hickman's council did was to hire a new principal. And a year later, when that administrator resigned, the council hired another one. Making these choices proved challenging to teachers unaccustomed to dealing with public controversy, Clifton said. Nevertheless, she enjoyed working with the other members of the council, and she appreciated their dedication as they endured many long meetings and late-night telephone calls to respond to all the new state mandates. Serving on the school council also helped her understand the conflicting demands within a school and appreciate the difficulty of keeping everyone focused on the same goals.

"I remember my principal wrote on my evaluation one time that 'Sue Clifton is a good teacher, and she's a strong advocate for students, but sometimes she needs to look on the other side of the issue,'" Clifton said. "In other words, he was trying to explain to me that I needed to sometimes look from the administrator's perspective instead of the teacher's. . . . When I became a site-based council member and saw that, yes indeed, there are issues from all areas, I knew he was right."

Clifton said one of Hickman's toughest jobs was figuring out how to implement the new primary school program. Although Kentucky did not require elementary school teachers to work with children from kindergarten through third grade in the same classroom, the state encouraged teachers to use flexible groupings, visual aids, and practical applications of basic skills. Unfortunately, Kentucky created the organizational model before it provided the curriculum details, which confused teachers already coping with a dizzying array of schedule changes and new responsibilities. Hickman's teachers tried to adjust, Clifton said. They traveled to other school districts to see recommended practices in action, then returned to report to their colleagues and try out new techniques. The increased attention to professional development invigorated the faculty, she said. But for Clifton the greatest energy boost came from seeing students thrive in the new elementary environment.

"As we began to get the units together, and began to stretch ourselves and stretch our students, and I watched a five-year-old begin to read, I had a guilt trip wondering how many kids I didn't give this opportunity," she said. "One parent came to me and said something about KERA, and I said, 'You know, I was really wrong about KERA.' And he said, 'Well, I was really concerned because I knew that if you were against KERA that it couldn't be good for kids.' He said his children had succeeded with it."

Such a response underscores the power individual teachers have to make or break education reform, in Kentucky and elsewhere. Research on a national level shows that teachers typically are the first—and sometimes the only—source of information that parents turn to when confronted with changes in their children's schooling. So a teacher's sphere of influence is not just limited to the students in her charge but extends to the students' families and to the people with whom those families interact.

Clifton said she realizes now that her negative attitude about Kentucky's reforms had a ripple effect in the community. She tried to make amends by discussing her change of heart with as many parents as possible.

"I really felt bad because I want what's best for kids, and if I thought I had stopped that or impeded that in any way, I went around to all the parents I could and told them," she said.

Her own children's attitudes were among the hardest to bend. Clifton said her daughter, who graduated from high school in 1994, and her son, who graduated in 1997, absorbed her early pessimism and remained skeptical of Kentucky's classroom changes. As honors students, they were accustomed to acing simple recall tests, and they resented the detailed answers, written explanations, and expansive thinking their teachers started requiring after the state reform law passed. Clifton said her daughter wanted to just "fill in the blanks" of worksheets with the right answer "and be finished."

"She thought all the [mandated] writing was ridiculous. What was really funny, though, about two years after she graduated, I overheard her talking to our son . . . telling him, 'You better do as they say because you won't believe it but you really do have to write [in college]. You really do have to be able to tell them what you think when you're filling out that job application.'"

Clifton believes many Kentuckians share similar feelings of ambivalence about school reform. They'd like to improve; they just wish they had more time to perfect the process. So although they respect the goals of educational excellence, they question whether a test can accurately measure student success. That's why, despite feeling proud of the state's accomplishments in the past decade and hopeful about the future, Clifton knows how much work remains to be done.

"What you're doing is changing the whole educational system that you had," she said. "It's a whole different way of looking at education and the way we operate. When you take into account site-based councils and family resource centers and all the things that came through, ten years is just a very short amount of time. We in education tend to want to say, 'Okay, here's the problem, here's the fix for the problem,' and move on. But we weren't able to do that with KERA."

13

A SCHOOL LEADER'S VIEWPOINT

"I DIDN'T REALIZE HOW FAR-REACHING
THIS ONE WOULD BE"

Holly Holland

AFTER FORTY-TWO YEARS as an educator, including stints as a teacher, principal, and superintendent, Dan Sullivan said he'd seen just about every new program and strategy available to improve Kentucky's beleaguered public schools.

So when legislators passed the Kentucky Education Reform Act of 1990 (KERA), Sullivan, superintendent of the Newport Independent School District in Northern Kentucky, didn't give the restructuring plan much chance of succeeding. Like many veteran educators, he thought this latest pledge for change would be as fickle as a politician's promise.

"I suppose at the onset I wasn't too enamored, only because I had been in the business for such a long time and had probably been through a couple of reform movements in Kentucky," said Sullivan. "I didn't realize at the time how far-reaching this one would be."

What surprised Sullivan more than the reform plan's endurance, however, was the way it shook up the status quo.

"You know, it kind of compelled you to cleanse your mind of the way things had been done before, on how we were to approach educating the child. That was a real challenge to me," he said. "Not having the elementary [school] instructional background—I was a secondary [school] person for my entire career—I really, really had to struggle, and grasp, and be trained, and just try to keep up with what was coming out of the new legislation. And this district did, too."

Although Newport lies across the Ohio River from Cincinnati in a bustling economic region that is part of Kentucky's "Golden Triangle," the city is a pocket of Appalachian culture. After World War II many eastern Kentucky families migrated to the area in search of better-paying industrial jobs in factories and steel mills. When those jobs disappeared during the 1970s and 80s, poorly educated workers had few employment options that could support a family. Home ownership and property values declined while poverty and crime rates soared. For the Newport public schools, the result was fewer financial resources to educate a tougher group of students who needed higher levels of achievement than ever before.

On a purely financial level the Kentucky education reforms provided much-needed relief to struggling school districts like Newport. By equalizing the distribution of state tax dollars for public schools, the reform law gave Newport additional money for staff training, technology, and after-school tutoring, among other things. The family resource and youth services centers that the state provided to schools serving high-poverty populations also made it possible to eliminate some of the barriers to learning that fall outside a teacher's control.

But new money did not instantly produce new attitudes about education. Sullivan said teachers, principals, and parents resented outsiders telling them how to run their schools—despite a history of low achievement in Newport. Many educators continued faulting their students and their families for the district's high number of failures instead of evaluating their own weaknesses in instruction. And they were not alone. Statewide, nearly a third of Kentucky's teachers still disagree with one of the reform law's basic tenets—that all children can learn, and most at high levels—according to the 1999 Statewide Education Reform Study, conducted by the independent Kentucky Institute for Education Research.

"At least in a district such as this, [the reform law] almost became a threat to their careers," Sullivan said. "Because we always like to blame everybody else: 'Oh, if you knew how tough that I have to work with these poor kids, and we have to do all these things just to get them ready to come to school.' We used that [excuse] for years."

To Sullivan, moving past finger pointing to finding solutions means "breaking down that insecurity that we have in our own minds"—the kind that, as he said, makes you tell yourself, "Hell, I can't get it done with what I'm doing, but I'll never tell anybody. And now they're putting this new stuff on me that I don't understand." The obvious solution, he explained, is to "blot it out, give lip service, and try to say, 'Yeah, we're on the reform wagon.'"

An experienced administrator, Sullivan chafed at the reform law's requirement that he return to school. He had been the superintendent in Newport from 1977 to 1984 before leaving to lead Campbell County Public Schools, a neighboring school district. After the Campbell County Board of Education voted three to two to fire him in 1990, Sullivan worked as an interim administrator in Dayton, Kentucky, before returning to Newport and the superintendent's job in 1992.

Kentucky's education reforms initially required all superintendents to spend ten days in formal training sessions focusing on school management, school law, school finances, school councils, and curriculum and assessment. Afterward they had to pass a series of written exams on those topics. In addition, all superintendents had to spend several days at an assessment center where management specialists helped them evaluate their strengths and weaknesses and develop professional growth plans. Although he initially resisted the regimen, Sullivan said he learned to appreciate it.

"There are things, many things, when you get into the superintendent's chair, and I don't care what size district . . . you really lose command of a lot of things," he said, adding that the training reminded him about the importance of "things I wasn't committed to or had lost control of. And then there were some things that were totally new and foreign to me."

School management was a comfortable fit for Sullivan. Instructional leadership was not. He was both impressed and confused by the recommended new teaching techniques, such as asking students to write in classes other than English and to solve complex problems instead of merely react to a textbook lecture. He was thrilled that the state gave schools access to high-speed computer networks so children who didn't have such resources at home would not be left behind. He was grateful for the extra state funds that enabled teachers to do more than attend the traditional once-a-year training workshop led by a "banjo-pickin', motivating" speaker who would leave town as soon as the session ended.

What Sullivan didn't like was the state's switch to local school councils. He struggled mightily—then as now—with the wide-ranging responsibilities the law took from school boards and gave to school councils. For example, 65 percent of state money earmarked for staff training can be used at the council's discretion. In theory, the funds should help each school select training suited to the faculty's particular needs. The downside is that each council must develop enough expertise to identify both the skills that teachers and students lack and the best training to provide them, a task made more difficult by the two-year terms most parent and teacher members serve before being replaced by others.

Sullivan said the five school councils in Newport have had varied degrees of success improving instruction. Some have not made good hiring and training decisions, he said, yet seem not to understand how those choices affect students' performance on Kentucky's achievement tests. He assigned district liaisons to each school to try to open communications, reduce overlapping expenditures, and bring some consistency to the curriculum.

"But basically, unless all your schools agree, let's say, on the same type of reading program or the same type of math program—which they do not have to do—that doesn't happen," he said. Elementary instruction "may then go in three different directions, which I don't necessarily agree with." With the district's high transience rate, he said, students often move from one school to another during the year and miss critical skills because of inconsistent instruction.

Sullivan's concerns are reflected in the conflicting opinions Kentuckians have about imposing a statewide curriculum for each grade level. The 1999 Statewide Education Reform Study found that most parents on school councils favor using the state's core content as a guideline whereas principals, teachers, and the general public believe it should be a requirement.

In addition to his frustrations with school councils, Sullivan regrets that the resources Kentucky's reform law provided to help parents become more active participants in their children's education have not paid off. In Newport, parent involvement specialists from the school district visit parents at home to nurture the family-school connection. The Newport schools also sponsor student mentoring programs, adult literacy classes, and telephone hotlines so children can get help with homework.

"KERA has given us the ability to do more things to be able to reach more parents through various mechanisms, one of which obviously is financial in nature," Sullivan said, adding, "We haven't put the key in the lock that opens the door yet because, as I said, we don't have a lot of parent involvement."

Asked to evaluate the impact of Kentucky's school reforms ten years after they began, Sullivan vacillated between giving an overall grade of C-plus or B-minus. Not a bad assessment, actually, but he had hoped for more.

"I don't know that I can blame the state. That's too easy. Maybe we haven't taken everything and sorted it out. . . . There's been so doggone much transition and things going on for the last nine or ten years," he said. "I'm not blaming KERA exclusively. Lots of the blame has to be taken by us"—for making poor choices, using bad instruction, and being reluctant to change.

At age sixty-four, Sullivan knows he won't be around much longer to shepherd the Newport school district. He wonders whether shifting political winds will set Kentucky schools on an entirely new course in the next decade, whether future politicians and educators will finish what others have started, and whether Kentuckians will have the courage to learn from their early mistakes and press on. However, one factor makes him particularly optimistic about the days ahead.

"I think the universities are doing a much better job in sending young teachers to us, and I think it's a direct result of KERA," Sullivan said. "I think they are probably better prepared than any group that I've seen. So that's got some salvation tied to it, I think."

PART FOUR

DEVELOPING
NEW FORMS
OF GOVERNANCE

14

EDUCATORS AND PARENTS AS PARTNERS IN SCHOOL GOVERNANCE

Jane L. David

"IF CENTRAL OFFICE makes all the decisions," said one district administrator, "it is too easy for schools to say 'I did what they told me to.' There was a time when I didn't think site-based [decision making] was a good idea, but now I think it is very important. When done right, it helps schools be clear about what they want for kids and how to go about doing it. It takes a while to learn to do it well."

The new education system created by the Kentucky Education Reform Act of 1990 (KERA) significantly altered many aspects of public schooling. Among the most radical of all the changes was placing decision-making authority at the school level. School-based decision making (SBDM) shifted significant authority from the district level to the school level and at the same time legally required participation of parents in the decision-making process. These two elements, coupled with the accountability provisions of KERA, sent a powerful message that the new education system was not to be business as usual.

The findings reported in this chapter draw largely on the author's study of school-based decision making for the Prichard Committee for Academic Excellence from 1992 to 1995, based on school and district interviews in eight districts across the state and follow-up interviews from 1996 to 1999 in five of those districts. In addition, the author reinterviewed representatives of the major stakeholder organizations in 1999.

According to the Task Force on Education Reform (1989), "School accountability and school-based authority are two intertwined parts of the same proposition." The architects of KERA sought to balance accountability and authority by rewarding and sanctioning schools based on student achievement on the one hand and delegating substantial decision-making authority to schools on the other. Among policymakers it was described as a "horse trade": schools are held accountable for student performance and in exchange get the freedom to figure out how best to raise test scores. The logic was that those closest to the classroom should have control over decisions most directly related to teaching and learning. In Chapter Three Jack Foster relates that the original goal of SBDM was to enable teachers to make collective decisions about their professional practice. Others saw the opportunity to give parents a formal voice as equally important, believing that parents historically had little say and that reform cannot succeed unless the community values it.

The legislation specified a particular school-based structure for engaging teachers in decision making. Each participating school was to have a school council composed of two parents, three teachers, and the principal or administrator (or multiples of those ratios). And all schools, except those rewarded for test-score gains or single-school districts, were to have councils in place by 1996. The principal was to chair the council, and teachers and parents were to be elected to the council annually by their peers. All teachers were expected to participate through committees that would submit recommendations to the council.

The legislation also delegated to school councils the authority to hire (but not fire) the principal and to consult with the principal on filling other staff vacancies. In addition, school councils were required to set school policies on curriculum, materials, instruction, assignment of staff and students, the schedule within the school day, use of space, discipline and classroom management, and selection of extracurricular programs and criteria for student participation in them. These were viewed as the key elements of school management that most directly influence the quality of the instructional program and, in turn, student achievement (see Chapter Three).

Together these requirements not only set up decision-making councils at each school but also gave them major responsibility for setting school direction and policy. The law was silent on the implications of these shifts for local boards, superintendents, and their staffs. The law was also silent on how such groups would acquire the necessary skills and knowledge to launch their school on a path of continuous improvement. As one education reform advocate noted, "It was easier to write about councils than curriculum and instruction."

How Site-Based Councils Developed

Although KERA was launched at the beginning of the 1990s, SBDM did not fully come into its own until 1996—the state deadline for virtually all schools to join in. Prior to the deadline schools signed on when their faculty, by a two-thirds vote, chose to do so. As of 1994 roughly two-thirds of eligible schools had established councils; the final third waited until the deadline. Consequently, conclusions about statewide implementation of SBDM rest on a very short three-year history.

Perhaps the most striking result of SBDM to date is what has not happened. After passage of KERA the word on the street about SBDM was, "This will never happen here." Yet there has been little conflict surrounding the introduction and spread of SBDM. The universal expectation was that power struggles and resistance would consume enormous amounts of time and energy. That simply has not happened. Some complaints have been filed, but far fewer than anticipated. One case, which reached the state supreme court in 1994, led to a key decision reaffirming the authority of school councils (*Boone County v. Bushee*, 1994). Although some complaints of interference and district stalling on allocating funds to schools were heard early on, formal complaints have all but disappeared. Most districts made and continue to make good-faith efforts to carry out the law.

Structurally, SBDM is working. Procedures are in place across the state and school councils exist in every school in which they are required. Over nine hundred principals have been hired by school councils. Councils have created bylaws and policies as required by law. They have set up committees, hired staff, and developed improvement plans as required by the state.

There are problems, to be sure. Many councils are run totally by the principal; others have parents or teachers with personal agendas. Many superintendents would like more say in the selection of principals; parents would like a stronger voice. Yet, overall, a new structure is in place that seems to be working as smoothly as, and in some cases more democratically than, the structure it has replaced.

Nevertheless, there remains a large gap between the vision held by KERA's architects and the reality of school councils. KERA's architects overestimated the ability of school councils to lead improvement in curriculum and instruction. The vision that school councils would take charge of diagnosing needs and planning and implementing changes in curriculum and instruction has not been realized on a wide scale to date. In light of the history of reform efforts that attempt similar changes, this is no surprise. And for those who imagined that such authority would unleash creative energy leading to radical restructuring of schools, the answer is clear: it does not. The task of setting schoolwide policies and making decisions that might lead to improved curriculum and instruction is a formidable one, even for the experts who devote their careers to these issues. The notion that this could be accomplished by three teachers, two parents, and a principal, with minimal training and little or no experience in collaborative decision making, strains credulity.

A middle school teacher remarked, "My sense of councils is that most are not functioning as they were intended to function. The concept sounded real good, but it is not teacher-parent togetherness. Even teachers don't realize the power the council has in making a difference in the school—even in the school day. They don't lobby for their ideas." An elementary school parent described a similar situation from his perspective: "When I got on the council, I thought parents would contact me with issues, but they haven't."

In spite of these problems, no one imagines returning to the pre-KERA governance structure. Some support changes in council responsibilities and concomitant changes in the district role. Others worry that councils may become still another organizational structure that operates in name but has little impact. Yet there is no effort to undo SBDM. The debate is over adjustments, not over whether or not SBDM should exist. And there is optimism about the future. "The longer we do this stuff," a middle school principal asserted, "the more schools will understand their own muscle."

How Councils Increase Participation

According to one legislative staff member, "Even if SBDM doesn't have an impact on student achievement, it's the way to run schools—it is democratic." There is no doubt that, overall, SBDM has increased the participation of teachers and parents in important decisions affecting their schools. As of fall 1999, 1,224 schools had site-based councils; only 19 did not, either because they were one-school districts not required to have councils or schools that exceeded student performance thresholds and chose to opt out. Over 3,700 teachers and 2,500 parents are council members across the state, and thousands more serve on committees established by councils (Office of Education Accountability, 1999). In many schools teachers and parents had not participated in any form of school decision making, so SBDM represents a radical change. In others, even under SBDM, the principal continues to call the shots. Principals are usually the recipients of information from the state and the district; hence the decision about what to share with teachers and parents is in their hands. Moreover, teachers are not likely to challenge the person responsible for their evaluation. But, in general, in contrast to decision making prior to KERA, schools have many more decisions to make, and many more teachers and parents are involved.

Louisville, the largest urban district in the state, is a somewhat different story. With their own history of participatory management, Louisville schools resented the intrusion of the state, which told them they could no longer decide the composition of their councils and who would chair them. And because Louisville had the only collective bargaining unit in the state, the legalities of hiring were more complicated than in other places. Even here the early conflicts have all but disappeared.

SBDM has also created new players and lines of communication. From 1994 to 1996, owing to changes in the law, minority representation on councils increased from sixteen to over seven hundred. State officials report increased contact between state and school representatives, including parents. As one state-level official said, "In the last five years I have had more contact with parents than in the previous ten years." School councils are also becoming a political force in their own right with a statewide association that includes over 480 councils. The association provides training, produces a monthly newsletter, and holds an annual conference, all directed toward disseminating information about legal and educational issues concerning what councils do.

Besides offering the opportunity to influence decisions at a school site, the experience of serving as a site council member is educational for those involved. Council members not only learn the ins and outs of how a legal decision-making body operates; they also become intimately acquainted with how the state-required planning process works, what it means to create bylaws and policies, and what is involved in hiring personnel. In the process, they learn a great deal about how their school operates. Thus, across the state, thousands more parents and teachers now know what school budgets look like.

One result of SBDM is that parents who sit on councils have more positive judgments about the educational programs in their schools than parents in general or the public at large. These differences are as much as 30 percentage points. When asked how well Kentucky's content standards were working to improve teaching and learning, 77 percent of parents on school councils answered "very well" or "moderately well," compared with 57 percent of parents in general and 52 percent of the public. Asked the same question about school councils, 85 percent of parents on school councils held positive views, compared with 64 percent of all parents and 56 percent of the public (Wilkerson & Associates, 1999).

Although such positive responses could be attributed to self-selection, interviews with parent council members suggest that their positive views are influenced by their firsthand knowledge of the school. As a middle school parent on one council put it:

> As a parent, if you just drop your kid off, you don't understand what goes on when they are here. When you are on the council and you start looking at what teachers do, you see what happens. . . . I don't think parents realize how hard teachers work. . . . I would recommend to anyone to be on committees and [a site-based council]. . . . I don't think the general public really understands what it takes to run the school financially and otherwise.

Clearly, more decisions are being made at the school level, and more folks are involved. More decisions do not necessarily mean better decisions leading to school improvement. Yet, prior to SBDM, district-level decisions did not guarantee school improvement. Similarly, involving more teachers and parents is no guarantee that all participants will have an equal voice. Yet, prior to SBDM, teachers and parents had virtually *no* voice.

What Councils Do

Across the state, school councils have created bylaws and developed policies for discipline, curriculum, hiring, and professional development, among other things. For many schools this is the first time written policies have existed—no small accomplishment for a group of people typically unfamiliar with what it means to set policy. Councils are making many important decisions, including decisions about the hiring of principals, the creation of a school's improvement plan, the organization of the primary school program, and the creation and filling of new staff positions.

Hiring the principal is viewed as the most important decision that councils make, and they are doing so more often as the number of vacancies increases each year. The hiring process now is generally viewed as more rigorous and sophisticated, as well as more open, than before councils were involved. Although this aspect of SBDM raises considerable debate among administrators, the fact is that councils have selected over nine hundred principals, and few cases have had serious problems. In addition, the percentage of minority principals, though still small, has increased, suggesting that councils are no worse than superintendents in minority hiring. During 1998–99 alone councils hired 182 principals. Over three-quarters of these councils involved other teachers and parents in the process. Only thirteen reported any interference in the process (Office of Education Accountability, 1999). "I would not have been hired had it not been for site-based [decision making]," one high school administrator attested. "They looked at my credentials and not my politics."

Council discussion and decisions tend to focus on personnel issues, extracurricular activities, discipline, and facilities. Most council time is devoted to issues not directly related to curriculum and instruction. Kannapel, Aagaard, Coe, and Reeves (in press), however, found such issues among the most frequent topics on council agendas, which they attribute to the role of the council in hearing reports and approving school improvement plans, not in debating issues. The issues that engender discussion are the hiring decisions councils are obliged to make and those that council members care about, which reflect the values of many communities across the nation where concern for sports is higher than for academic issues. Hence decisions about athletic issues, especially hiring or determining extra pay for those who coach, can be contentious and time-consuming. Similarly, issues that matter a lot to parents, such as student uniforms, and to teachers, such as discipline codes and report card format, take considerable time (David, 1994).

An elementary school principal noted, "The issue of shared governance comes down to the amount of work and how much effort you give to allowing everyone to have input, and the other is good faith. Good faith is easier." It is not only a lot of hard work, but it also asks the principal to play a role unfamiliar to most. Although leadership occasionally emerges from the faculty, it is typically the principal who is the key to collaborative decision making, a role for which most are not trained and which they do not necessarily want to play. Yet without such leadership, teachers and parents, both on the council and on the committees that do the work, are unlikely to make the serious commitment of time and energy that the responsibilities demand.

Because it is a legal body, much time goes into making sure they are doing things by the rules—rules on announcing meetings, public input, the kinds of questions asked of applicants, how rulings are appealed, and so on. For teachers and parents, as well as principals, things such as making sure the council operates legally, gathering and absorbing information on a range of issues, communicating with one's constituents, and holding meetings all take considerable time for which they are not reimbursed. Moreover, it is work that often goes unappreciated or, worse, generates criticism from those not pleased with the resulting decisions.

Few councils have taken on a major role in changing curriculum and instruction, although that has begun to change somewhat as councils take on more responsibility for preparing (or at least approving) the school's improvement plan. A few schools have made significant changes through policies that influence classroom practice, but these are the exception (Kentucky Institute for Education Research, 1997).

How Effective Councils Operate

Some schools have site-based councils that operate well and manage to focus their attention on issues that affect student learning. These schools are typically led by strong principals, most of whom have always practiced some form of participatory management and prefer that style of management. The principal keeps the school council and faculty focused on student learning. As one principal said, "For every issue that comes up we ask, What does it have to do with student learning?"

In these schools, committees made up of teachers and parents serve as the backbone of the council. Here is where ideas are generated and information is gathered. In order to present well-supported recommendations to the council, committee members gather information through calls and visits to other schools, surveys of faculty, and ongoing discussion with school staff and parents. One elementary school teacher explained, "We quickly learned how important the committee structure is. The council cannot do it all."

For example, in one school the assessment committee identified weaknesses in writing, based on test score results and interviews with teachers. The curriculum committee recommended that all teachers maintain writing portfolios, not just those in the grades where portfolios are required by the state. The professional development committee recommended training for the whole faculty on scoring and proposed using professional development days to score student writing. Finally, the budget committee ensured that funds were available. Then the council approved the plans. After this it is the principal's responsibility to see that policies are translated into action.

Even in schools with effective councils, decisions rarely involve major reorganization of the instructional program. Yet there are examples of changes, unique to individual schools, that probably would not have resulted from district-level decisions. For example, one school council chose to hire a retired teacher to provide tutoring to students struggling with their writing. In another school the council agreed on a schoolwide policy for assessing student progress during each grading period, together with a significantly different report card that described progress toward standards. In one high school, council policy required that teachers of the same courses meet to analyze student work. Coe, Kannapel, Aagaard, and Moore (1995) describe an unusual case in which instructional decisions were made by a strong council under weak leadership, including the introduction of advanced placement classes and a portfolio requirement for graduation. In this instance, the principal did not follow through with council recommendations until the council contacted the local board.

In general, it takes several years for schools to develop ways of organizing that work for them. It takes trial and error, and it takes experience. Experience is hard to build as council members change from one year to the next and have poor mechanisms for developing institutional memory. One elementary school with twenty teachers once had ten committees, which, according to the principal, meant "people were spread way too thin and the right hand didn't know what the left hand was doing." So the council reduced the number of committees to three: curriculum, budget, and professional development. Schools that had prior experience in projects that called for site-based management teams found the transition to SBDM easier than those that had not, as did many schools in Louisville with a history of participatory management.

Schools serious about involving parents are strategic in their outreach efforts. For example, they hold elections for parent council members on nights when a popular school activity is being held. These schools also operate with scheduled meeting times, clear time lines, and well-defined tasks on each agenda. Parents sit on each committee, and meeting times of committees and the council follow a set schedule.

Communication—the flow of information in and out—is a cornerstone of effective councils. Principals ensure that they have the latest information from the state and the district that might affect their deliberations. Schedules and agendas for meetings are set well in advance. Finally, meetings are run efficiently, with set start and stop times and clear rules and time limits that allow participation by all while also ensuring that meetings do not go on and on.

Not surprisingly, then, the most effective councils are those in schools with strong principals committed to participatory decision making—the very people who would operate this way without the requirement for a council. However, even these principals might put out less energy to engage parents and to operate from a shared set of policies without the SBDM requirements.

Challenges and Lessons

The basic rationale behind KERA was that the state would set high standards for students and hold schools accountable for achieving them. In exchange, schools would receive considerable autonomy to determine how to help students meet the standards. The legislature went a step further, however, and specified in some detail the governance structure that would manage this autonomy. By including parents, the law signaled that the voice of the parent community was important in determining a school's program. By naming the principal as the chair, the law signaled that the principal retained authority. And by requiring more educators than parents on each council, the law signaled that professionals were to have the greater say.

Creating a school policymaking body composed of teachers, parents, and the principal presents major challenges to all the players. To function smoothly and, beyond that, to make positive contributions to the school community, calls for fundamental changes in roles and relationships, especially for the principal. Such role changes in turn require a broad array of learning opportunities for council members and their constituencies. In addition, the balancing act between schools and districts requires continuous attention and adjustment.

A New Definition of the Principalship

Few council members have experience working as collaborative decision makers in their daily lives as teachers, parents, and principals. Working as a group asks even more, requiring council members to overcome historical, often adversarial, relationships. Parents are accustomed to thinking about their own children, not an entire school, and they are usually uncomfortable challenging educators. Teachers are accustomed to thinking about their classroom and are often uncomfortable working collegially with their own peers, let alone parents. And teachers have reason to be wary: the accountability provisions of KERA fall on the school, not on the parents.

Principals face perhaps the biggest challenge. They need to lead the way to collaboration and to educate their councils, yet neither their conception of their job nor their training speaks to these needs. As previously described, effective councils are led by principals who maintain a focus on student learning, encourage broad participation in planning and decision making, and facilitate ongoing discussion of instructional issues.

These are principals who know something about teaching and learning (at least enough to recognize sound instructional practices) and who know how to mobilize their faculties and communities to seek improvement. They use the state-required planning process as an opportunity to set realistic goals and to assess progress through a variety of measures. And they listen to what teachers and parents have to say.

This conception of the role of principal is not how most principals view their jobs. They became principals to run a school: to make sure that the building is in working order and all staff, from custodians to bus drivers to teachers, are doing their jobs, to handle discipline problems, and to deal with complaints from parents and teachers. They did not expect to share this authority (although some might have chosen to do so), nor did they expect to lead an instructional reform effort.

Moreover, few principals are trained to enact these new roles. Most principals are trained to be building managers, not to be instructional leaders and facilitators of change. Hence they are ill prepared to take on the role of chairing school councils and leading thoughtful planning efforts in their schools. Many are autocratic, a style that served them well in the past. Only recently has the state begun to provide training that helps build the capacity of principals to play these new roles (see Chapter Ten).

Such role changes cannot happen quickly. Administrator preparation programs need to be redesigned with these new roles in mind. Practicing principals need access to a much richer array of learning opportunities than currently exists to develop their skills and knowledge as instructional leaders, as facilitators and mediators, and as builders of learning communities for their councils and their faculties—not quick fixes through occasional workshops. Like teachers, principals also need on-the-job access to assistance and support through networks of peers.

A Broader View of Training and Assistance

Teachers and parents elected to serve on councils typically have no special knowledge about policy development, school operations, or planning. They are elected for one-year terms (and on average reelected once) and are required to take six hours of training (three hours for incumbents). These six hours focus almost exclusively on the legal and technical aspects of councils, although some trainers have begun to ground the training in school plan development. And the quality of the training varies considerably. This amount of preparation barely scratches the surface of the knowledge needed to review data, diagnose problems, and set schoolwide policies.

Simply understanding what policy means—for example, creating a schoolwide policy for field trips rather than reviewing individual requests—is a learning process. In addition, most council members have never had experience working as a team and representing diverse interests. Similarly, few principals have experience in chairing such a group or in the kinds of facilitation and mediation required to run efficient meetings and reach decisions.

Teachers and parents also have little experience in interviewing candidates and making hiring decisions. Some training exists, but again it tends to be legalistic, focusing on the kinds of questions you can and cannot ask, for example, with little attention to determining the kind of person you are looking for and the qualities you should be seeking.

An important lesson from the Kentucky experience is that creating effective councils requires more than one-shot technical training sessions for council members. Their training needs to provide a deeper understanding of the purposes of schoolwide decision making and its relationship to teaching and learning. And it needs to be tailored to the particulars of their school, its history, and its leadership. The training also needs to be bolstered by making mentors or facilitators available to schools on issues of both substance and process. Without these supports a council's effectiveness ebbs and flows as leadership and members change (Coe et al., 1995).

At the same time it is also important that the larger community of teachers and parents understands the purpose and functioning of school councils. Without the understanding and support of the broader community, councils are not likely to work well. To the extent that an ongoing committee structure is in place and the larger community understands the role of the council, problems created by council member turnover are lessened. For this reason training a much larger proportion of the school community than simply council members is needed.

More training puts more time demands on busy people and requires a much larger supply of qualified trainers. Teachers are already stretched trying to implement new practices, and parents often have full-time jobs. At the same time they are taking on new leadership roles that are demanding and time-consuming. As an elementary school teacher on the school council said, "They put me in there to teach, and this eats up all my time." Without being reimbursed for their time, councils must rely on a small number of highly committed people. Without investments in creating a supply of quality trainers, needs for training cannot be met.

A New Balance of District Leadership and School Authority

The law is clear on the responsibilities of site-based councils. However, it was left to district leaders and staff to determine for themselves the implications of this delegation of authority for their roles. When SBDM became law and was reaffirmed by the courts, local boards and superintendents adopted a hands-off approach, fearing they would be accused of interference if they gave strong direction. Yet, to be effective, even decentralized systems need strong central direction (Murphy, 1989). With little guidance or training available to district administrators, they have had little sense of what their new roles should be. Consequently, district administrators have had a hard time shifting from a mind-set of power, mandates, and monitoring to one of inspiring, guiding, and supporting instructional improvement and generally providing support and assistance.

In a few districts central office staff have learned not only that they can exercise leadership but also that schools and their councils need and want guidance and support. For example, in the area of professional development strong district leaders communicate a clear districtwide focus on instruction and stick with specific priorities over a period of several years. These district leaders also strategically engage schools in high-quality professional development through persuasion, stipends, and making good trainers available. Moreover, they do this without stepping on school councils' toes (David, McDiarmid, & Corcoran, 2000). As an elementary school teacher described it, "We were given the wonderful opportunity to govern ourselves with no training. We threw everything away and started all over. Now we need guidance—what strategies work—people to come in and show you what works with these kids."

Balancing the interests of all stakeholders is a perennial challenge to policymakers at all levels of the system. There are districtwide needs that individual schools cannot meet, such as finding a place to house a special program or linking curriculum from elementary through high school. At the same time there are individual school needs that are not well met by a districtwide solution, such as organizing the staff and planning the daily schedule.

Under a decentralized system, superintendents have a more complicated role than before. They deal not only with their boards but also with school councils. Similarly, local boards must now communicate directly with schools as well as with the superintendent. Few districts have created effective mechanisms to do this, although a growing number of boards invite presentations from school councils at each meeting.

Superintendents and school board members frequently worry that their authority is diluted by that given to schools. Many superintendents would like to hire principals (they have the authority to screen and recommend candidates and to fire principals), and many board members would like to have ultimate veto power over school councils.

The tension between centralized and decentralized authority is most evident in the selection of principals. Superintendents screen candidates and recommend at least three to the school council. If the council does not like any of the applicants, they may request additional candidates from the superintendent. Some superintendents, particularly from larger districts, believe that selecting principals is their primary management tool. Others point out that superintendents retain the upper hand through their power to choose candidates and to dismiss principals.

In one unusual case a site-based council could not agree on a principal, kept requesting additional applicants, and took almost a year and a half to make their decision. This situation clearly had negative effects on both the school and the larger community. However, such negative examples appear to be no more numerous than accusations against superintendents of forwarding only names of cronies and not those best qualified. It is easy to confuse the particulars of what people fight over (in this case, selecting principals) with the larger issue of balancing authority. As the primary symbol of school council authority, the selection of principals can easily become the focal point of the debate.

In fact, the selection of principals poses a far greater problem than who has the upper hand in the choice: the challenge of finding qualified candidates. Although a few superintendents may try to control the selection process by recommending only certain candidates, there is not in fact a large pool of highly skilled administrators seeking principalships. Across the country the pool of qualified candidates is small in relation to the demand, and the job is becoming more difficult. Kentucky is no exception, and SBDM makes the job of being a principal even more difficult than before. Moreover, under SBDM some sitting principals are hesitant to apply to other schools for fear of alienating their own council, which further reduces the pool. One district has begun to increase its supply of principal candidates by establishing assistant principal positions open to interested teachers in their schools. The lesson here is the need to focus on increasing the pool of qualified candidates for principalships.

Balancing centralized and decentralized authority rests on an exercise of goodwill, together with the skills, knowledge, and experience to embrace new roles both in schools and in the central office. Even under current SBDM law some superintendents and boards are able to exert considerable influence over their principals and school councils. Without approval authority for school plans the law still allows for boards and superintendents to exercise a strong hand in each school's implementation of their improvement plan. In addition, some superintendents set the climate for change in all schools simply by visiting schools regularly to ask what they are doing and how the central office can help. When local boards and superintendents take a proactive role in leading and helping school councils create and carry out strong plans, conflicts over power and authority rarely arise.

Conclusions

Like all complex reforms, SBDM in Kentucky is a mixed story. On the one hand, given the short three-year history of full implementation, it is a major success. Virtually all schools have functioning councils that have brought parents and teachers into decisions formerly left to principals and district staff. Councils have created bylaws, policies, and school improvement plans and have hired hundreds of principals. Parents have gained a deeper understanding of, and as a result more appreciation for, the job of teachers and principals. Although many councils are still dominated by the principal and distracted by some members with personal agendas, most of them have met the letter of the law and operate in good faith. And all this has been accomplished with a surprising lack of conflict while significant authority has been shifted from the district level to the school level. "I think there is room for abuse," one middle school teacher concluded, "and I'm sure [SBDM] is abused. . . . It can be abused by a council member or a principal. Some people get on because they have their own personal agenda. . . . But overall it is good. The former system was abused."

SBDM has created new norms for decision making about schools. Parents now have an official voice in school affairs. In addition, it is now the norm that teachers have a voice—the majority voice—in decisions that affect the school. At a time when civic knowledge is low, councils serve to model the democratic process, warts and all. As a state administrator pointed out, "Democracy is hard and messy. It is tedious and time consuming, but it is democracy. And in America that is what we like—getting everyone to participate. . . . A lot will be quick to say it is hard; but they do not want to give up their right to participate. This is not a 'feel good' kind of thing, but it can be a very effective system; and I think it is working well in Kentucky."

On the other hand, few councils have met the ambitious goal of leading improvement in curriculum and instruction. In all fairness, neither have local school boards. In fact, across the country local boards pay little attention to curriculum and instruction (Elmore, 1993). It is easy to point to the failures of councils and the problems created by the ones that do a poor job of decision making. But the real question is, Compared to what? Student achievement, minority hiring, qualified principals—these were all issues across the state before SBDM. Getting folks to run for office and to vote in an election is as much a problem for school boards as for parent council members. Given that school boards are the only model, it is not surprising that many councils reflect the same problems as beset their boards.

SBDM was not designed to operate in isolation from the other elements of KERA. KERA is a sweeping reform effort that encourages changes in curriculum and instruction and holds schools accountable for improved student achievement. Across the state, teachers struggle to make sense of the reforms and to change their practices accordingly. SBDM is but one piece of this larger effort. As such, it is hardly surprising that councils have not become a forum that empowers teachers to make collective decisions about their professional practice.

From the perspective of what it takes to change teaching practices in classrooms, councils can at best provide some structures and remove some barriers to this process. As Chapter Nine points out, improvements in teaching practice result from teachers' opportunities to learn more about their subject matter, to understand better how students learn, and to work with colleagues on issues of curriculum and instruction. These are professional activities that can be influenced by schoolwide goals, by a focus on instruction, and by district leadership and direction. But they are not likely to occur in a legally bound setting under the watchful eyes of parents and the principal.

Nevertheless, school councils can contribute to creating conditions that foster improvements in curriculum and instruction. Seeking principals who are instructional leaders, developing school plans that focus on student learning, setting up committees that discuss curriculum, and measuring student progress in multiple ways are all means by which effective councils can influence the instructional program in their schools. When councils have their own conversations about how students learn and the quality of their work and when they stimulate others to have these conversations, their impact can be significant.

Beyond curriculum and instruction, councils may be achieving goals that are equally important and difficult to measure. Reforms in schools will not persist without the support of their communities. The fact that parents who are on councils have more positive attitudes toward their schools than those who are not, and more positive attitudes than the general public, suggests that councils are playing a constructive role in generating support for school reform.

Some of the details of SBDM policy might benefit from review: whether the composition of councils should be more flexible, whether councils might choose their own chair, and whether terms of office should be longer. But these policies are not the real obstacles to effective councils. The major barriers transcend the legal requirements for SBDM. These include the need for leadership, clarity of purpose, and the skills, knowledge, and willingness to take on new roles.

Like other elements of KERA, SBDM was well thought out in structure, but less so in regard to the amount of training and support needed. Kentucky has begun to address these needs. For example, through the efforts of the Kentucky Leadership Academy (created by the department of education) and the Commonwealth Institute for Parents (founded by the Prichard Committee for Academic Excellence), principals and parents are now acquiring new skills and knowledge to lead school improvement. At the same time the state is now providing clearer direction on its expectations for curriculum and is offering subject matter–based professional development for teachers. To the extent these efforts are effective, they will contribute to strengthening site-based councils and school improvement efforts.

SBDM in Kentucky has strengths that set it apart from the many attempts across the country to implement site-based decision making. One strength is that the state delegates authority to school councils by law. This means that council authority is not at risk each time the superintendent, school board, or state commissioner changes.

Another strength is that the state has stuck with the basic structure of SBDM for an entire decade and continues to support it through legislation, legal opinions, and administrative actions. This persistence is critical. It takes a long time for a school community to grasp what it means to run their school's instructional program. The kinds of changes in roles that SBDM calls for are enormous and take well over a decade to achieve. Councils typically begin with a focus on technicalities and small issues; but over time, with leadership, professional development, and assistance, they can move on to tackle more substantive issues of school performance.

Whether most councils ultimately become a functional asset to schools rather than an added layer of bureaucracy and politics remains to be seen. SBDM has brought in new players, the people with the greatest stake in school outcomes. It provides an opportunity for folks to think about the collective needs of a school beyond individual students and individual teachers. To the extent that teachers and parents now have a real voice, this is an important achievement in its own right. To the extent that these folks also have the direction and knowledge to make informed decisions, SBDM can help pave the way to a stronger educational program that directly influences student achievement.

REFERENCES

Boone County Board of Education v. Bushee, 889 S.W.2d 809 (Ky. 1994).

Coe, P., Kannapel, P. J., Aagaard, L., & Moore, B. D. (1995, April). *Non-linear evolution of school-based decision making in Kentucky.* Paper presented at the annual meeting of the American Educational Research Association, San Francisco.

David, J. L. (1994). School-based decision making: Kentucky's test of decentralization. *Phi Delta Kappan, 75,* 706–712.

David, J. L., McDiarmid, G. W., & Corcoran, T. C. (2000). *The role of Kentucky districts in professional development: Exemplary cases.* Lexington: Partnership for Kentucky Schools.

Elmore, R. E. (1993). The role of local school districts in instructional improvement. In S. H. Fuhrman (Ed.), *Designing coherent education policy: Improving the system* (pp. 96–124). San Francisco: Jossey-Bass.

Kannapel, P. J., Aagaard, L., Coe, P., & Reeves, C. A. (in press). *Elementary change: Moving toward systemic school reform in Kentucky.* Charleston, WV: AEL, Inc.

Kentucky Institute for Education Research. (1997). *School-based decision making: Shared findings and insights of researchers* (Research Informing Policy and Practice Series). Lexington: Author.

Murphy, J. T. (1989). The paradox of decentralizing schools: Lessons from business, government, and the Catholic Church. *Phi Delta Kappan, 70,* 808–812.

Office of Education Accountability. (1999). *Kentucky General Assembly, Office of Education Accountability annual report.* Frankfort, KY: Author.

Task Force on Education Reform. (1989). *Statement of principles.* Frankfort, KY: Legislative Research Commission.

Wilkerson & Associates. (1999). *1999 statewide education reform study: Final report.* Louisville: Kentucky Institute for Education Research.

15

A NEW MISSION FOR THE DEPARTMENT OF EDUCATION

Susan Follett Lusi, Patricia Davis Goldberg

THIS CHAPTER FOCUSES on the experiences of the Kentucky Department of Education (KDE) and its decade-long effort to implement the Kentucky Education Reform Act of 1990 (KERA). We based our findings on research and practice, including forty interviews conducted during the latter half of 1999. Our sample included five groups: KERA "historians," individuals both inside and outside of government who have been involved with KERA since its inception; KDE staff in Frankfort and in the regional service centers (RSCs); distinguished educators (DEs); practitioners who have worked with DEs and the RSCs; and representatives of professional associations. Distinguished educators are selected and highly trained educators (mostly teachers and school leaders) employed by the state under KERA to assist schools with declining test scores. In 1998, DEs were renamed highly skilled educators. Under KERA, eight regional service centers were created that decentralized field services to schools.

Our sample of practitioners included superintendents of districts served by four different RSCs, and the superintendent, principal, and DE of five different schools. The RSCs and sites served by DEs were chosen with the advice of individuals knowledgeable about these programs, with an eye toward regional and programmatic variation. We concentrated on these two programs because they are directly focused on helping schools and districts better implement the KERA reforms. Our interviews focused on

KERA and whether or not it was generally on track, the RSC and DE programs when the individual had knowledge of them, KDE and its role in KERA, and lessons that others should learn from the Kentucky experience. In addition, we reviewed research and other documentation on KDE and KERA.

Setting the Course for Systemic Reform

Every four years from 1838 through 1990, Kentuckians had elected a new superintendent of public instruction. The newly elected superintendent was able to fill key leadership positions in the department of education and implement new policies and programs. The position was used as a stepping-stone to higher office. Local superintendents were treated as political constituents, and the direction of KDE changed with each electoral cycle. By 1990 "the Kentucky Department of Education had gained a reputation as an ineffective bureaucracy heavily populated with political appointees who were perceived to be inept, and who had long since 'retired on the job'" (Steffy, 1993, pp. 199–200).

That changed on July 1, 1991, when KERA terminated all positions in the department and stripped away the authority of the superintendent. A new commissioner of education, who reported to the gubernatorially appointed Kentucky Board of Education, replaced the superintendent of public instruction. (The Kentucky Board of Education, formerly the State Board for Elementary and Secondary Education, is an appointed lay group that sets educational policy and provides oversight for elementary and secondary education. The Kentucky Department of Education, under the leadership of the commissioner of education, implements educational policy and answers to the board of education.) The commissioner was charged with building a new department of education and eight new RSCs to provide more direct service to practitioners. The new KDE's mission was "to ensure for each child an internationally superior education and a love of learning through visionary leadership, vigorous stewardship, and exemplary services" (Steffy, 1993, p. 204).

Armed with substantial new funding, KDE had the responsibility of implementing reform through seven initiatives that directly affected instruction in every classroom in the state: school-based decision making, preschool programs, primary school programs, family resource centers, after-school programs, high-stakes assessment, and technology. Traditional, routine relationships between the department and schools were no longer acceptable. In addition to transforming itself into a service organization, the department was supposed to promote new relationships between district personnel and schools. Schools were to be supported and held accountable for student learning, with the goal of nearly all students achieving proficiency by 2014. The decade of the 1990s required major change from all involved in Kentucky education, and KDE was the agency given the responsibility to make it happen.

Assembling at the Starting Line: Creating the New Kentucky Department of Education

Kentucky's first commissioner, Thomas C. Boysen, started on January 1, 1991. All positions in the department were abolished at the end of June 1991, and a reorganized department opened on July 1. The new KDE was organized to reflect the components and priorities of the KERA reforms and was staffed by a number of people unfamiliar with the agency; this was particularly true of those in top leadership positions. Only 18.5 percent of top-level managers came from the old department, and 35 percent came from out of state. Much less turnover occurred at the lower levels, with more than 80 percent of KDE's merit employees (civil service) returning to the department, although in many cases not in their previous positions (Boysen, 1992).

The mandated opening and closing of KDE had both positive and negative aspects. Starting with the positives, many new, high-caliber people were attracted to the department. Department leaders were allowed to go outside the regular state personnel system and deviate from the established salary structure for new hires. Although the alternative hiring structures created their own set of negative consequences in the agency—such as new people earning more than longtime KDE staff members in similar jobs— they did help the agency attract talent. (See Lusi, 1997, pp. 32–34, for a detailed description of the different hiring structures and their strengths and pitfalls.)

However, the major upheaval caused some good people to leave and placed the department in limbo for an extended period of time. One KERA historian explained that writing the legislation was awkward in part because the position of superintendent of public instruction was still in the state constitution, and the person holding the job was legally there until the term expired. So the KERA framers statutorily stripped that position of its legal responsibilities and gave them to the new commissioner of education. They subsequently provided for a phase-in period of the new governance structure: six months to search for a commissioner and six months for the new commissioner to become acclimated and reorganize the agency. The KERA framers did not specify any of the features of the

reorganization; they wanted the new commissioner to have as much latitude as possible. As this historian said:

> We effectively told everybody in the department that they have their
> job for one year and the new commissioner will determine whether
> you are going to be part of the organization after that. . . . We were
> hopeful that there would be a major turnover [and there was]. . . . But
> the difficulty was that . . . some of the best people that we had on
> board who would have served us well afterwards left. . . . They were
> not going to . . . wait and see if [they got rehired]. I don't know how
> we could have avoided that, but that was something we should have
> given more thought to. . . . What we ended up doing then was we dis-
> abled the very organization that we had to depend upon so much in
> the early stages to implement what we wanted. . . . and one should
> never do that.

Organizing and Reorganizing to Better Run the Marathon

As KERA unfolded throughout the 1990s, staff members at KDE had to
shift their activities from jump-starting the system and outlining the
course to running the marathon of systemic change. During this time the
agency experienced a number of noteworthy shifts in structure as well as
leadership.

The new KDE was headed by the commissioner and had four bureaus
supervised by deputy commissioners: chief of staff, management support
services, learning results services, and learning support services. Some divisions were named after specific components of the KERA reforms: the
Division of the Kentucky Instructional Results Information System,
the Division of School-Based Decision Making, the Division of Early
Childhood Education, and the Division of Student and Family Support
Services. Although authorized at the outset of the reform, the eight RSCs,
designed to provide professional development and assist with the local
implementation of KERA, were actually up and running only in 1992–93.

After the opening of the "new" KDE in 1991, the department went
through two relatively major reorganizations in 1994 and 1998. The 1994
reorganization eliminated the Bureau of the Chief of Staff, sought to more
closely align curriculum and assessment development by placing them
together in one division, and streamlined the number of divisions focused
on assessment and accountability. The number of deputy commissioners
was reduced from four to three, associate commissioners from eleven to

ten, and Frankfort-based directors from thirty-three to thirty. (These numbers count Frankfort-based leadership staff only. They do not include leadership of the RSCs or of the schools for the deaf or blind.) Wilmer S. Cody became Kentucky's second appointed commissioner of education in 1995. (During the writing of this chapter Commissioner Cody resigned his position and the Kentucky Board of Education made plans to appoint Kentucky's third commissioner of education by autumn 2000.)

The 1998 reorganization reduced the number of deputy commissioners from three to two and divided KDE into three functional areas: the commissioner (with some offices reporting directly to the commissioner), the Bureau of Management Support Services, and the Bureau of Learning Support Services. The Bureau of Learning Support Services was merged with what had previously been the Bureau of Learning Results (Lumsden, 1999).

According to Lumsden (1999), the Bureau of Learning Support Services was organized to focus KDE and the RSCs on developing teacher content knowledge and further clarifying the curriculum. The bureau was also organized to support and ensure the assessment system's credibility by creating a unit that focused on defining, executing, and evaluating the assessment contract, guided by a new gubernatorially appointed committee. This reorganization also was designed to mitigate the effects of the personnel losses since 1991. Consecutive governors, for both financial and political reasons, had reduced the size of state government, leaving uneven, fragmented staffing patterns throughout the structure (Lumsden, p. 3).

KDE also had experienced a reduction and redistribution of personnel since the passage of KERA. KDE had a staff of 520 people based in Frankfort and 49 people in the RSCs (Boysen, 1992). The comparable numbers, as of July 2000, were 421 in Frankfort and 63 in the RSCs. The department also has had substantial turnover in leadership positions (defined as Frankfort-based commissioners and directors). Using the fiscal year 1991–92 as the baseline, 47 percent of KDE's leaders were new to their positions in 1993–94. Turnover has been reduced since that time but remains significant. On average, 22.4 percent of the people in leadership positions were new to their jobs each year from 1994 to 1999. (These percentages are based on our analysis of KDE staff directories for the years in question. Again, these numbers count Frankfort-based leadership staff only and do not include leadership of the RSCs or of the schools for the deaf or blind. The chief of staff and similar positions over time also were not counted.)

Adjusting the Strategy for Winning the Race

The structural changes just described signaled changes in the work and emphasis of KDE over the 1990s. The people we interviewed consistently described KDE and its RSCs as being focused primarily on getting the structural aspects, or "strands," of the state's reforms in place during the early years of KERA. This included developing and implementing the assessment and accountability system and helping schools adopt school-based decision making and the ungraded primary school program, for example. By 1996 researchers agreed that the structures mandated by KERA had been implemented and that the processes the law required for developing the new school reform initiatives had been followed for the most part (Kentucky Institute for Education Research, 1997).

Raising test scores was also an early priority beginning in 1994–95, after the first accountability cycle. Accountability cycles are two years in length. Schools are held accountable for improving test scores over the period of each cycle. KDE focused on schools whose scores had declined or that had failed to meet their performance goals, providing direct assistance to help them raise test scores (R. Pankratz, personal communication, March 17, 2000). Informants agreed that as the KERA strands became clearer in people's minds, KDE shifted its focus to building capacity for improving teaching and learning. The department and its RSCs began to concentrate on content, curriculum alignment, and instruction—the guts of KERA's larger reforms. A KDE official explained, "We have heard more and more messages from teachers, and we have also experienced this problem of moving students beyond proficient to distinguished; that's caused us to rethink how we deploy resources in the department. And we have shifted a lot of our regional support base and a lot of our [Frankfort] staff . . . [to] helping teachers understand curriculum and how to teach that curriculum."

The second effort to build capacity is a very recent one. Because teacher education programs were not explicitly addressed in KERA, school faculties have adopted the recommended changes unevenly. The state did not pay enough attention to coordinating teacher preparation with the reforms and goals or to making sure practicing teachers had sufficient training. A KERA historian noted, "The accountability consequences through [the assessment system] have not worked, and teachers who have not made the change remain on the job. There is a new effort, the Teacher Quality Task Force, in the legislature to look at teacher competency. New kinds of consequences may be invoked."

In the late 1990s it became evident to KDE staff and other educators across the state that achievement of Kentucky's high expectations for all children was directly related to the improvement of teacher quality in the state. This prompted Governor Patton in January 1999 to establish by executive order the Task Force on Teacher Quality, which was charged to make recommendations to the 2000 General Assembly. Chapter Eleven describes the legislation developed in the Kentucky 2000 session (Senate Bill 77) to improve teacher quality. This bill was passed after much controversy and debate about experienced teacher evaluations. It raises the standards for teacher preparation and provides new initiatives, including funding for professional development of teachers. Although the provisions of Senate Bill (SB) 77 did not address some of the key recommendations of the task force, it did include some new measures to improve teacher quality. Also, more than $17 million was appropriated for the next biennium to support teacher development mandates in SB 77.

Assessment of Progress at the Ten-Year Mark

KERA and the KDE have received mixed reviews over the past decade. With only two exceptions, however, everyone we interviewed reported that KERA was on track and had resulted in extremely positive changes for education in Kentucky. This said, everyone also concurred that the reform was not where he or she wanted it to be, particularly as measured by student achievement. Student achievement has increased but not as dramatically as was originally hoped.

It is clear that student achievement in Kentucky has improved. Exactly how much it has improved and KDE's contribution to higher school performance are difficult to assess, however—particularly since the assessment system changed significantly in 1999, making it impossible to compare this year's scores to those from the earlier state tests, and causing the state to extend the deadline for getting nearly all students to standards from 2010 to 2014. (See Chapter Five for description of the changes in Kentucky's assessment system.)

Both bad and good news are contained in the assessment results of subpopulations of students. The bad news is that while achievement has improved for all subpopulations, the gap that exists between some subpopulations—such as between African Americans and whites, and between males and females—has not been reduced. The good news in Kentucky is that there is evidence that the state is breaking the predictable pattern of low socioeconomic status paired with low test scores. According to a KDE official, a number of high-poverty schools are achieving more not only relative to other high-poverty schools but also relative to schools in wealthier communities.

Kentucky has reached the halfway point in the marathon of systemic reform. Whether or not it has achieved the midpoint in getting all children to a "proficient" level is difficult to determine at this time. Assessing the performance of KDE is difficult because of the size and "loose coupling" of the system it is trying to influence. (A system is "loosely coupled" when its linkages are indirect, making it difficult to predict how change in one part of the system will influence activity in other parts of the system; see Weick, 1976.) Three factors on which KDE might be evaluated emerged from our interviews: leadership, service to the field, and results.

Leadership

Our sources assessed the performance of KDE in part by discussing its two commissioners, but their views differed as to the effectiveness of the two leadership styles. One person described the first commissioner, Boysen, as too involved. A superintendent said Boysen's micromanaging led to "having your hands tied and not getting to use your own imagination." Conversely, a KERA historian stated emphatically that Boysen was "the right person at the right time . . . because he had that incredible energy level and salesmanship. . . . [He] traveled all over the state and . . . he was excited and enthusiastic about implementing [KERA]." Another person described the second commissioner, Cody, as "not managing enough." Yet, a different source said, "[Cody] is more down to earth. Probably more practical . . . he can generally apply some common sense to the solution of the problem."

Service to the Field

Sources also offered evaluations of KDE's effort to shift from a bureaucracy to a service organization that can assist schools with student achievement. Although many people still see KDE as bureaucratic, they did report that the agency now provides more service. No practitioner we interviewed stated categorically that KDE had served them poorly, and the RSCs received particularly high marks for their service orientation. One superintendent reported:

> I personally interact with the RSC about two or three times per month.
> I would estimate that someone from our school, either building or

classroom level, interacts with the RSC on a weekly basis. . . . Often, the RSC will send me an e-mail or a fax about information that is pertinent to something happening. . . . People at the building level . . . are generally . . . in contact with the RSC concerning curriculum issues. . . . They're always very informative. I have found the RSC to be very timely in their response to both myself and my staff.

One RSC director described the breakdown of staff time: 40 percent was spent on technical assistance to specific schools, 50 percent on "broad-sweep" training for information in areas such as writing cluster training and curriculum development, 5 percent on short-term professional development such as code of ethics training, and 5 percent on meetings, including meetings with university committees to keep them informed and involved. According to the director, "Time with any one district varies because of what is needed. Some work is for everyone; other work is targeted. The center always honors requests."

There is some evidence that staff turnover during the past decade has negatively affected KDE's service. One principal said of the early days of KERA, "You could never get a clear answer from anyone. . . . There was a lot of the right hand not knowing what the left hand was doing." A superintendent commented that you knew everyone in KDE personally prior to the reforms. Another added, "You would call up someone to ask them for information and be told they don't work in this department anymore." A third superintendent stated, "A main strength [of KDE] is people with expertise and knowledge—especially those who have been there longer. A weakness is that another group of people have come in who have only been there two years or so. It takes a couple of years to build integrity, credibility, and a knowledge base."

Results

There are two KERA initiatives in which the presence of KDE can have a direct effect on student learning results: through the DE program (in which the designation of "highly skilled educator" has now replaced "distinguished educator") and through RSC consultants working with high-need schools. Kannapel and Coe in Chapter Ten of this book describe the positive impact of the DE program on test scores of the schools that received assistance in accountability cycle 1 as well as the School Transformation and Renewal (STAR) program in cycle 2. The authors of Chapter Ten also cite evidence of longer-term impact on student learning, school personnel, and development of school leadership. As a result of the success of the DE program in raising test scores and focusing attention on student achievement, school leaders across the state made requests to KDE to train principals and superintendents in the skills and strategies used in the STAR program. This prompted the development of the Kentucky Leadership Academy, which now serves more than three hundred participants who voluntarily have signed up for a two-year training program at a cost of about $1,000 per person to be paid by local districts.

With respect to the RSC consultants who can have a direct effect on school performance, there has been a priority established for 1998–2000 to assist targeted schools with low test scores in their region. RSCs have assumed responsibility for higher achievement in these schools, but as of this writing, test scores to measure their impact were not available.

Supporting the Runners So All Children Can Win

State departments of education around the country are struggling to sustain systemic reforms and provide practitioners with sufficient support so that these reforms fundamentally change teaching. KDE is no exception. Its biggest challenges are keeping the system focused on the reforms and providing practitioners the help they need to develop the hows of reform now that they have articulated the whys.

People interviewed agreed that the framers of KERA dramatically underestimated the amount of training, assistance, and, especially, time that educators throughout the system would need in order to enact the KERA reforms. One KERA historian said:

> The core vision is that the state is to set expectations and to provide direction . . . and then let schools decide what to do. . . . [However,] there wasn't as much capacity at the school level as the legislature assumed. The other problem was that they put in a lot of support for professional development but it wasn't enough. . . . One of the visions . . . , and this was a political compromise, was that teachers would do this with the time they had. That was just wrong. So we have been trying to make up for that.

As KDE has worked to change the inner workings of teaching and learning, it has encountered a number of problems that surround this type of work. Negotiating these dilemmas has required, and will continue to require, the department to make a number of strategic choices as it tries to determine how to build local capacity to improve student learning—how to get all the runners across the finish line. The choices are familiar to those of us who have worked in education reform over time, but it is instructive to examine them in the Kentucky context. Following are three critical choices Kentucky must grapple with as it continues on the marathon of reform. We recognize that we present the choices more starkly than they exist in practice. None of the choices is mutually exclusive, and the challenge for state agencies may well be to find the best balance.

CHOICE 1: To make whole schools the primary focus of state change efforts *or* to make individual teachers the focus.

At the outset of KERA, KDE primarily worked with schools to bring about change. Now the department has shifted to working more with individual teachers. One KDE official outlined the difficulties inherent in this choice as he described changes in the DE program. This official did not see the shift as all bad but wondered if the timing was right:

> Initially the mission [of the DE program] was very clear. It was . . . to help schools be successful as measured by the state assessment system. . . . The major strategies were around [developing and] aligning the curriculum. . . . What we found was that schools were not teaching what was being assessed . . . and that is still true today. . . . [We focused on] lesson design . . . [and giving] feedback on instructional strategies that were being used. . . . We also worked, in those days, a lot on writing because we identified writing as the gatekeeper for children demonstrating what they could do on that assessment. . . . We also paid a lot of attention to school culture and leadership development and focused on working with the principal. I would say that we worked more . . . on schoolwide issues because that's where the bang for the buck is ultimately going to come. . . . I think the major change that we've seen since the last legislative session is a much greater emphasis on working teacher by teacher. My concern there is that you'll do that and you won't get the schoolwide movement that shows that you're being successful. It's not to question how important it is to work teacher by teacher. It's just that when the legislature meets in 2001 and wants to look at the 2000 data, will our schools have moved forward in the [highly skilled educator] program like they had in the past?

This statement points up a classic debate or dilemma in school reform. To what degree will working on schoolwide reform bring about changes in the practice of individual teachers and vice versa? And what is the right combination of these two approaches in the face of limited resources?

CHOICE 2: To broaden the state focus to include inputs *or* to maintain a focus purely on results.

No one questions the fact that Kentucky has focused on results. There also is very strong implied agreement that the business of reforming schools so that virtually all students achieve proficiency is a much more difficult task than originally thought. Given these observations, however, experts disagree about what should be done, and they are concerned about the degree to which KDE can broaden its attention and focus to include inputs, or the processes of teaching and learning, without losing its primary focus on results. Two examples illustrate the dilemmas of this choice.

The first example is KDE's shift to focusing on content. Although there is agreement that practitioners need more help than was originally foreseen and that content and curriculum alignment are part of the help they need, there is disagreement, or at least concern, over the degree to which KDE's new focus on content will detract from its unremitting emphasis on results. One interpretation is that focusing on content and curriculum is a natural progression in the implementation of KERA. This interpretation was put forward by Commissioner Cody:

> The Department's initial role during . . . the first four years . . . was to implement . . . the various strands of KERA. . . . And then beginning . . . four years ago . . . it seemed to be obvious that [these strands] were becoming institutionalized and that what was needed was an increase in time and attention on school faculties . . . [and their] academic disciplines. So it sort of shifted from strands of KERA to the academic core content itself. And with that, focusing more of our time and energy on what students are to be taught and how they should be taught.

A second interpretation of this shift to a content focus is that KDE may be backing away from its focus on results and must be careful not to shift back to providing unfocused professional development. This perspective was put forward by another KDE official:

> It's taking a real close look at student performance and what students need in school; then design [professional development] that is going to help those students move forward as measured by the state assessment system. . . . [For example,] teachers don't know how to give [students] strong open-response questions, which help with critical learning, thinking, and writing. Now, these are things, in my estimation, that the teacher needs [professional development] in, not in some very curricularly related issue, be it technology or whatever she might be interested in. . . . With the strong emphasis we have on [professional development], it can't be for it's own sake.

The second example is the varied responses to 1998 legislation that introduced scholastic audits as part of assessing whether or not a school was in decline or crisis, rather than relying only on the results of the accountability index. Some states (including Rhode Island, where one of the authors works) view assessment data as one set of important indicators of a school's progress but as insufficient by themselves to make comprehensive judgments about a school. From this perspective, the introduction of scholastic audits—in which a team headed by a highly skilled educator visits a school and makes judgments about the school's student performance, learning environment, and efficiency—provides another important set of indicators that should help to determine a school's status. In the minds of some, this sort of dual-level examination honors the complexity of changing schools in the fundamental ways called for by KERA and other similar state-level reforms.

However, others believe the scholastic audits signal that Kentucky may be beginning to waver on its commitment to results. According to one KERA historian, the shift has a lot of stakeholders and school officials asking if the game has changed. One KDE official said:

> It was pretty clear in the last legislative session, especially with the scholastic audit, that the legislature was starting to waver on holding schools accountable only to a score. . . . That's why they brought an independent team to come in and verify whether or not that score accurately reflected what was going on in a school. You can see we're starting to equivocate here. The authority for the designation is put in the hands of the team rather than the state. That is significant because . . . the team . . . [is] not looking solely at results anymore, it's going to be looking at inputs. . . . As long as you can indicate that you've had the right kind of inputs and that you have some other things in place, then you would be considered not [to be in] crisis [or] decline.

This set of issues was brought to the forefront by schools that were strong performers relative to other schools in the state in terms of absolute achievement but were designated as in decline because they did not make progress. The legislature concurred that these schools might not deserve the "in decline" label, especially if they had achieved high scores over the last several years.

CHOICE 3: To work with schools that are the lowest performers in absolute terms *or* to communicate the necessity of continuous improvement by working with schools that have not improved, regardless of their absolute performance.

This choice relates to the foregoing discussion. The accountability system constructed in the early days of KERA was driven by the assumption that all schools needed to improve to the point where virtually every student reached proficiency. Using the accountability index, a baseline score was developed for each school, and each school had to improve over time, no matter how high its initial score was in comparison to other schools in the state. Schools that did not improve sufficiently were designated as in decline or crisis and were assigned a DE regardless of their relative performance.

The focus of the DE program has shifted to the lowest-performing schools. Although the legislature advised KDE to make this shift, some of our informants objected strenuously to this change. One KDE official said:

> [Improving schools] is about continuous progress . . . and lessons learned. . . . I always saw the DE program as a learning process to share with everyone, not just an intervention piece [that focuses on low-performing schools]. [By focusing on low-performing schools], we're not . . . on the issue of continuous progress. We're no longer [holding] all schools . . . accountable. . . . It's only when you place accountability throughout the infrastructure, causing the entire system to move, [that] you create the kind of energy I think that got us to the progress to date.

The dilemma for all states is that they have limited capacity with which to work with schools. Given this limited capacity, the question arises whether or not the state can afford to enact the vision of holding all schools accountable for improvement regardless of their relative performance. Put in its strongest terms, is it moral or ethical to work with a high-achieving "school in decline" if it means not working with a low-performing school even if that school is improving? Clearly, there are multiple ways in which states or their partners can work with schools, but it is not clear that states can work with all schools that are not improving at the same rate. How states can work within their limited capacity, while at the same time maximizing their learning in order to better help other schools in the future, is a true dilemma.

Staying the Course on the Change Marathon

A review of the earlier work of one of this chapter's authors (Lesser & Wilson, 1999) challenged that author to pursue further what state departments of education had to teach and learn as they engaged in systemic reform. Lesser and Wilson cited the work of Cohen, McLaughlin, and

Talbert (1993) and referenced their notion of the "pedagogy of policy." Cohen et al. argue that policymakers need to give careful thought to how policy can be implemented in ways that help educators change their instruction as envisioned—in other words, to think through how and what the policy "teaches" practitioners.

When Cohen et al. (1993) first introduced the idea of the pedagogy of policy, they found that policymakers' efforts to help policy enactors change were often didactic whereas the policies themselves called for constructivist teaching with frequent application of knowledge. The pedagogy of the policy did not mirror the pedagogy sought in classrooms. Lusi (1997) concluded that what happens inside state departments of education is reflected in the relationships they have with schools. Their agenda and their implementation strategies should model the desired results of state-level reform efforts. In other words, they need to learn how to practice what they preach so that they can teach these practices to the field.

Here we examine KDE's success in learning how to model the practices it was trying to teach. In many respects KDE appears to have modeled the kinds of strategies and approaches that it wanted educators to pursue. The RSCs work with schools in ways that are based very much on their individual needs. One RSC staff member specifically discussed the importance of modeling appropriate pedagogy for teachers participating in the content academies. The DE program has focused on the needs of individual schools; the training provided to DEs prepared them to work with schools in a hands-on, participatory way. One principal commented, "[The DE] was one of us. . . . She came in; she'd say, 'Okay, well, let's look and see what we've got and then go from there,' and she was right in there with us, you know. We were working late; she was working late." Another principal said, "[Our DE] was a heck of a resource. Anything you needed—if you needed her to go observe one teacher . . . or sit down with a whole department and help align their curriculum [she could help]. . . . I learned a lot from [her]. . . . [She] and I would sit down [together] and determine areas that . . . we needed to work on."

The fact that district and school administrators see the extensive training provided to DEs as highly valuable further demonstrates that practitioners view the program as teaching what they need to learn in the ways they need to learn it. The Kentucky Leadership Academy was developed to provide similar training for instructional leaders in schools and districts and is funded largely by local dollars.

There are different opinions about whether or not KDE has modeled desired behavior for the field in the areas of goal setting and planning. One KDE official said:

[There has never been] a real definition of what success was for the
state agency. Never in the state agency has there been a measurable goal
for expected student achievement across the state. . . . The state agency
. . . doesn't have . . . a strategic plan, but each of the regional service
centers has a strategic plan. . . . I do think the reorganiz[ed] structure
now has the potential to deliver better service, but it won't work unless
there is a shared definition of success and that vision is held . . . from
the top of the leadership [and] throughout the infrastructure.

Other KDE staff members spoke of the goals and milestones established
by the state board of education as providing the agency with strategic
direction. But the larger point of the importance of modeling in the pedagogy of policy remains.

The challenge of getting a state department of education to model
desired behavior should not be underestimated. It is difficult to get the
multiple pieces of bureaucratic agencies to work together cohesively, a
problem that has persisted within KDE throughout the KERA reforms.
When Lusi (1997) studied KDE in 1992–93, she found it to be a seg-
mented organization: "KDE is still organized into bureaus, offices, and
divisions, and these are divided along the strands of the reform. . . . While
some work takes place across offices and divisions in the department, the
implementation process still reflects this segmentation" (p. 72).

Likewise, a KERA historian noted Commissioner Boysen's struggle to
make KDE work as a unified whole:

[Boysen] made a very strong effort to convert a bureaucracy to a service organization. . . . He talked a great deal . . . about the systemic
nature of the reform . . . and he wanted his organization to function
in ways that would communicate . . . to people . . . [that] all of these
things fit together in some kind of a meaningful way. . . . [But] bureaucracies just don't work that way. People get committed to . . . the
things that they're responsible for, and consequently, he was forever
reorganizing to try to somehow or other get people's attention that this
is an overall effort. . . . I think he felt at times that he touched it and
got it but he couldn't hang on to it. It was one of those things like trying to catch smoke.

Commissioner Cody confirmed that this is an ongoing issue, saying, "It's
a continuous effort to . . . build a common understanding among all the
people in the department, not only of their particular mission and role but
for them to see the larger picture of what needs to be accomplished."
Another KDE official said:

> We try to make . . . being a resource to the local districts to reach high
> achievement for all students [our mission]. But I worry from time to
> time about the dynamic tension between each of the program offices
> and their individual mission and the overall department vision. . . . I
> think it's a constant problem, both of understanding and of pull. It's
> much easier for a staff . . . [to make its own] program work . . . [than
> to make sure all of the department's programs are linked]. . . . It is a
> constant issue . . . of trying to keep everybody aligned and informed.

A number of forces push KDE back into its traditional, bureaucratic
behaviors. These forces come from the field as well as from the legislature. One source described the "compliant culture" of Kentucky educators and their long history of looking to the state for directives. A KERA
historian described both the local and the legislative forces that push KDE
to remain bureaucratic:

> This may be unfair, but I think [KDE] has turned back into the kind
> of bureaucracy that we were trying to get rid of. . . . But . . . some of
> that was almost unavoidable because the schools kept insisting that
> the state do things for them. . . . and then that led to someone going
> back and saying, "Well, we really ought to have a regulation for this."
> And . . . people were again looking back to Frankfort . . . which was
> against the philosophy of [KERA]. . . . [So] there were organizational
> pressures put upon [KDE]. [Pressures also came] from the legislators
> who got jumpy, for example, when they got complaints about the
> implementation of the primary program and the complaints of the
> teachers that they didn't know what they were doing. . . . Well, that
> scared a lot of the legislators, and they immediately said to the depart-
> ment, "Get that straightened out." Well, what that means is passing a
> regulation. And so trying . . . to be responsive to the legislature while
> at the same time trying to carry out a philosophy of being in a support
> role . . . just didn't square.

KDE has learned to be more service oriented and model many of the practices it wants educators to emulate. However, it has not learned how to
pull together as an institution; nor has it learned to overcome the forces
that lead it away from the vision of a decentralized, service-oriented
agency.

This raises the question of whether such learning is possible for state
departments of education. Timar, Kirp, and Kirst (1998) raise serious
questions as to whether or not state departments of education can ever
sustain these far-reaching reforms given their political and institutional

contexts: "The central problem . . . is whether existing institutional roles and relationships are consonant with the magnitude of change reformers envision. Is the current infrastructure that supports policy change capable of sustaining large scale change?" (p. 4). Timar et al. point out that the number of state department of education staff members has dwindled over the past fifteen years and that "the state role is often defined by budgetary considerations rather than a self-conscious effort to build an institutional architecture that connects state policy goals" (p. 215).

The irony is that systemic reform requires these agencies to play pivotal roles but does nothing to ensure that state departments of education have the capacity to fulfill these roles. State departments charged with implementing systemic reform tend to have fewer people to do more work, rely on targeted funding streams that pull against the cohesion needed to enact the reforms, and have no greater control over the reform agenda than they had in the past.

State departments of education can influence, but not control, the social, political, and institutional forces that surround them. This creates conditions that can be tantamount to running the marathon of systemic reform in weather conditions that change every thirty minutes. Runners can remove their raincoats, but they cannot change the temperature. Whether or not state departments of education have the capacity to complete the marathon is a question that ultimately will be answered by watching these agencies over time. For those of us running the marathon in state agencies, however, it is crucial to learn lessons and strategies from states such as Kentucky, so we can run smarter, faster races and eventually complete the course.

REFERENCES

Boysen, T. C. (1992). *Organization design for the new Kentucky Department of Education*. Frankfort: Kentucky Department of Education.

Cohen, D. K., McLaughlin, M. W., & Talbert, J. E. (1993). *Teaching for understanding*. San Francisco: Jossey-Bass.

Kentucky Institute for Education Research. (1997). *1996 review of research on the Kentucky Education Reform Act (KERA): Executive summary*. Lexington: Author.

Lesser, J. A., & Wilson, S. M. (1999). *The role of state departments of education in complex school reform* [Review of the book]. *Anthropology & Education Quarterly, 30*, 398–400.

Lumsden, R. W. (1999). *The continued reorganization of the Kentucky Department of Education* (Draft No. 1). Unpublished manuscript.

Lusi, S. F. (1997). *The role of state departments of education in complex school reform.* New York: Teachers College Press.

Steffy, B. E. (1993). *The Kentucky education reform: Lessons for America.* Lancaster, PA: Technomic.

Timar, T., Kirp, D., & Kirst, M. (1998, August, Draft). *Institutionalizing mathematics and science reform: Do state education agencies matter?* San Francisco: WestEd.

Weick, K. E. (1976). Educational organizations as loosely coupled systems. *Administrative Science Quarterly, 21* (1) 1–19.

16

ENGAGING PARENTS AND CITIZENS IN SCHOOL REFORM

Robert F. Sexton

PEOPLE WHO WRITE about school reform and people involved in school reform have come to agree that comprehensive reforms like Kentucky's must have support from the larger public to be successful. There is a rapidly growing interest in how the public can be "engaged" or, even better, how the public can assert itself. Because of this and my experience as executive director of the Prichard Committee for Academic Excellence, the editors of this volume asked that I reflect on the role of citizens in Kentucky's school reform experience.

The request that I write this essay invites immodesty. I will acknowledge up front that all citizen engagement in Kentucky education is not driven by the Prichard Committee and that I cannot be a detached observer. I hope that the attention the Prichard Committee has received is not solely because of its endurance. But endurance should not be discounted either. I remember that some military historians saw George Washington as a general without brilliance. His greatest achievement, one wrote, "was keeping his army in the field" (Noland, 2000, p. D3). Those who nurture civic engagement will, I am certain, know that Washington's accomplishment was not a small one.

My experience on the Prichard Committee is the source of these observations, and I make no claims to research beyond that experience. Therefore I tell little here about other engagement efforts, such as parent organizations like the Kentucky Congress of Parents and Teachers, business groups like the Kentucky Chamber of Commerce and the Partnership for Kentucky Schools, or official outreach from the Kentucky Department of Education. Focusing on our own lessons does not presume that the Prichard Committee acted alone. Far from it. Others' support was critical. But I concentrate in this chapter on what I know about: the Prichard Committee.

Engaging Citizens in Reform: The Prichard Committee's Role

The Prichard Committee was established as an independent, private corporation in 1983. Before that, from 1980 until 1983, it was a commission of citizens appointed by the Kentucky Council on Higher Education called the Committee on Higher Education and Kentucky's Future. After they issued their report on higher education, the thirty citizen members of that group, chaired by attorney Edward F. Prichard, decided to re-create the group as an independent organization. They did so out of frustration with the indifference of elected officials toward education and because they felt that Kentucky's historic educational deficits would not solve themselves.

These days, when people discuss "public engagement," they often focus on what schools or school districts need to do. The belief is that school administrators need to reach out to the public, inform the citizenry, and urge consensus around their agendas. A recent Wingspread Conference report provides a good example: "Schools should make continuous efforts and provide endless opportunities to get parents involved—always invite" (Duggan & Holmes, 2000, p. 15).

The Prichard Committee's volunteers were not "invited." They invited themselves. Their approach was from the outside in, not from the inside out. Back in the 1980s the committee fit a model espoused recently by David Mathews (1999): "Those trying to reconnect the public schools and the public by bringing the community's agenda to the schools rather than bringing the schools' agenda to the community will be worth watching. They stand a better chance of returning ownership to the public and benefiting from that reclaimed responsibility in the community" (p. 24).

In 1983 the original members established the Prichard Committee as an independent, nonpartisan, nonprofit corporation and increased their number to about seventy volunteers. They set out to make education quality the central public concern for other Kentuckians. Ed Prichard was fond of saying that the committee's job was to "afflict the comfortable and comfort the afflicted."

Until 1990 the committee's staff consisted of a director (myself) and a secretary. Financial support came entirely from Kentucky businesses, individuals, and, after 1990, national foundations. Funding, not surprisingly, was a constant struggle. As of this writing, the committee itself has a staff of eighteen, plus ninety-five volunteer members, and an extended family(its contact list) of several thousand more.

Before 1990 the committee rallied other citizens, raised Cain about poor-quality education, and made recommendations based on public deliberation. Following the passage of the Kentucky Education Reform Act of 1990 (KERA), the committee's volunteer members decided to carry on and to redesign their agenda. They knew that passing a reform law was one thing—but implementing it in thousands of classrooms quite another. They saw their new job as keeping the public involved and vigilant, promoting the thoughtful implementation of the reform, informing the public and the business community, monitoring the reform's progress, and making recommendations for either additional reforms or for changes in the Kentucky Education Reform Act. This postreform role was vastly different and much harder than complaining about Kentucky's historic deficiencies. "It's easier to throw stones than catch them," said Wade Mountz, the committee's volunteer chair in the late 1980s.

The Prichard Committee is, more than anything else, a citizen voice. It has a staff, offices, publications and the like. But it is, first and foremost, a group of citizens. It cannot, of course, be all citizens or speak for all citizens. However, it can speak for the citizens who voluntarily give it their time, endorsement, encouragement, or financial support. Its extended family is open to all who agree with its stated purpose: the improvement of education for Kentuckians of all ages.

Someone once said that the Prichard Committee translates ideas to the public. This is partly true but not fully accurate. The committee operates at both the grassroots and policy levels, at the top and the bottom, at the same time. Whenever possible, the committee tries to get citizens to do the work themselves. As activists, the volunteer members of the Prichard Committee concluded that the state's seemingly intractable problems in education could not be solved solely through governmental actions. They reasoned that the state also needed a reinvestment in civic capital; their fellow citizens needed to speak up. They were willing to consider new questions and alternatives, to reeducate themselves, and to practice the skills of citizenship, teach those skills to others, and encourage them to use those skills. They decided to take personal responsibility for changing the state's direction in education instead of viewing it as somebody else's job. And they decided to stick with the job over time—to keep their army in the field.

One of the most unusual features of the implementation of Kentucky's school reforms is the presence of this organized public voice. Of course, the period leading up to the 1990 reform required citizen engagement too. Engaged citizens have been central to what has happened in Kentucky education. I will start with an illustration—a real person's story.

If she had grown up during a different time, Karen Jones might have become another nameless victim of low expectations for public education. Instead, she came to symbolize how ordinary citizens used a citizens' school reform lobby and Kentucky's school reform law to demand a better future for themselves and their children.

A native of Kentucky's Appalachian region, Jones was married and bore her first child at age fifteen. Although she managed to stay in high school with support from her parents and in-laws, Jones did not dare dream of college and a career. She held a series of low-wage retail and secretarial jobs. She divorced, remarried, moved to a different region of Kentucky, and gave birth to two more children.

As a young mother, she became a regular volunteer in her children's elementary school yet never thought to question the school's long-standing practices and policies. "I was involved in the [Parents and Teachers Association]," Jones said. "I volunteered on field trips when I could find the time. I was a homeroom mother." On November 15, 1984, Jones assumed a much larger role in shaping Kentucky's system of public education. And in the process, she demonstrated the tremendous power and potential of teaching and mobilizing citizens and parents to be advocates for education.

In 1984 the Prichard Committee decided to organize a statewide town forum to highlight the need for reform and to rally other concerned citizens. Jones volunteered to help set up the forum in her community, one of 145 sessions like it held across Kentucky that night. In the end twenty thousand citizens came together across the state and addressed a single question: What do you want your schools to do? Local organizers recorded more than six thousand individual comments and collected fifteen thousand written statements from participants. The (Louisville) Courier-Journal, the state's largest newspaper, described the event as "the most massive extravaganza for better schools Kentucky has ever seen." The town forums sent politicians a signal that in a state where citizens supposedly did not value education, many people did indeed care (Wilson, 1984).

The forum moved Karen to a new point in her development. She was one of the most inspired students in this 1984 classroom of civic activism.

"That's when I really started understanding that there was more to education than just what happened in your local area," she said. "We had people from other counties come to our town forum. Just sitting there listening to people talk about public education, and nepotism, and all the problems . . . made you do some deep thinking, which as a parent, I had never done before."

Jones stayed involved with the Parents and Teachers Association (PTA) and started taking courses at a community college. She kept in touch with the staff of the Prichard Committee and eight years later, in 1992, was hired as a regional staff member to teach other citizens about the intricacies of school reform. "And, boy, did my life change," she said. "I learned so much." Mainly, her job was to organize and coach local volunteer community committees. The idea was to keep parents and citizens informed and involved as complex reforms unfolded. By 1996 about seventy of these local groups existed, involving about two thousand people. They were supported by seven part-time Prichard Committee regional coordinators—people like Karen Jones.

With encouragement from the Prichard Committee, she also applied to be a "KERA Fellow," one of 250 people trained by the Kentucky Department of Education to understand the reform law's recommendations and spread information throughout the state. Jones says she was the only parent who participated in the training; the rest were educators. "We went through the assessments, and the [academic] expectations, and the performance events," she said. "I sat there and listened to all these wonderful ideas. I was so fortunate to be part of that. I didn't even have a college degree, and I wrote my own rubric and my own [curriculum] unit—a history lesson on Christopher Columbus. Those people worked together with me as a team. It was amazing—the things I learned from them and the things they learned from me as a parent."

While employed by the Prichard Committee, Jones attended college, eventually earning a bachelor's degree in library science. In 1996 she was elected to a three-year term as president of the state PTA. Although she no longer works for the Prichard Committee, Jones continues to use the knowledge she gained from the group to teach other Kentucky parents that they have a right and a responsibility to make sure their children achieve.

"I was truly the at-risk parent. Who would have ever thought I would have amounted to anything?" Jones said. "But I know now what can be accomplished. I've seen the best. I've seen students moved ahead in life because of good teachers. And, by gosh, don't tell me you're satisfied with

what you've got. We should never be satisfied with what we have." Jones had indeed come a long way. "I'm proud of where I came from," she said. "But I know there's so much more that we can do."

Jones's story represents just one part of the citizen engagement picture. In her case, an interested parent armed with good intentions found the encouragement, knowledge, and skills she needed to make a difference. Jones's story is exceptional but not unique.

The expanded story, however, is about building public support and political will to enact reform and to sustain reform over time. "Buying time for the system to ingest the reforms" is the way a friend describes what organized citizens have done since 1990. Kentucky's record shows that a continuous civic voice is critical for implementing reform.

These days, when school reform is discussed, the talk moves quickly to how the public needs to be connected, or reconnected, to the schools. Terms like "public engagement," "constituency building," "public will," and "business involvement" are common. No matter what it is called, the argument is that an engaged and knowledgeable public is essential for successful systemic reforms.

One of the first researchers to focus on independent citizen and business groups was researcher Susan Fuhrman with the Consortium for Policy Research in Education. Her research examined external groups in Kentucky and South Carolina. She argues convincingly that independent external organizations can overcome the four characteristics of the political system that block coherent reform: fragmented organizational structure, election cycles, policy overload, and specialization. Fuhrman (1994) concluded that "the Prichard Committee and the [South Carolina] Business-Education Subcommittee provide many lessons about the role of constituency-bridging groups in building and sustaining support for reform" (p. 6). If experience is a guide, it is true that broad-based citizens' coalitions are essential. Citizens matter. My own firsthand experience confirms Fuhrman's conclusions.

But there is another reason that public engagement is critical to school reforms that are driven by standards, assessment, accountability, and school performance data. The Kentucky reform sets academic standards and measures school (not student) progress. Test data are periodically sent to schools and published in newspapers. Financial awards based on performance are distributed. Students are tested, and the data are provided to teachers and the public, for a serious purpose. It is provided so something will happen. That something, the theory goes, is improved student achievement. It is an old-fashioned democratic ideal: give people knowledge, and in some form or fashion they will react. Reform theorists often talk about this reaction as the schools' responsibility. They are only partly right. We believe the reaction also has to come from voters, taxpayers, parents—the *public* in *public schools*. Part of our strategy has been to help the public react. If their schools get better, they should encourage them; if they do not, they should apply pressure.

As reforms based on standards unfold across the nation, the pivotal importance of information and how citizens and educators use that information becomes more apparent. The report *Testing, Teaching, and Learning* from the National Research Council (1999) points out that successful reform "relies on information and responsibility." The report says, "Everyone in the system—students, parents, teachers, administrators, and policy makers at every level—needs high-quality information about the quality of instruction and student performance. At the same time, everyone needs to be responsible for fulfilling his or her role in improving results. The key is transparency: everyone should know what is expected, what they will be measured on, and what the results imply for what they should do next" (p. 3). Our Kentucky experience confirms this. But how difficult it is to do! In Kentucky this was because parents and the larger public did not know they had this role, and they were not prepared for it. Helping other parents and citizens understand their job and carry it out seemed a logical task for the Prichard Committee.

The importance of a powerful public role in shaping and sustaining school reform in Kentucky cannot be overstated. At ten years old, the Kentucky Education Reform Act is the nation's longest-running model of comprehensive school change. Its tenure owes much to a high degree of citizen commitment and involvement and to successfully representing public views to policymakers. Acting as a surrogate for other citizens, the Prichard Committee achieved results like these:

- ○ Creating a sense of urgency and reminding the public continuously why the reforms were needed

- ○ Persuading the public that reform was a long-term change, not a quick fix, and asking Kentucky citizens for patience, thereby buying time for implementation and adjustments

- ○ Representing the public in state policy discussions, assuming an aggressive monitoring role, and countering the tendency to veer from the reform's original intent

- ○ Helping parents become stronger advocates for their children

○ Reinforcing the commitment of the business community to
   Kentucky's school reforms
○ Keeping the public focused on the big picture

These results are one way to frame a more detailed examination of citizen engagement in Kentucky. Let us look at these results in greater detail.

Helping Kentuckians Remember Reforms Are Needed

Without the public's general support for change, Kentucky's school reform law would not have endured. Across the country education reforms are tossed out when voters and parents fail to see quick and measurable results. Shortly after KERA was passed, Frank Newman, then president of the Education Commission of the States, offered advice I will always remember. "Never forget," Newman said, "that this may be a massive solution for a problem the public doesn't know it has" (personal communication, June 12, 1990). Although there have been significant pressures to abandon school reform in Kentucky, from those who objected on partisan grounds and from educators, the basic model for change remains in place. There was a backlash, but it has not been powerful enough to derail the reform from its basic direction.

Creating a sense of urgency had been the committee's objective in the 1980s. The idea was to build and maintain a movement. After the reform passed, reminding people about the original problem became the challenge. The strategy was to remind people about Kentucky's historically low educational level and inject into the public bloodstream a compelling new vision—that of all children learning at high levels.

The entrenched myth that there had once been a golden age of fine schools had to be debunked. In a 1999 column carried by many of the state's newspapers, I recalled a conversation with a friend who lamented Kentucky's elementary reading problems (Sexton, 1999). "When I was in school in the 1940s, everyone learned to read," he said. We challenged our friend's selective memory: "Kentucky's reading problems have been with us since the beginning of recorded history. Our volunteer group alone has been raising Cain about reading since our first report in 1981," we wrote. "Today, Kentucky schools are teaching a larger portion of the same population to read than they did fifty years ago and a considerably smaller fraction—probably under 20 percent—is not learning to read. But we're saying that number is still too high, even though it's the best Kentucky schools have ever done." The Prichard Committee has also concentrated on making high student achievement the center of public attention. This was the vision of the reform and someone needed to drive it home to the public. In every forum and publication student academic achievement has been the focus.

We have used a variety of tools to teach citizens about school reform, including

- Mass mailings on the responsibilities of school councils and the new state achievement tests
- A toll-free telephone line that enabled anyone in the state to call with a question
- Publications explaining school policies and laws in user-friendly language
- A quarterly newsletter sent to local and state activists
- A monthly column about key reform topics distributed to two hundred newspapers throughout Kentucky
- A series of short radio spots that small stations routinely broadcast
- A network of regional organizers
- A massive parent engagement program—the Commonwealth Institute for Parent Leadership

Between 1990 and 1999 the members and staff of the Prichard Committee made approximately three thousand public appearances before civic and business groups, showcasing successful schools, reminding people of new possibilities, and suggesting alternative policy directions.

Keeping the public focused on the overarching goal of Kentucky's school reforms—academic success for all children—has had the effect of persuading a substantial portion of the public to be patient with the inevitable fits and starts.

Involving the Public in Policy Discussions

Few policymaking bodies involve the public in substantive ways. Obtaining public feedback, much less reaching public consensus, is difficult and time-consuming. But if the entire public cannot be present in person, it must be present in spirit, and that is the role the Prichard Committee has assumed in Kentucky.

In some ways the committee was symbolic and inspirational. As one local activist said, "Seeing you speaking out at the state level shows me we can do it down here" (J. Rosenberg, personal communication, November 12, 1986).)We also used action. We testified and lobbied. We published position papers. Our members and staff served on state boards and commissions. We met regularly with governors, legislators, and education organizations. We held high-visibility forums for candidates. In sum, the committee was directly involved in the legislative and political processes.

After the passage of KERA the committee tried to position itself as an unbiased adviser to anyone who would listen. This was difficult because the committee had supported the reforms in 1990 and was presumed to be biased. It was a "cheerleader," some said. Our goal, though, was to take part in policy discussions so we could suggest continued changes without destroying the reform's fundamental strategies.

As expected, adjustments in the reform were needed. When they were, we wanted to be part of the discussions. We also wanted to influence the pace of the discussions and to see that topics were raised in a nondisruptive way. It is easy to shove complex changes off course, so the pace at which more change is introduced is important. In the case of Kentucky's school reform, it was clear that teachers, for instance, could tolerate only so much change at one time.

We also forced to the surface topics that concerned many citizens. The committee convened task forces on emerging topics or those not initially addressed in the reform law. These included, for example, reading, postsecondary education, early childhood education, teacher preparation and professional development, and more effective use of school time. We held events to highlight topics and stir up interest. For instance, in cooperation with the Partnership for Kentucky Schools, we brought together representatives from about twenty of the state's consistently improved schools to share lessons and demonstrate that such sharing was valuable.

Deep, lasting changes do not just happen. They must be pushed and maintained by people who are invested in, but not directly responsible for, implementing reforms. Through intensive lobbying the Prichard Committee continually reminded state officials that the concerned public was expecting results. At the state level the growing national stature of KERA had the effect of keeping elected officials on their toes. Jacob Adams (1993) noted that the attention steeled "the resolve of Kentucky legislators and other policy makers to stay the course regarding KERA implementation. As one observer described this effect, 'when a nationally prominent figure slaps you on the back and says that Kentucky is the envy of the nation, you walk away anxious to continue the program.'" Adams went on to say that "intangible contributions to reform brokered by the committee," such as those I have described, counterbalanced state and local efforts to scuttle the reform law (p. 27).

Helping Parents Become Strong Advocates for Their Children's Education

KERA carved out a major role for parents by requiring schools to include them on elected school councils responsible for school governance. But the law did not specify how parents should be trained and supported in these new roles. Early in 1991 the committee decided that someone needed to recruit parents to run for school councils and train those elected. Initially the committee planned to recruit and train those parents itself. But it soon became clear that this job was too big and too specialized for a small organization. Our revised strategy was to use our "bully pulpit" to stir up interest in school councils but to encourage others to do the training. That training need was gradually (but never completely) filled by the department of education and by a new organization, the Kentucky Association of School Councils, which was created by Susan Weston, a skillful and determined civic entrepreneur encouraged by the Prichard Committee.

The Prichard Committee was not alone as it encouraged parents. By 1998 almost twelve hundred schools had school councils with substantial powers. With two parents on each council, this meant that 2,400 parents were now in the field, facing considerable new challenges. Over time they constituted a significant statewide force for maintaining school-level decision making, participating in important decisions, such as the hiring of principals.

Likewise, the PTA worked to engage parents in a way that supported reform. Representing approximately five hundred out of about thirteen hundred schools, the PTA encouraged voting in council elections, provided training, and taught parents about reform in its conferences and publications. Unlike some other statewide PTAs in other places, which mobilized opposition to reform, the Kentucky PTA was a positive force for maintaining the Kentucky Education Reform Act on its original trajectory.

In more direct actions the Prichard Committee kept a variety of constituents involved and made it easier for them to participate in their schools. For example, to build a stronger grassroots understanding of school change in the early 1990s, we organized dozens of community committees for education. These local volunteer groups included some of the same volunteers who had been mobilized for the committee's successful 1984 Town Forum on Education.

Another initiative was a carefully packaged and prepared discussion format called "Parents and Teachers Talking Together." These are four-hour dialogues for small groups of teachers and parents, led by a trained volunteer facilitator. Parents and Teachers Talking Together was designed to help school communities move beyond topics that tended to divide teachers and parents and instead find common agendas for school change. The idea was to foster candid and effective face-to-face communication. From 1995 to 1999, more than 7,300 Kentuckians participated in these sessions.

In 1997 we launched the Commonwealth Institute for Parent Leadership, a new strategy for stirring up parent engagement. Bev Raimondo, creator of the institute, said that "we needed to raise expectations for parents just like they were raised for educators" (personal communication, April 17, 1999). Each parent participating in the institute spends a minimum of six days in interactive training that helps them understand Kentucky's academic standards and accountability system so they can explain it to others. They also practice civic engagement skills and develop strong networks with other parents. This training helps parents understand student achievement data and use it to evaluate instructional practices and lead improvement.

One parent from a rural county cites the institute as her inspiration to be an activist in her community. She has served on the school council at her elementary school for six years. "I couldn't have done what I've done without being involved in the Commonwealth Institute. And I say that because it's taught me where the resources are," she said. "I'm a person who hates conflict . . . but once you learn that these are only people and they work for you, you can stand up to them" (Prichard Committee, 1999, p. 4).

Encouraging the Business Community to Support Kentucky's Reforms

Building strategic alliances has always been a Prichard Committee strategy. These existed, formally and informally, with the social service community, academics, the media, other educational groups, and the business community.

The leadership of Kentucky's business community has been committed to improved schools since the early 1980s. Business support was essential to building reform sentiment and later passing the reform act. Ashland Inc., for example, purchased television and radio advertising for the 1984 town forum. The Kentucky Chamber of Commerce and a smaller, elite group of CEOs, the Kentucky Economic Development Corporation, were the most prominent advocates from the business community in the 1980s. The chamber of commerce was at the table as a reform consensus was crafted during the period from 1987 to 1989, and it lobbied hard for the reform's passage in 1990. The chamber continues in that supportive role, helping to ensure a coherent business voice.

Since the early 1990s, however, the most visible business presence has been the national Business Roundtable's Kentucky affiliate, the Partnership for Kentucky Schools. At the national level the Business Roundtable resolved in 1990 to establish state-level advocacy groups, each chaired by a Business Roundtable member. These organizations exist in many states, including Maryland, Washington, and Ohio.

In 1991 the three Kentucky Business Roundtable members, as part of the national initiative, decided to create a Kentucky presence. But what about the Prichard Committee? It already existed, included prominent businesspeople, was financed by business contributors, reached out to business audiences, and established alliances with groups like the chamber of commerce. The committee, though, had never presumed to speak for the business community.

The Business Roundtable's Kentucky initiative could have been either an opportunity or a problem—a well-funded, powerful business leadership group or a scattered and divided enterprise. Opportunity won out. The Prichard Committee's membership overlapped with that of the Partnership for Kentucky Schools, and the committee's history of alliance building meant we were open to working together. From the start, we strategized with the business leaders who were creating the Partnership; they ultimately decided to join forces with the Prichard Committee. The Prichard Committee in turn helped create and incubate the Partnership as a fully independent corporation with its own staff and leadership, sharing office space and support staff with the Prichard Committee.

The inherent messiness of having two separate organizations seemed a small price to pay for a strong business voice. The leaders of the Partnership, from United Parcel Service, Humana, and Ashland Inc., concluded that separate but linked organizations would result in two effective voices, rather than just one. We all decided cooperation, not competition, would benefit everyone.

Through the Partnership, business leaders made a ten-year commitment to support the reform law's implementation by providing timely information, training, and assistance to educators and the public. Their agenda included a multiyear study of professional development, for instance, and building a leadership roundtable on that topic. It also included launching an advertising campaign to help explain the reform, dispatching a school bus outfitted with easy-to-read literature and interactive displays to hundreds of county fairs each year, and giving employees time off to volunteer in their local schools. "Whenever the reform law appeared to be growing more controversial in the halls of the state Capitol, full-page advertisements would almost instantly appear in the state's newspapers reiterating the importance of the law to companies with headquarters in Kentucky—Ashland Inc., Humana, Inc., and United Parcel Service of America, Inc.," wrote reporter Lonnie Harp (1997, p. 116).

The Partnership's business leaders also helped encourage the political and educational communities to maintain a common front. Members of the Partnership included school board members, teachers, school administrators, Kentucky Educational Television, the PTA, legislative leaders, the commissioner of education, and publishers of the state's largest newspapers. The support of some of the state's top business leaders also encouraged smaller companies to keep the faith and push their local schools.

The Partnership for Kentucky Schools, aligned with the Prichard Committee, kept the pressure on state politicians to stick with the state's model of school change. Citizen activists on one side and major corporations on the other acted as a pair of bookends to prop up Kentucky's school reform law. During the 1994 General Assembly, and again in the 1998 General Assembly, this coalition beat back an organized effort to repeal the law. The antireform push had begun in the 1992 legislative session and was similar to the movements against outcomes-based education that had emerged in states like Pennsylvania. By 1994, fueled by national organizations such as Focus on the Family, the backlash effort against reform had enough legislative champions, savvy, and grassroots support to be a serious threat. The most difficult and controversial part of reform, the testing system, was the target. Parental confusion, as well as teacher opposition and misinformation (embodied in statements like "The state won't let me teach your child to spell"), helped fuel the opposition's passion.

Legislative leaders who wanted to stick with the reform needed support. The Prichard Committee and the Partnership teamed up with the Kentucky Chamber of Commerce. Partnership funds were used to hire a full-time lobbyist and organizer. Her efforts generated hundreds of letters to legislators. She organized a student speakers bureau. She used her own considerable reputation to persuade individual legislators. Advertising dollars were used too. Now and then, corporate lobbyists let legislators know where their companies stood. In one volley fifty-five heads of Kentucky's largest businesses, unions, and education groups signed a letter in support of the reforms that ran as a full-page advertisement in newspapers reaching more than one million readers.

Keeping the Focus on Children's Learning

Compared with many other states, Kentucky has been able to debate complex reform topics and not throw out core concepts. The initial focus on all children learning at high levels, via standards, assessment, accountability, and local decision making has, by and large, been maintained. All of the strategies I have mentioned thus far converge at a single point: staying focused. In a rough and general way this focus has been maintained. There has been disagreement. There have been changes. Some legislation has strengthened and some has weakened the initial program. But all in all, the implementation of reform has stayed on the trail that was marked in 1990.

This continued focus has been maintained by several factors: a largely united educational community, a core of committed legislators, continuity of viewpoint in the governor's office, a generally supportive and attentive media, support from mainstream civic organizations, and consistent public support. All of these conditions were present in enough force to maintain focus. All depended on the public and voters. Since the early 1990s, opinion polls have shown that a public plurality supported reform. Although a small portion of the public saw reform as ideal and a smaller portion saw it as evil, most thought that reform would result in better schools. No candidate for governor in the 1991, 1995, or 1999 election made opposition to reform the center of the campaign; opposition was present but guarded. (Both parties' candidates in two of these elections had at one time been members of the Prichard Committee.)

Other strategies helped maintain the focus. Alliances that had been established in the 1980s were nurtured through the 1990s. The media was provided with extensive information. Consistent themes were maintained; distractions were minimized. Bridges were built between political administrations and between leadership transitions in the Kentucky Department of Education. Citizens were at the table when changes, such as those in assessment and accountability, were suggested and made. Radical and destructive changes were countered with less harmful alternatives. New items were added to the reform agenda: teacher preparation and professional development, stronger reading instruction, and early childhood reforms, for example.

The focus was also influenced by research. The committee was not a research organization. It sponsored a few low-budget studies early on, but funding and capacity were inadequate for high-quality research. But research was needed, so the committee decided to play a catalytic role. When it became clear that the Kentucky Department of Education could not establish a research agenda (routine data gathering was inadequate), the committee helped create the Kentucky Institute for Education Research. Keeping that institute strong over time became an important part of our agenda. The committee was also a much used source for other researchers, providing background information, guidance, and encouragement to numerous projects from outside Kentucky. In cooperation with the Partnership for Kentucky Schools, the committee secured foundation support for a major study of professional development.

In short, Kentucky politicians, educators, and the media stayed focused on the ends and the means that were established in 1990. The dominant discussion was about finding solutions within the existing reform framework, not starting over. There were steps forward and steps backward, but compared with reform efforts in many other states, in Kentucky the focus was maintained.

Conclusion

Many people believe that Kentucky's passage of KERA was solely the result of the state supreme court's 1989 decision. This interpretation is too simplistic. A more complex collection of forces was at work through the 1980s, long before the court ruling. These forces set the stage for the ruling and the comprehensive reform that resulted. Conditions were favorable after six years of media and public outrage about the palpable inadequacies of Kentucky's educational system. There was enough public support for a high-stakes political action, a difficult and complex reform, and a large tax increase. The Prichard Committee was a focal point—for many the symbol—of that outrage. Its advocacy fed on the outrage and also reflected it.

But after the reforms were enacted in 1990, the situation changed. There is no point in advocating something unless you are willing to defend it. Outraged people are more passionate advocates than satisfied people. Before 1990 poor schools were the enemy, the source of outrage. After 1990 the reform became the enemy, although for a different outraged constituency.

Advocates and organizers know that maintaining energy can be a problem in the face of defeat—or victory. Somehow, a sufficient number of Kentucky citizens concluded that passing a reform law was not good enough and that classroom improvement would be harder than legislative change. "The dragons are back in their caves," said a parent in 1991. "But they'll come out again" (E. Plattner, personal communication, July 7, 1991). Our experience shows that the public does not rise up to confront dragons easily. Someone has to carry the flag—to organize, synthesize, strategize, bring coherence, keep the focus. That is what the citizens on the Prichard Committee and their like-minded friends have attempted to do.

I conclude with an often asked question: What went well and what went poorly for public engagement in Kentucky reform? We would have hoped for greater gains in these areas:

o *Parent participation.* Parent participation increased, but not enough. About 2,400 parents serve on school councils and many more on council committees. But voter turnout for school council elections (just as for local school board elections) is usually under 10 percent, and parent participation in school activities seems to have increased little.

o *Public awareness.* Too large a portion of the public still knows little or nothing about the reform.

o *Understanding of the concepts.* The concept of absolute academic standards (what a student knows and can do) as opposed to what parents remember (students ranked relative to one another) is still not widely understood.

o *Dissemination of good information.* There is never enough thoughtful, parent-friendly information available, distributed so it competes with the relentless flow of information from the mass media. (I will never forget a woman who, at the peak of the O.J. Simpson trial, was asked by a reporter about the 1995 governor's race. "I don't know who's running," she said. "I've been too busy with O.J." [Sexton, 2000].)

o *Political and policy changes.* Not all political battles were won, and not all policy changes were for the better. In a highly charged political environment it was difficult to make thoughtful midcourse corrections.

o *Response to low student achievement.* Not enough teachers use school performance data to adjust teaching practice, and parents do not respond to poor achievement results as strongly as was hoped initially.

As we reflect on these shortcomings, we have to ask, Were our standards too high? Probably so.

What were the successes? Here are a few:

○ *Sustained focus.* Reform stayed roughly on track; focus was maintained. Transitions in political and educational leadership were bridged.

○ *Public support.* Opinion polls have shown more public support than opposition over the entire decade of the 1990s, with support increasing as time passed.

○ *Lack of successful opposition in the gubernatorial campaign.* In three elections no gubernatorial candidate launched an effective campaign against the reform.

○ *Parent involvement in school-based decision making.* About 2,400 parents serve on school councils, and thousands more serve on school council committees.

○ *Parent education.* Thousands of parents attend training each year as school council members. Through the Commonwealth Institute for Parent Leadership, several hundred parents have mastered the complexities of school achievement data and are working with their teachers to apply that knowledge to improving instruction.

○ *Parent-school partnerships.* There are shining examples of schools that welcome parents.

○ *Strong networking.* A supportive network of several thousand individuals remains active and energized.

○ *Partnership with the business community.* The business community remains committed to the reform's objectives and continues its campaign through the Kentucky Chamber of Commerce and the Partnership for Kentucky Schools.

○ *Media support.* The Kentucky media by and large remains committed to reform.

Engaged citizens and parents matter when controversial and confusing standards-based reforms are implemented. But helping citizens matter is "steady work," to borrow Richard Elmore's phrase (Elmore & McLaughlin, 1988) about school reform itself. Citizens and parents need information, encouragement, and support over the long haul. And they need to keep foremost in their minds the low opinion of Tammany Hall's George Washington Plunkitt concerning the staying power of reform movements: "I can't tell you how many of these movements I've seen started in New York during my 40 years in politics, but I can tell you how many have lasted more than a few years—none. . . . They were like mornin' glories—looked lovely in the mornin' and withered up in a short time, while the regular machines went on flourishin' forever, like fine old oaks" (Riordon, 1963, p. 17).

By the yardstick of comparison with other states, I believe that Kentucky citizens who cared about good schools have done well. Like General Washington, they kept their army in the field.

REFERENCES

Adams, J. E., Jr., (1993). *The Prichard Committee for Academic Excellence: Credible advocacy for Kentucky schools*. Philadelphia: Consortium for Policy Research in Education.

Duggan, T., & Holmes, M. (2000). *Closing the gap*. Washington, DC: Council for Basic Education.

Elmore, R., & McLaughlin, M. W. (1988). *Steady work: Policy, practice and the reform of American education*. Santa Monica, CA: RAND.

Fuhrman, S. (1994). *Politics and systemic education reform* (Policy Brief). Philadelphia: Consortium for Policy Research in Education.

Harp, L. (1997). No place to go but up. *Quality counts*. Washington, DC: Editorial Projects in Education.

Mathews, D. (1999). Whose schools? Reconnecting the public and public schools. *American School Board Journal*, June, pp. 22–24.

National Research Council. (1999). *Testing, teaching, and learning: A guide for states and school districts*. Committee on Title I testing and Assessment, R. F. Elmore, R. Rothman (Eds.). Board on Testing and Assessment, Commission on Behavioral and Social Sciences and Education. Washington, DC: National Academy Press.

Noland, T. E., Jr. (2000, January 2). Washington, Lincoln and Lee. *The (Louisville) Courier-Journal*, p. D3.

Prichard Committee for Academic Excellence. (1999, November). Commonwealth Institute propels parents into powerful position. *Parent leader* 1 (2), 4.

Riordon, W. L. (1963). *Plunkitt of Tammany Hall*. New York: Dutton.

Sexton, R. F. (1999, September). Fighting illiteracy in Kentucky schools. *Changes in our schools*. Lexington, KY: Prichard Committee for Academic Excellence.

Sexton, R. F. (2000). Whose poor scores are they? *Changes in our schools*. Lexington, KY: Prichard Committee for Academic Excellence.

Wilson, R. (1984). One Warren official said, "I think (the forum) will bring into focus the value of schools to a community." *The (Louisville) Courier-Journal*, p. B1.

17

A PARENT'S VIEWPOINT

"IT'S GOING TO TAKE A
WHOLE LOT OF PEOPLE TO DO IT"

Holly Holland

IN 1990, WHEN JUDY KASEY first heard about the Kentucky Education Reform Act (KERA), she felt hopeful that her children and other public school students would soon benefit from the plan's bold pronouncements. The multiage primary school program and its promise of active, hands-on learning seemed a good idea to a mother who had enrolled her children in one of Louisville's most progressive public schools. As a regular school volunteer, she also felt inspired by the reform law's call for greater parent involvement in everything from school governance to homework assistance.

She remembers attending an informational meeting in Louisville sponsored by the Prichard Committee for Academic Excellence. A panel of speakers, including new education commissioner Thomas C. Boysen, discussed the reforms, and Kasey became energized when he described the important new roles for parents in helping to ensure that all children succeeded in school.

"There was a sense of excitement because it seemed so right," Kasey said. "I tried writing articles for the school newsletter so parents could learn about it because I knew I couldn't begin to effect the changes on my own; people needed to be informed if anything was going to happen at all."

What Kasey didn't anticipate, however, was the widespread resistance from educators in Kentucky's largest school district. Headed by the onetime national Superintendent of the Year, leaders of the Jefferson County (Louisville) Public Schools considered themselves a cut above their counterparts throughout much of the state. Over the years, Jefferson County had hired a large number of national education consultants to lead workshops for teachers—although these limited training sessions rarely led to substantive changes in classrooms. The school system also had pioneered a highly regarded shared governance model, known as participatory management, which involved a partnership between the teachers' union and the administration. Because they had fought so hard to be involved in school governance, Jefferson County's teachers were concerned that they might lose some of those rights under Kentucky's school council setup.

In the first few years after the passage of Kentucky's school reform law, many people in Jefferson County paid little attention to the new directives. The state's accountability system, which distributed rewards and sanctions based on school performance standards, forced them to take notice. Over several testing cycles it became clear that Jefferson County wasn't a cut above the rest of the state—it was home to some of Kentucky's worst schools.

But back in the early 1990s these developments weren't clear to Judy Kasey, a homemaker, mother of three, and Parent-Teacher-Student Association board member at the J. Graham Brown School. This K–12 school had opened in 1972 as a haven for self-motivated students who chafed under the highly structured, authoritarian classroom model typical of the time. Teachers and students communicated on a first-name basis, and teachers had a great deal of freedom to choose their own curriculum. Based on their early understanding of KERA, many of Brown's teachers thought the reform law would lend support to their progressive education practices. Later they complained that the state's high-stakes accountability provisions required so much paperwork and so many checks on their course content that they had few opportunities to make professional judgments about instruction (Holland, 1997).

One of Kasey's first indications that Brown was not eager to jump on the state's bandwagon was the faculty's initial decision to reject the school council model. Until July 1996 Kentucky did not require all schools to establish a council (which consisted of a principal, three teachers, and two parent representatives). Two-thirds of the teachers in each school had to vote to accept the new format. After 1996, faculties could opt out only if they had met the state's performance goals for the previous biennium.

At Brown, Kasey said, former principal Lennie Hay's efforts to demonstrate the benefits of the state's reform model included bringing in the executive director of the Kentucky Association of School Councils (KASC) to speak to teachers and parents about the self-governance format. Kasey, who served on Brown's participatory management committee and later on the board of directors of KASC, said she began to realize the importance of forming a school council at Brown. In her view participatory management seemed to focus more on resolving differences between teachers and administrators whereas the school council setup encouraged faculties to take a tougher look at their instructional practices and determine if they were making the best decisions to improve student achievement. But that distinction was not clear to many people at the time. It was difficult for teachers to vote to make the switch from a model they knew to the time-consuming process of establishing new bylaws and policies while simultaneously learning how to respond to a slew of state mandates. Jefferson County school leaders compounded the challenge by doing a generally poor job of helping faculties understand the rights and responsibilities of councils.

Once Brown's faculty adopted the school council model in 1994, some underlying tensions surfaced. Kasey, who was elected to serve on Brown's first school council, soon became involved in education issues statewide by participating in activities sponsored by the Prichard Committee for Academic Excellence. She joined the first class of the Prichard Committee's Commonwealth Institute for Parent Leadership, which helps parents understand the state's education reforms and work to integrate them into their children's schools. In 1999 she was invited to join the Prichard Committee.

As she attended meetings throughout Kentucky, Kasey said, she gained a firmer grasp of the education reform law's purpose and realized how slowly Brown's faculty was responding to the recommended changes. Traveling around the state, she said, "really did start opening my eyes to a bigger picture. I guess it helped me see things beyond my own children's school or my own children's community. It was discouraging, though, because I'd come back home and not see these things happening, or if they were happening, they certainly weren't being done with the same degree of enthusiasm as in other places.

"And honestly, I hold the leadership of our [school] district responsible in large part for that. They were, and still are I believe, struggling with their new advisory role. I don't think they were willing to relinquish control so they could help an individual school learn to self-govern. Part of it is financial, I'm sure, but it's my sense that they continue to resist these changes and, instead, strive to put their own spin on things. At least that's how I see it. I believe our children—as well as parents and teachers—suffer as a result of this resistance at the top."

At Brown, Kasey said, some teachers seemed to be trying very hard to improve their instruction, but others ignored the state's recommendations altogether. She mentioned asking one teacher about plans to incorporate the state's recommended subject content into children's lessons. "And this teacher said, 'I don't *teach* the core content.' I'm staring with my mouth open," Kasey recalled. "This is a good teacher! There was just this dismissive tone."

Another time, Kasey and other parents joined with the school's teachers and an outside education specialist to learn how to help students revise the writing portfolios Kentucky requires as part of its annual assessments. The training was designed to encourage a writing process that involves multiple drafts, feedback, and revisions. It also conveyed the need to hold students to high standards. As part of their pledge to help, the parents invested time at school and at home asking children questions aimed at stimulating their thinking, such as, "Who is the audience for this paper?" and "What is the evidence to support your position?"

Kasey said parents later were disappointed to find that some teachers had not taken the training to heart. They continued bunching up the writing assignments near the state's portfolio deadline, providing limited feedback to students, and expecting few revisions beyond the first draft. To Kasey the process was another example of an intended school-family partnership that did not live up to expectations.

Brown's faculty paid a heavy price for resisting such changes. In 1994 the state assigned a distinguished educator to work with the high school teachers after Brown failed to meet its performance standards. And in 1996, when the middle school fell from the rewards (the top) category to the crisis (the bottom) category from one testing cycle to the next, the state assigned a second distinguished educator to evaluate and coach the staff. Although some of Brown's teachers praised these interventions for helping them examine their practices and make improvements, others attacked the accountability measures and the distinguished educators who sought to enforce them (Holland, 1997).

Kasey believes many teachers and administrators in Jefferson County misunderstood the KERA mandate for full collaboration with parents and viewed increased parent involvement as interference. Although she recognizes that working with committees is difficult and that educators might be justified in wondering whether parents will commit to following through on their proposals, Kasey says schools must do whatever it takes to help children.

"I don't think any one group can do it alone," she said. "I don't think the principals or the superintendent can. The teachers and parents certainly can't. I think it's going to be a lot of people working together and appreciating the skills of one another. . . . If you're going to make those sweeping reforms, it's going to take a whole lot of people to do it."

Looking back, Kasey realizes some of Brown's growing pains probably resulted from the tensions that follow rapid change. She has been heartened by recent efforts to improve the relationship between the faculty and parents—and the potential for boosting student achievement. Earlier this year, for example, parents from the Commonwealth Institute for Parent Leadership, the school council, and the Parent-Teacher-Student Association all worked with the faculty to weave family involvement initiatives into the school's consolidated plan, making them integral parts of the plan rather than add-on projects to which people may or may not respond. To Kasey this emerging partnership represents a huge stride from where things stood a decade before.

"These latest changes are really exciting," she said. "I have been working so long for parents to be viewed as partners in education. And other people have, too. What really excites me is that because we've embedded this in the consolidated plan, it's not going to die on the vine. That's really, really nice. So it doesn't matter if we stay or go—other people will be here. The collaboration will continue."

REFERENCE

Holland, H. (1997). Brown vs. the department of education. *Louisville* magazine.

CONCLUSION

INSIGHTS FROM A DECADE OF SCHOOL REFORM

Roger S. Pankratz, Joseph M. Petrosko

THE PASSAGE OF the Kentucky Education Reform Act of 1990 (KERA) was a critical event in Kentucky history. It marked an unparalleled commitment to elementary and secondary schools in a state that had previously ranked near the bottom on almost every indicator of educational accomplishment. Although improvements during the past ten years have not met all expectations, there is clear evidence of progress. The majority of the reform structures and processes created in 1990 are still in place a decade later, demonstrating that Kentuckians have put a much higher priority on education than in years past. They have chosen to learn from the successes and failures and to continue improving teaching and learning for future generations.

A majority of educators who bore the brunt of the work of putting KERA's initiatives in place acknowledge that it was a difficult and stressful time they would not wish to repeat. Some teachers and administrators responded by leaving the profession. Yet significant numbers of educators have labeled the decade of the 1990s as a time of personal and professional growth.

The chapters in this book contain reflections about the critical events of the nation's most comprehensive statewide plan to improve public schools. The writers were charged with examining the intended and unintended consequences of Kentucky's reform law and sharing information about policies and practices that can improve or impede the ability of all children to learn at higher levels. Based on the collective findings, the editors of this book will highlight some of the most important lessons from the Kentucky experience.

> INSIGHT 1: Persuading government leaders and power brokers that their actions will benefit society is critical to gaining the commitments, compromises, and decisions needed to enact difficult but desirable reforms.

Kentucky's education reforms stemmed from several politically unpopular actions: suing legislative leaders, the governor, and top state education officials because they failed to provide an efficient and equitable education for all children; striking down all laws creating common schools and ordering the General Assembly to re-create Kentucky's schools in a single year; asserting that past efforts of the legislative and education establishments were woefully inadequate; and proposing to raise taxes to improve education for all children. Despite the controversy and the potential political fallout, key individuals in the Kentucky courts, the governor's office, and the legislature persevered to push reform ahead. And on April 11, 1990, when Governor Wallace Wilkinson signed House Bill 940, Judge Corns, Judge Stephens, and legislative leaders from both the House and Senate were convinced that their roles in this great achievement had been the most critical. That belief—and their subsequent commitment to KERA—gave leaders from all three branches of government strong feelings of ownership and personal pride in the law.

It is important to recognize the courage and leadership demonstrated by the judges, the governor, and the lawmakers. But it is equally important to recognize the staff members and other people who worked behind the scenes to see to it that difficult and unpopular decisions were made. If Arnold Guess had not reminded former governor Bert Combs of his obligation to the poor children of eastern Kentucky, there might not have been a lawsuit. If Kern Alexander had not developed such a compelling and persuasive financial analysis demonstrating the huge disparities in funding among Kentucky's public schools, Judge Corns and Judge Stephens might not have had a factual basis for their bold rulings. If Representative Greg Stumbo had not persuaded Governor Wilkinson that he would lose his chance to reform Kentucky's schools unless he agreed to compromise on the $.01 sales tax, House Bill 940 might not have survived. If Speaker of the House Don Blandford had not taken personal responsibility for shepherding the reform package through the General Assembly, he might not have called a critical legislative recess to thwart an amendment that would have scuttled the reforms.

Time and again, these players made critical choices because they believed their actions would help Kentucky's children. In addition, they were advised by people in support roles who understood the importance of sharing ownership of a common goal—the opportunity for all children to have an adequate education.

> INSIGHT 2: Providing an "adequate education" for all students requires more than creating a fairer system of distributing state and local tax dollars to schools. It also depends on the state's ability to use financial resources and professional support to promote higher academic achievement and greater educational accountability.

As Adams points out in Chapter Two, the new Support Education Excellence in Kentucky program, which distributes financial resources to schools, has narrowed the gap between the poorest and most affluent districts. This represents real progress in creating a more equitable system of public education. However, as Adams also noted, the marginal increases in base funding will never be sufficient to address what the Kentucky Supreme Court defined as educational adequacy. Both Judge Corns and Judge Stephens ruled that an adequate education for every child must include seven learned capacities (Loftus, 1989, p. A13). This "transforms school finance into a catalyst for student performance, linking school finance to the fundamental purposes of education" (p. 42).

Although Kentucky has moved closer to financial equity in education, it must do more. Legislators, educators, parents, and citizens should examine existing policies to ensure that they are achieving maximum results. Adams recommends experimenting with different forms of school-based budgeting and linking finances to education programs. The legislative Task Force on Education Reform, which designed KERA, asserted that "the school should be the primary unit of measurement" (Legislative Research Commission, 1990, p. 16). This focus on schools, instead of school districts, as the center of financial distribution and spending might place Kentucky once again on the cutting edge of advancing the notion of educational adequacy. Tying costs to performance—to what it takes to achieve adequacy—is critical. States must invest in the research and development to get this done, or they will never know how to invest in adequacy.

> INSIGHT 3: To keep education reform on track the designers of the various initiatives must regularly communicate their intentions to the people charged with implementing them, and the practitioners must provide ongoing feedback about the outcomes.

The legislative Task Force on Education Reform employed expert consultants in curriculum, governance, and finance to create a new blueprint for education in Kentucky. House Bill 940 charged the Council on School Performance Standards with defining six school goals to guide assessment and curriculum development and authorized national experts to design Kentucky's system of performance assessment. KERA also created a new state department of education to implement the designs. However, it did not link the architects of the reform initiatives with those who had responsibility for implementing them. As a result, the purpose and intended structure of various components often were not communicated to the practitioners or the public.

A prime example was the failure of many teachers and parents to understand the purpose of the ungraded primary school program, which aimed to provide continuous progress for all children and ensure that they gained basic academic skills. Instead, many parents believed the recommended multiage groupings would hold back the best students and simplify the curriculum for everyone.

The inclusion of noncognitive indicators of school success was another example of an important idea that failed to reach its potential. David Hornbeck, curriculum consultant to the Task Force on Education Reform, believed that removing the barriers to learning would make it possible for all children to achieve, especially those with excessive absences and physical or mental conditions that put them at risk of failure. Initiatives such as improved school attendance, family resource centers, and extended school services were some of the legislative responses. But the successful models that Hornbeck had in mind were not communicated to the implementers of these new initiatives.

A third example of where better communication between the designers and the implementers might have improved the results concerns the curriculum framework. The original academic expectations that defined what all students should know were created over the first eighteen months of KERA by the Council on School Performance Standards and eleven task forces composed of 125 public school, department of education, and university professionals. In December 1991 the council and task forces presented to the State Board for Elementary and Secondary Education a technical report describing the seventy-five key concepts students should know, then the council and task forces disbanded. During the next eighteen months a different group of people created the framework that was to guide the development of curriculum in schools. As a result, the materials that filtered down to teachers for the most part did not build on the work begun by the council and task forces. Former members of the Council on School Performance Standards believe there would have been more continuity if the creators of the framework had communicated more with the practitioners, especially regarding the goals of thinking, problem solving, and integration of knowledge (Foster, 1999, pp. 235–236). One of the authors of this chapter served as executive director of the Council on School Performance Standards and can corroborate this belief.

A fourth example concerns the implementation of the Kentucky Instructional Results Information System (KIRIS), the state testing and accountability system. Five national consultants designed the system. Afterward they turned the plan over to a private contractor and the department of education. The five consultants as a group did not review the progress of implementation, share insights, or make recommendations. As a result, schools did not know how to develop the continuous, authentic assessments envisioned by KERA's designers.

How much involvement and what role the designers of the reform should have had is speculative. But policymakers in Kentucky who have monitored the implementation of KERA believe that more continuity between the design and the follow-through might have produced outcomes more in line with what the framers of KERA envisioned as the central purpose of school reform.

INSIGHT 4: Performance assessment and school accountability can be powerful forces for improving student learning.

Chapter Five makes a strong case that KIRIS has led to meaningful change in Kentucky. At the same time, it has carried a high price tag. KIRIS has been the single most controversial feature of Kentucky's reform law. For example, between January 1997 and April 1998, when legislators were debating revisions in the law, the Kentucky Department of Education clipped more than four hundred articles from the state's leading newspapers about the accountability system—many of them negative—to share with key staff members to monitor public and press reaction.

The precise effects of KIRIS have been debated. However, most observers would credit the assessment and accountability systems with motivating educators to focus on improving learning for all children. Although some schools have been far more successful than others in helping all students learn at higher levels, white children have improved more than African American children, and females have made more progress than males (Smith, 1997; Johnson, 1998). Nevertheless, many educators and researchers believe that, in general, students are writing more and thinking at higher levels than before KERA.

It should be noted that after more than a year of fierce debate in 1997 and 1998, the legislature created a new assessment, the Commonwealth Accountability Testing System (CATS). However, performance assessment and school accountability remain the foundation of CATS because both policymakers and educators believe these components will continue to improve teaching and learning in Kentucky.

> INSIGHT 5: In addition to setting high academic standards and designing sophisticated assessment and accountability systems, states must commit substantial resources to curriculum development and professional training if they expect to achieve significant increases in learning.

The designers of KERA believed that if they defined learning goals in measurable terms, developed performance-based assessments, and held schools accountable for improving student performance, teachers and administrators would find a way to realign their curricula to address these standards. KERA clearly stated that local schools would decide the curricula and that the state would design the testing measures. The problem was that few resources were available at the state level for helping educators to learn how to match the curricula to the assessments.

A 1995 statewide research study showed that school practitioners wanted much more clarity from the state about what students should know and be able to do at each grade level (Wilkerson & Associates, 1995). Over the past ten years it has become apparent that most schools and school districts do not have the resources or the time to redesign curricula. They need outside assistance. Schools that have acquired the leadership expertise and funds to conduct ongoing alignment of curriculum with Kentucky's core content for assessment achieved the best results. Teachers and administrators of schools that have consistently improved their test scores confirm that building a curriculum that engages students in in-depth learning requires a high level of professional effort for most schools. In most cases local leadership and outside expertise have been essential to significantly changing classroom experiences. However, expert resources for curriculum alignment and development have been limited. This was especially true in the early years of KERA.

A repeated finding in the 1990s in Kentucky was that faculty at schools judged to be successful and faculty at schools judged to be unsuccessful were both working hard but getting different results. In 1999, when the Prichard Committee for Academic Excellence assembled teachers, parents, principals, and superintendents of twenty-one of the thirty-eight schools in that state that had received rewards in each testing cycle, the organizers found that most of the schools went well beyond superficial coverage; they were well into the process of thinking through how to actually teach the different topics and judge whether students had met the standards (David, 1999). Likewise, when distinguished educators were deployed to work with underperforming schools, they found that superficial attention to curriculum alignment was a common problem (David, Kannapel, & McDiarmid, in press). Working harder is not the answer. Schools that continually earn rewards work smarter.

> INSIGHT 6: Unless educators have "adequate time" to develop different instructional and assessment methods, they will intentionally or unintentionally impede mandated education reforms.

Two major initiatives, KIRIS and the ungraded primary school program, suffered greatly because Kentucky leaders expected too much too soon. In both cases the time lines for implementation were unreasonable, and this had negative consequences.

In the first instance the department of education made the decision to implement a statewide, performance-based assessment system on an accelerated schedule. House Bill 940 required the new system to be in place by 1996, but the system was fully operational by 1994, with rewards dispersed to successful schools and intervention strategies used with schools "in crisis." Kentucky's new assessment system included the creation of tests in five (eventually seven) content areas as well as writing portfolios, open-response items, and performance events that required students to demonstrate their understanding of key concepts. The state collected baseline data for the high-stakes accountability provisions in 1992. Getting such a complex and innovative system running in record time was remarkable and unprecedented nationwide, but the downside was that Kentucky did not spend enough time testing different elements of the system and making proper adjustments. Because of the high stakes involved, educators immediately questioned the validity and reliability of the tests.

After five years of controversy over KIRIS and three independent evaluations by national experts, public confidence in the system had completely eroded. The 1998 General Assembly ordered a complete revision of Kentucky's tests, establishing new baselines of performance. The designers of the new system, CATS, benefited from the rich experiential data from the first eight years. Yet assessment experts, educators, and policymakers agree that Kentucky would be farther ahead if the Kentucky Department of Education had taken the time to test the former system before using it as the foundation for high-stakes accountability provisions.

In the case of the ungraded primary school program, the initial plan developed by the Kentucky Department of Education called for the new multiage, multiability elementary schools to be "fully implemented" in the 1995–96 school year. This new teaching configuration required not only a significant reorganization of classrooms but also a different way of thinking about the continuous progress of individual students. Because there were no other statewide models of multiage groupings, Kentucky had to implement an innovative and ambitious mandate without a guide or a transition period from the old to the new. Concerned that educators would not take the initiative seriously, the 1992 General Assembly amended the law to move implementation up a full two years earlier than originally scheduled. Ready or not, many elementary schools had to regroup kindergarten through third-grade students with little understanding of why they were doing it or how multiage, multiability classrooms might increase learning. In addition, although they might have been expected to be among the primary school program's biggest supporters, parents were so confused about the new arrangements that many jumped to the opponents' camp.

Statewide surveys in 1994 through 1996 showed that the primary program was widely unpopular, particularly with fourth-grade teachers who believed it left students unprepared for the state tests (Wilkerson & Associates, 1994, 1995, 1997). Complaints from teachers and parents increased, and many of the criticisms reached the ears of legislators. In 1994 the General Assembly amended KERA to allow each school council to choose the multiage groupings it considered best for students. As mentioned in Chapter Seven, a 1999 survey found that only 5 percent of primary school programs in Kentucky had an age span of three or more years, 71 percent had only two age groups in one classroom, and 24 percent had returned to predominantly single-age groupings (KDE, 1999). Clearly, the design intended by KERA's chief authors has not been implemented statewide. Proponents of Kentucky's primary school program are convinced that given more time to explain and try out new strategies for continuous assessment and grouping of students, schools might have had very different results.

INSIGHT 7: Ongoing dialogue and collaboration between
researchers, policymakers, and school practitioners can be
a productive strategy for overcoming barriers to effective
implementation of education reform, especially in regard
to designing better professional development practices.

In chapter Nine, McDiarmid and Corcoran describe the conditions that made it difficult to introduce more productive forms of professional development in Kentucky schools. For one thing, KERA's authors assumed that defining what students should know and be able to do was sufficient information for teachers to understand how to change their instructional practices. Also, the framers of KERA assumed that by creating a market economy (a high demand for services and more money for professional development), they would spur the growth of high-quality training programs and technical assistance. Neither expectation was fulfilled. Defining what students should know was not sufficient to show teachers what they needed to know. And making more money available for professional development did not lead to the creation of high-quality training.

In spite of these limitations, over time groups have worked to fill in the gaps. Through a project initiated by the Prichard Committee for Academic Excellence and funded by the Pew Charitable Trusts and the Partnership for Kentucky Schools, researchers (including the authors of this chapter) have brought their findings to a forum consisting of legislators, state department of education officials, university professors, and school leaders. The ongoing dialogue, followed by responsive actions, has spurred the creation of more innovative models of professional development designed to help teachers adopt new strategies. Slowly, these efforts are changing the nature of professional development in Kentucky.

> INSIGHT 8: Targeted intervention to assist schools with declining achievement scores can be highly effective in focusing their attention on measures that improve student test scores. However, the impact of the intervention depends on a good match between the skills of the consultant and needs of the school, as well as the intensity and duration of the assistance.

In Chapter Ten Kannapel and Coe describe the effects of Kentucky's distinguished educator program (now the highly skilled educator program) on the improved performance of schools with declining test scores. This program is KERA's primary vehicle for providing direct and focused assistance to underperforming schools. With some exceptions the program has been so successful that the department of education has created the Kentucky Leadership Academy to share proven and promising practices with school leaders across the state.

Since the beginning of the distinguished educator program in 1992, more than 200 people have been selected and trained. Of these, more than 150 have been deployed to about three hundred schools around the state. Experiments with focused, high-quality technical assistance to schools have been very promising but also very expensive. Kentucky currently employs fifty-eight highly skilled educators at an average annual salary of $81,100 (D. Allen of KDE, personal communication, March 22, 2000). State officials are not able to predict the number of highly skilled educators they will need to serve schools in the next decade, but they will be under pressure to show that past expenditures have paid off in higher student achievement.

The authors of Chapter Ten suggest making more careful matches between distinguished educators and the schools they serve and taking into account the specialist's length of service and the school's specific needs. They also suggest finding ways to minimize the amount of fear and suspicion between highly skilled educators and school staffs. Given the cost of the highly skilled educator program, the authors of Chapter Ten also recommend that the state consider offering varying levels of assistance along a continuum from the intensive assistance of a highly skilled educator to the less intensive, less expensive assistance of the Kentucky Leadership Academy.

> INSIGHT 9: Addressing issues of teacher quality and preparation are essential to ensuring that all children learn at high levels, and strong leadership is needed to implement new policies and programs that compete with the self-interest of educators who are required to implement the changes.

After a decade under KERA it has become more clear that school leadership and teacher quality can lead to successful schools, especially in the case of schools that serve children from poor families. Because results show teachers do make a difference, the Prichard Committee for Academic Excellence has put a high priority on ensuring the presence of a highly qualified teacher in every classroom (Honeycutt, 2000, pp. B1, B13). To accomplish this Kentucky has adopted higher standards for new teachers and is considering raising standards for practicing teachers. However, as two governors' task forces discovered in 1993–94 and 1999–2000 when their efforts were opposed by organized teacher groups, raising standards threatens teacher security. In both instances advocates of teacher quality were surprised that their proposals were not supported by school leaders, teacher educators, or classroom teachers. Although most people believe that improving teacher quality and raising teacher standards are important, they have not figured out how to counter the self-interest of groups that must implement the changes. School districts and states that expect higher levels of performance from all children must address teacher quality as an integral part of the reform program. However, they must also be prepared to work through issues of higher teaching standards that run counter to the self-interest of educators and teacher educators.

INSIGHT 10: Education reform works best when it blends the strengths of past practice with the potential of new initiatives.

Mandating that all employees of the old Kentucky Department of Education would have to reapply for their jobs under the leadership of a new, appointed commissioner sent a message to many Kentuckians that nothing from the past was worth preserving. As time went on, it became clear that those who refined past practices and added new initiatives, while keeping in mind the purpose of the innovations, were far more successful than those who pushed for radical changes or did nothing new. Educators who believed KERA was a top-down mandate to do away with traditional professional practices were more likely to feel threatened, become resistant, and undermine the framers' intentions. In the early years of KERA many false rumors circulated: that teachers could not group students in certain ways, that teachers no longer should teach spelling and punctuation, that students would not take multiple-choice tests, that teachers were required to focus on students with the lowest level of ability.

Researchers who have studied elementary, middle, and high schools over time (Craig & Kacer, 1999; Petrosko, 1999) have found that schools that produce higher test scores continue to teach the basic skills, use different types of assessments, and group and regroup students in ways they believe produce the best learning environment. In other words, the most successful school leaders and teachers use their professional judgment to identify what to keep, what to discard, and what new practices to adopt. They blend the old with the new and help their colleagues feel less threatened by change.

INSIGHT 11: Site-based decision making gives teachers and parents more ownership of and responsibility for their schools but requires strong democratic leadership and preparation for new roles for schools and districts.

As David points out in Chapter Fourteen, the Kentucky school council arrangement is only one model for shared decision making. The designers of KERA expected school councils to have a much greater influence over school curricula. This has not happened to the degree hoped for. However, KERA's mandate for school councils has brought more teachers and parents into school decision making than ever before, and many councils are focusing on planning for improvement and selecting high-quality school leaders. Successful changes are characterized by two main elements. One is the ability of the principal, as leader of the council, to use democratic processes and keep members focused on teaching and learning. Another is mutual respect for and understanding of the roles and responsibilities of council members, school boards, and school district officials. KERA changed the roles of the local board of education, the district superintendent, and the central office staff but did not redefine these roles sufficiently. The shift in power away from the centralized bureaucracy to the local school has created contentious relationships in many communities. In some instances, however, school councils and school districts have found ways to delegate responsibilities and create support for common goals. Decentralized governance takes considerable time, but it presents many opportunities for district and school leaders to learn different ways of working together.

INSIGHT 12: Organized citizen and business groups can help sustain reform and counter attempts by opponents who want to weaken or sabotage changes.

The Prichard Committee for Academic Excellence grew to be a recognized force in advancing public education in Kentucky. Under the leadership of Executive Director Robert F. Sexton (author of Chapter Sixteen), a support group for KERA, the Partnership for Kentucky Schools, was formed with about twenty business partners, including the chief executive officers of Humana, Ashland, Inc., and United Parcel Service. The Prichard Committee used grassroots support, coupled with an aggressive public relations campaign through the new Partnership for Kentucky Schools, to advance the cause of education reform. In addition, these groups generated funds from private foundations whose resources enabled people around the country to learn from the extensive research conducted on KERA.

Although the Prichard Committee and the Partnership for Kentucky Schools have served a variety of functions, none has been more important than influencing policymakers to stay the course of reform in the face of strong opposition. Kentucky has had the longest sustained statewide school reform in the country. Most researchers, educators, and policymakers in Kentucky would agree that a key ingredient has been the organized citizen and business support for change. Other states may not be able to duplicate what the Prichard Committee and the Partnership for Kentucky Schools have done for Kentucky. But certainly they can learn from the successful practices of these two groups.

IF YOU HAVE JUST FINISHED reading the twelve insights set forth in this chapter, you may be wondering, "So what?" Or if you have turned to the back of this book to read "the bottom line," you are likely looking to see whether KERA was judged a success or a failure.

Four of our insights were derived from successes in KERA: insights 1 (the important role of key individuals in initiating reform), 4 (the power of assessment and accountability for improving performance), 8 (the effectiveness of positive school interventions to assist failing schools), and 12 (the strength of support from citizens and business groups to sustain education reforms). Three insights—2 (an "adequate education" is more than equity of resources), 7 (sharing research with practitioners and policymakers can transform professional development), and 11 (shared school governance can increase ownership but requires new roles and relationships)— were drawn from chapters in which the authors reported both successes and failures of KERA initiatives. The remaining five insights—3 (communication between the designers and implementers of reform is important to achieve the intended outcomes), 5 (accountability must be balanced with resources for curriculum development for improved school performance), 6 (mandating reform without time to develop new strategies often impedes progress), 9 (addressing issues of teacher quality is essential to improved school performance), and 10 (progress of school reform is enhanced by blending past strengths with new initiatives)—resulted from experiences with reform initiatives that failed to meet policymakers' or educators' expectations.

For readers who want or need a summary evaluation of KERA over the past ten years, we offer the following response. The improvement of test scores, the positive results in schools that received state assistance, and the continued support for schools by key citizen groups, parents, educators, and policymakers all provide evidence that Kentucky has made progress toward the goal of achieving high levels of learning for all children. Although the results have not been what the designers of the reforms expected or what many Kentucky educators hoped for, the progress is a matter of record. As for the mistakes and failures, these too can represent progress: because of them, we know today much that we did not know ten years ago. The trials and tribulations will be useful both to Kentucky and to other states that choose to use Kentucky's experiences to guide education policy and practice in the future. For example, Kentucky is continuing to weather the storms of performance assessment and school accountability that have caused other states to give up or start over. Ten years of experience with reform initiatives that for the most part remain in operation puts Kentucky at a distinct advantage if it uses the lessons of the past to guide future actions and efforts.

Some of the lessons we have learned have taught us to build better assessments, communicate results through better school report cards, design more in-depth learning tasks for students, create more productive professional development for teachers, and design more effective school councils. Other lessons have brought Kentuckians face-to-face with tough challenges. KERA has taught us that reform is a process that requires harder work and far more time than we originally estimated.

The central goal of KERA was to create schools that enable all children to learn at high levels. Over the past two to three years Kentucky has identified a few schools in impoverished areas that have been able to raise achievement levels to rank among the best in the state. In other words, these schools have proved the central thesis of KERA. Yet the hard reality is that very few schools have the right leaders, teachers, or support to do what Kentuckians want for all children. To achieve this, additional resources, coupled with exceptional ingenuity and strong leadership, will be needed to achieve Kentucky's performance goals for schools.

Chapter Eleven quotes Governor Paul Patton's address at the tenth anniversary of the signing of KERA, in which he affirmed that "we must continue the difficult course of excellence and not take the easy path of mediocrity." If Governor Patton indeed speaks for the citizens of Kentucky and they stay the course, the efforts of KERA reformers will be rewarded. We believe it is possible for the goals of KERA to be achieved if enough policymakers, educators, and citizens choose to act. Only time will reveal the real success or failure of the Kentucky reform experience.

REFERENCES

Craig, J. R., & Kacer, B. A. (1999). *A longitudinal study of eighteen selected middle and high schools in Kentucky.* Lexington: Kentucky Institute for Education Research.

David, J. L. 1999. *Creating successful schools: A continuous commitment.* Paper prepared for the Partnership for Kentucky Schools and the Prichard Committee for Academic Excellence (pp. 2–4).Lexington: Partnership for Kentucky Schools.

David, J. L., Kannapel, P. J., & McDiarmid, G. W. (in press). *The influence of distinguished educators on school improvement: A study of Kentucky's school intervention program.* Lexington: Partnership for Kentucky Schools.

Foster, J. (1999). *Redesigning public education: The Kentucky experience.* Lexington, KY: Diversified Services.

Honeycutt, V. (2000, July 11). *The Lexington Herald Leader,* p. B1, 13.

Johnson, L. (1998, December 4). Big gap from best to worst gets wider. *Lexington Herald-Leader,* p. B9.

Kentucky Department of Education. (1999). *Demographic survey of primary programs 1999: Data Summary 10–16–99.* Frankfort: Author.

Legislative Research Commission. (1990, February 3). *Recommendations related to curriculum* (adopted by the Task Force on Education Reform 2/23/90) (p. 16). Frankfort, KY: Author.

Loftus, T. (1989, June 8). *The (Louisville) Courier-Journal,* p. A13.

Petrosko, J. M., & Lindle, J. C. (1999, April). *State mandated school reform in Kentucky: Year three of a longitudinal study.* Paper presented at the annual meeting of the American Educational Research Association, Montreal, Canada.

Smith, D.C. (1997). *Assessing race and gender subgroup performance differences in KIRIS accountability cycle 2 results.* Office of Curriculum, Assessment, and Accountability. Frankfort: Kentucky Department of Education.

Wilkerson & Associates. (1994, October). *The 1994 statewide education reform survey.* Frankfort: Kentucky Institute for Education Research.

Wilkerson & Associates. (1995, October). *The 1995 statewide education reform survey.* Frankfort: Kentucky Institute for Education Research.

Wilkerson & Associates. (1997, January). *The 1996 statewide education reform survey of teachers, principals, parents, and the general public.* Frankfort: Kentucky Institute for Education Research.

INDEX